Girls and Violence

Qualitative Studies in Crime and Justice
Mercer L. Sullivan, series editor

Girls and Violence
Tracing the Roots of Criminal Behavior

Judith A. Ryder

LYNNE
RIENNER
PUBLISHERS

BOULDER
LONDON

WITHDRAWN

Published in the United States of America in 2014 by
Lynne Rienner Publishers, Inc.
1800 30th Street, Boulder, Colorado 80301
www.rienner.com

and in the United Kingdom by
Lynne Rienner Publishers, Inc.
3 Henrietta Street, Covent Garden, London WC2E 8LU

Library of Congress Cataloging-in-Publication Data
Ryder, Judith A.
  Girls and violence : tracing the roots of criminal behavior /
Judith A. Ryder.
      pages   cm. — (Qualitative studies in crime and justice)
  Includes bibliographical references and index.
  ISBN 978-1-58826-838-9 (hc : alk. paper) 1. Violence in adolescence.
2. Violence in women. 3. Teenage girls—Psychology. 4. Youth and violence.
I. Title.
  RJ506.V56R93 2014
  303.60835—dc23
                                                              2013016463

British Cataloguing in Publication Data
A Cataloguing in Publication record for this book
is available from the British Library.

Printed and bound in the United States of America

The paper used in this publication meets the requirements
of the American National Standard for Permanence of
Paper for Printed Library Materials Z39.48-1992.

5   4   3   2   1

If one regards the soul of the body as a blood-red membrane, let us say a curling helix of anxiously fragile tissue that connects all the disparate nameable parts of the body to one another, a scarlet firmament between the firmaments, touching and defining both, one might view the soul of Wade's or any other life as that part of it which is connected to other lives.

And one might grow angry and be struck with grief at the sight of those connections being severed, of that membrane being torn, shredded, rent to rags that a child grows into adulthood clinging to—little bloody flags waved vainly across vast chasms.

—Russell Banks, *Affliction*

Contents

Foreword

I am pleased to present this third volume of the series Qualitative Studies in Crime and Justice, Judith Ryder's compelling study of girls who have been confined in residential youth facilities for acts of serious violence while still only in their mid-teens. The goal of this series is to provide adequate space for the presentation of in-depth qualitative data on important matters of crime and justice in a way that is often difficult to achieve within the format of conventional journal articles. The issues addressed here are both important and, despite considerable recent advances in the study of female offending, still relatively understudied.

Like all good qualitative studies, this book provides something unique and essential in social research, namely the chance for readers to hear the voices of those being studied and to see how they represent their own experiences in their own words, to themselves and others. The stories here are riveting, shocking, yet they are presented not for sensational effect but in the spirit of scientific inquiry into the sources of serious violent behavior and the implications of better understanding of such behavior for prevention and treatment.

Two aspects of the study mark it as original and important. One is the in-depth focus not just on violence committed by females, but, more specifically, on females who are so young and whose violent behavior has already landed them in the deep end of the juvenile justice system. This close look at the intersection of early adolescence and severe violence among females has few precedents. A second distinguishing feature of the study is the way it is grounded in and furthers developmental theory. It connects victimization and neglect in childhood to violence during adolescence at the level of social process. The existence of some of the developmental pathways described here has been evident in prior research, but the black box connecting subsequent to prior experiences has remained opaque. This study takes us inside that black box in the best tradition of qualitative research. To be sure, much remains to be learned about girls who suffer similar experiences but do not progress to such extreme outcomes, but this study sets a benchmark for further progress in understanding a highly vulnerable and volatile population.

—*Mercer L. Sullivan*

Acknowledgments

I had a lot of support in writing this book. I wish to thank Rich Allinson for first encouraging me to publish, and Andrew Berzanskis and Karen Williams at Lynne Rienner Publishers for their diligence and enthusiasm in seeing the book through to completion. I am indebted to Mercer Sullivan, who read and reread the manuscript and graciously shared his thoughtful insights. Thank you to reviewers Nikki Jones and Christopher Mullins; their substantive comments made this a better book. A special thank you to Phyllis Schultze for extraordinary research assistance and guidance and for providing a sanctuary at the Gottfredson Library of Criminal Justice.

Writing a book is an arduous and time-consuming process. It is also a collective effort, and my task was lightened by those who both inspired me and offered practical help. Some are long-time friends and colleagues; others appeared at just the right time and place to challenge and encourage me. I am deeply grateful to all.

I thank Dawn Esposito and my colleagues in the Sociology and Anthropology Department at St. John's University in Queens, New York, for providing the space and time to complete this project. The research was supported in part by a grant under the university's Summer Support of Research program. Deirdre Matthews's assistance and efficiency in corralling references is much appreciated. My debts have multiplied over time and as the scope of the project shifted. Thank you to Susan Crimmins and the Learning About Violence and Drugs Among Adolescents (LAVIDA) research team for suggesting a path of investigation, and to Robin Robinson for stretching my thinking and writing about trauma and violence in a psychosocial context.

Gayle Olson-Raymer, Rehana Patel, and Rashi Shukla—my intellectual posse—thank you. Thanks to Diane Biondi Mukkala for long conversations on parenting and child development, and for years of friendship through the hills and the valleys.

My love and thanks to my large and extended family, which sustains and nurtures me, especially my parents, Louise and Paul Ryder. My dad did not live to see this book published, but his influence on its completion is immeasurable. I also want to thank my mother-in-law, Rae Langford Moran, for always asking detailed questions about my research. To Bill Moran, my husband and friend, thank you for listening when I needed to talk and giving me wide berth when I needed to be alone with the work.

Finally, to the girls who shared their stories: I changed your names, but not your voices. Thank you for speaking. I sincerely hope that others will listen.

—*Judith A. Ryder*

Girls and Violence

1

Girls and Violence

I know I won't have a perfect life. But, I wanna have a good
life. I wanna stay in college as long as I possibly can, and I
wanna own a house. I still don't want no kids yet. You gotta
spend a lotta time raisin' kids. I don't really have patience
with kids. I'm still a kid myself.
—Sherry, 15 years old

While researching and writing this book, I was acutely aware of the
media coverage of "girls' violence."[1] One exceptional news story
occurred in a bedroom community north of New York City. Eight
girls, aged 14 to 16 years old, allegedly beat and set fire to a 32-year-
old female counselor in a treatment center for troubled teens. The
police chief expressed his shock at the "viciousness" of the attack,
exclaiming, "it's hard to believe that we're dealing with children
here."[2] When the district attorney (DA) announced indictments on
charges of attempted murder and assault, she stated: "We cannot
excuse anyone, because of their age, from being held accountable or
responsible for their actions."[3] Neither the police chief nor the DA
mentioned gender or race—there was no need. The fact that females
were involved in such a horrific act was the story; that the (pho-
tographed and named) accused were African American and Hispanic
reinforced racial stereotypes of wild and unredeemable youth. It was
another disturbing story of out-of-control girls, another reason to fear
young women of color.[4]

That a violent offender is female elicits a collective sense of surprise, even alarm, in most sectors of the population. The seemingly

extraordinary event grabs our attention and rattles our assumptions about how girls are "supposed" to act. So many of us who are privileged by race, class, and gender also are granted "safe privilege"— what geographer James Tyner describes as the ability of some people to go about their daily routines free from the direct effects of community and interpersonal violence.[5] Thus freed, we turn away and avoid the need to confront and question the production of such violence. It is easier to condemn the violators: once the New York incident was publicized, the Internet erupted with sexist and racist screeds that called for severe and public punishment of the young "witches" and "monsters."[6]

Months after the original reports, a local newspaper investigation chronicled the life of Lidia, one of the 16-year-olds charged in the case.[7] Unlike the early, sensationalistic coverage, this account was based on several years of court records and child welfare reports, interviews with family members, and excerpts from the girl's journal. The newspaper story documented a history of parental alcohol and drug abuse, sibling incest, foster care placements, physical abuse, neglect, and abandonment. Eventually, because the girl was truant, ran away, and drank alcohol, she was placed in a residential center and treated for depression and alcohol abuse. Describing children at the center, one employee said, "They've just had horrific stuff thrown at them."[8] Clearly, Lidia had. But now she was charged with attempted second-degree murder. So, how does the victimized become the victimizer?

In my own research with adolescent girls, I have thought a lot about this duality of violence, questioning what violence even means for girls growing up in decimated, postindustrial inner cities.[9] The term *violence* is imbued with a host of meanings and, despite their official "violent offender" label, most of the girls I interviewed for this book did not see themselves as such. When asked, many girls described defensive maneuvers taken to counter the abhorrent acts of adults in their lives. I sat and talked with girls who were funny and caring and strong and resilient but who, in the same conversation, became tough, cynical, even menacing, as they told of their attacks on family members, peers, and strangers. How are these experiences connected, and how might girls' interpretations of violence be tied to family dynamics in the context of the larger community? These questions must be answered if we are to understand girls' experiences and violent behaviors.

To begin, we know that girls are targets of violence. A comprehensive 2009 nationwide survey of the incidence and prevalence of children's exposure to violence reported that 42 percent of girls had experienced a physical assault in the prior year, and 7.4 percent had experienced a sexual assault. Over their lifetime, 52.9 percent of girls had experienced a physical assault and 12.2 percent reported being sexually victimized.[10] Extensive evidence from national incidence reports consistently has found that girls are sexually abused at a rate more than five times that of boys; the incidence of psychological and emotional abuse is also higher for girls.[11] Girls who end up in state justice systems have much higher victimization rates compared with girls in the general population, including a disproportionate risk for incest and other child abuse as well as acquaintance and stranger rape as adolescents. Interview data have indicated that, within the national juvenile custodial population, nearly one-third of all youths reported a history of prior abuse. When custodial males and females are compared, females "reveal nearly twice the rate of past physical abuse (42 percent vs. 22 percent), . . . and more than four times the rate of prior sex abuse (35 percent vs. 8 percent)."[12]

We also know that girls do act violently. In addition to histories of victimization, research has documented young women's participation in disorderly conduct and street fights for at least the past century.[13] The expansion of historical work on incarcerated females provides evidence of a range of violent offenses including robbery, assault, and homicide.[14] According to Federal Bureau of Investigation (FBI) data from 1980 through 2010, 3,594 juvenile females were implicated in homicides in the United States (compared to 42,723 juvenile males), and nearly 30 years of self-report data reveal that, on average, girls account for about 15 percent of high-frequency assaults and about 35 percent of less frequent or minor involvement in violence.[15] In 1988, girls' arrests for violent crime (driven primarily by assaultive behavior) began to rise and continued to increase proportionately more than did violent crime arrests of boys; when overall violence began to fall a decade later, the female rate dropped proportionately less than the male rate.[16]

Prior to the late 1980s, the number of girls engaged in violence in the United States was low and their arrest rates were stable. News coverage was rare and unlikely to generate much social anxiety. But as the crack cocaine trade began to flourish in poor, African American, and Hispanic neighborhoods and girls' arrests began their ascent, media accounts of female involvement in drug-related crime and violence suddenly multiplied[17] and sensational headlines continued to inflate public fears over the next decade. The media used the national FBI arrest statistics that indicated a rise in female delinquency to frame extreme cases as typical: "the episodic rhetorically recrafted into the epidemic."[18] Stories of "vicious young women" engaged in extreme acts of violence (e.g., the "baby-faced butcher" of Central Park) or "joining gangs that fight and rob like male gangs" were effectively contrasted with hegemonic gender expectations to present girls as violent marauders.[19] Racialized images of gun-toting girls merged with stories of youngsters battling over drug product and turf to construct an urban (black) female "gangsta" ready to wreak havoc on a nation already in fear of its youth and a purported drug epidemic.[20] Misperceptions of juvenile crime and youths (boys and girls) as violent superpredators justified increasingly punitive state strategies, including sweep laws, zero-tolerance policies, waivers to adult court, and the extensive use of detention and incarceration.[21]

Subsequent analyses have discredited much of the hype surrounding girls' violent offending, and contentious international debates as to whether female arrest rates are up or down and by what percentage have substantially diminished. Indeed, research has indicated little overall change in girls' level of violence between 1980 and 2003, as well as little change in the female-to-male percentage of violent offending. Female violence may be rare, but it is overreported in the media. The supposed meteoric rise in serious juvenile female violence appears to be "more a social construction than an empirical reality."[22] Widened regulatory nets and punitive policies created in the wake of the ongoing dispute, however, continue to affect young women and girls, and lingering arguments about the *amount* of female violence distract from efforts to discern the *context* and the *processes* that may contribute to those behaviors.

Arrest and other official data outline delinquency patterns, but tell us more about law enforcement policies than the motivation for girls' actions.[23] We know that victimized children are more likely than others to become involved in violence, but a deeper understanding of mitigating factors is required—the "cycle of violence" does not sufficiently account for the fact that the majority of abused, neglected, and otherwise victimized girls do not always or necessarily turn to violence.[24] Further, calculating the number of offenses or sensationalizing individual acts fails to appreciate the contexts in which violence occurs or the underlying mechanisms that help to propel it.

To better understand girls' violent behaviors, we need to look wider and deeper than specific acts. Each of us invests our own experiences with meaning, as do girls who are perceived as deviant. Thus, it is important to explore how girls interpret acts of violence (both their own and those of others) and investigate the social and psychological contexts of girls' lives before they become violent criminals in the eyes of the law. What, for example, are the dynamics of their primary relationships? How have girls' experiences of trauma been addressed (or have they)? More broadly, we need also to consider the role of families, communities, and social institutions in the production of violence.

Lidia's story resonates with those told by the two dozen girls interviewed for this book. These are the narratives of girls who the newspapers write about only in the abstract as one-dimensional violent offenders. They are also those of girls who came of age in urban neighborhoods blighted by violence and abandoned by mainstream social, political, and economic institutions. Growing up in the context of banal violence, these mostly African American and Hispanic girls are without "safe privilege"; extraordinary violence is all too often quite ordinary. Prior to becoming wards of the state—at a time when the justice system was rapidly expanding its reach into the lives of minority youths—they inflicted varying measures of physical harm on others and committed a range of property- and drug-related offenses. Significantly, the girls also tell of broken relationships and losses, of neglect and maltreatment, often by the very persons and institutions responsible for their care. Each of them has tightly intertwined histories of violence: violence experienced, witnessed, and enacted at home, in school, and on the streets. They are wounded, but they are not monsters or modern-day witches. Like Sherry, who introduces this chapter, the girls have dreams of a better self and a better life.

Rather than condemn girls and their actions, we need to imagine what happens to a girlchild when families and other institutions fail to keep her physically and emotionally safe. What are the traumatic consequences of those failings, and how might the exposure to violence and experiences of loss contribute to the girl's alienation, stigmatization, and violent aggression?[25] Like Lidia, the girls whose stories form the basis of this book have troubles and they are often troubling—and they made decisions and took defensive steps that added to their troubles. Their stories affirm much of what is known about associations between female exposure to violence and violent offending; of greater import is what they reveal about the traumagenic effects of broken and disrupted primary relationships.

Rendering a Detailed Picture

This book focuses on 24 teenage girls adjudicated and remanded to custody for a robbery or an assault in the mid-1990s.[26] (The characteristics of the interviewees are included in Table 1.1.) It is a secondary analysis of the girls' one-time interviews conducted in 1996 in four New York residential youth facilities. In my analyses of the qualitative data, I integrate constructs of psychosocial theory, particularly attachment theory and the effects of chronic trauma, into a theoretical framework for understanding girls' violent behaviors. I was the senior project director of a federally funded study, Learning About Violence and Drugs Among Adolescents (LAVIDA), that examined relationships between juvenile drug use and trafficking and violent offending based on semistructured interviews with 363 boys and 51 girls in custody for a violent offense.[27] The current secondary analysis is based primarily on interview data from 24 of the 51 girls.[28]

A gender analysis of the LAVIDA quantitative data revealed significant differences, particularly in terms of family relationships.[29] Girls were much less likely than boys to report having someone in their household with whom they could talk about things that were bothering them, and they were significantly more likely than boys to have been sexually bothered or to have witnessed a family member sexually bothering someone. Girls were almost three times more likely than boys to have run away from home overnight and more than twice as likely to have ever been in foster care. But quantitative data alone cannot fully portray the nuances of an adolescent's world; as sociologist Andrew Abbott notes, "all social facts are located in contexts."[30] These quantitative data serve only as a starting point for a more in-depth analysis of the early lives of the incarcerated young women.

LAVIDA's semistructured interview format afforded the girls room to discuss events in detail and provided them with the opportunity and space to raise topics important to their presentation of self. Spontaneous offerings opened unexpected avenues of conversation and introduced new themes that clarified (and just as often muddied or complicated) the narrative and helped to "center and make problematic" diverse life situations.[31] Fourteen-year-old Elena describes a fairly typical violent event:[32]

> It was two of my cousins, my cousin's friend, and me. We was
> in the train station and I told this lady she looked nice and she

Table 1.1   Characteristics of Interviewees (*N* = 24)

Pseudonym	OCFS Offense	Age	Race/Ethnicity (recoded)	Last Grade Completed	Children
Adele	Assault	14	Black	7th	No
Alona	Robbery	15	Black	10th	Yes
Christine	Assault	14	Black	8th	No
Diane	Robbery	16	Black	9th	No
Donna	Robbery	15	Black	7th	No
Elena	Robbery	14	Biracial/Multiracial	9th	Yes
Gayle	Assault	16	Black	6th	No
Gina	Assault	14	Black	8th	No
Jackie	Assault	13	Black	7th	No
Jennifer	Assault	15	Multiracial	9th	No
Jill	Assault	14	White	7th	No
Joanne	Assault	15	Hispanic/Latino	8th	No
Kathy	Robbery	16	White	9th	Yes
Lauren	Assault	15	Black	8th	No
Lisa	Assault	15	Black	8th	No
Marcella	Assault	15	Hispanic/Latina	6th	No
Maria	Assault	14	Hispanic/Latina	9th	No
Michelle	Assault	16	Black	7th	No
Natalie	Assault	16	Black	9th	No
Paula	Assault	16	Black	6th	No
Rose	Assault	16	Hispanic/Latina	8th	No
Royale	Assault	16	Biracial/Multiracial	8th	No
Sherry	Assault	15	Black	8th	No
Valerie	Assault	15	Black	9th	No

Note: OCFS = Office of Children and Family Services.

was like fronting. She was like y'all black Bs. I was like what? I was already high but I didn't even pay her no mind. My cousin was like you heard what she said? . . . My cousin was like, she pulled the gun out. She was like, which one of you all wanna die tonight? . . . The lady was like, y'all kids. Y'all need to be home in your bed. I was like s'cuse me? She was like, you heard what I said. I said, "what?" and I just punched her. Then I slapped her when we got on the train. Then she was trying to get something outta her pocketbook.

> She pulled out a knife. And I was like, oh, say what? And I just smacked her with my gun and just started beating her up. . . . And after that, my cousin grabbed her purse. We just got off the train and started running.

High on marijuana and acting in concert with other females her age, Elena attacks a woman in her mid-thirties over perceived insults regarding race, gender, and age. A verbal exchange escalates to a physical beating; Elena characterizes the robbery (her official charge) as an afterthought.

How are these actions to be understood? Is this only about drugs and out-of-control girls? What else might be going on internally, beneath the described behaviors? A clue exists in the girls' responses to questions about trauma. It is at this juncture in the interviews, when we asked if certain, potentially traumagenic events had ever occurred, that the girls began to disclose the many and varied harms they had experienced in their young lives.

The other interviewers on the LAVIDA study and I strove to attend to what each girl said as well as to the silences, expressions (or lack thereof), fragments and repetitions—recognizing that the experience of trauma affects memories and consciousness and thus shapes its telling. This attentive stance is critical, especially because in disclosing a story of trauma, the teller relies on a "listening space" where not only is she able to speak and be heard, but she is believed. During the interviews, the girls stopped and started, added side comments, and jumped to new topics. Some descriptions are sharp and specific, others are vague, and in some the language breaks down completely: "these stories are not easy to tell, emotionally or linguistically."[33] This is a feature of recalling traumatic experience, made even more difficult perhaps by the speakers' gender, youth, and devalued status as wards of the state. Although the study did not formally use the narrative interview method that criminologist David Gadd describes, our assumptions were similar:

> The reality of the interviewee's biography is greater than the sum of the extracted parts; and that those parts elicited during the interview are an incomplete set. Memory loss, embarrassment, shame and the sheer inexpressibility of so much human experience delimit the interviewee's capacity (by some unknown quantity) to either "tell it like it is" and/or completely conceal their own emotional truths.[34]

In conducting this research, we could not expect the girls to be able or willing to reveal all the details of their lives, particularly lives saturated by trauma, or to explain all of the reasons for their actions. Each girl has her own unique tale as to how she came to be in state custody, and the medium of a transcribed interview can only represent it partially: "in what way could we mark the 'beginning' or 'end' of the [young] women's stories?"[35] Writer Joan Didion also reflects on the difficulty of expressing one's own story and suggests that all of us "interpret what we see, select the most workable of the multiple choices," and, when asked, try to impose "a narrative line upon . . . the shifting phantasmagoria which is our actual experience."[36] Collectively, the girls' circumstances, experiences, and behaviors belie the assumed clarity of their officially assigned labels of *robbery* or *assault* and tell us much more about *traumagenic* effects of broken relationships. Selective as they must be, the data disclose general patterns that help to explain complex journeys in the aggregate.

As I listened to the girls discuss their families and their neighborhoods, I was struck by the pervasiveness of violence and loss, of lives nearly devoid of personal supports. Revisiting Elena's story, we learn she is the 11th of 14 children. She is placed in foster care as an infant and does not return to her birth family until she is 7 years old. Reinserted into the family unit, Elena recalls fighting with and being beaten by her mother, who has a serious drug problem. At age 11, her father dies of a chronic illness; that same year she watches as a younger brother bleeds to death, stabbed by a neighborhood boy. She describes an older brother as lost to the family because of his lengthy prison sentence ("He 19, by the time he come out, what's gonna be the use?"). Summarizing her family life, Elena explicitly connects early experiences of broken attachments to later delinquency:

> We had so many family problems because I had just lost a little brother, just lost my father; I was really out of control. My family was really slipping away, oh God. It was just breaking off in pieces. It was so much drama, I can't believe it. We had cops in it too, oh man, it was so horrible. . . . I just started flipping and going wild, doing things I wasn't supposed to be doing, then got locked up and that was it.

For Elena (to whom I will turn frequently) and the other girls introduced throughout the book, violent behaviors are linked to the status and strength of their emotional bonds with others. My investigation of attachments with primary caregivers, considered within the context of family- and community-related trauma, helps to explicate the processes that draw some girls into violent behaviors.

Crack Cocaine and the Devastation of Community

To appreciate the reality of the girls' lives, it is important to ground their narratives in a particular time and place; their stories reflect interpersonal family dynamics and the nature of the environment in which they came up. Born in the early 1980s into neighborhoods with limited access to services, resources, and power, the girls grew up in the vortex of the crack cocaine era. Most lived at the epicenter of the trade— New York City—and several are the daughters of the first-generation of female crack users.[37]

Crack, a cheap new version of cocaine, flooded poor African American neighborhoods beginning in 1983. Its availability and use quickly expanded and, within only a few years, crack was entrenched in certain New York neighborhoods, where it remained popular throughout the 1990s.[38] The pervasiveness of crack cocaine only added to the social ills of neighborhoods already suffering the consequences of back-to-back recessions. In New York and other large East Coast cities, unemployment among urban African American and Hispanic males escalated when low-skilled jobs and manufacturing economies relocated and workers without the requisite service sector skills were forced to the sidelines.[39] Deindustrialization, coupled with discrimination in the labor market, also decreased demand for teenage African American and Hispanic employees and ended the long-run trend of rising youth employment.[40]

Economists Roland Fryer and colleagues argue that crack was responsible for much of the violence in urban neighborhoods. Specifically, they found that the rise in crack use between 1984 and 1989 accounted for the doubling of homicides of black males 14 to 17 years old, and an increase of more than 25 percent in weapons arrests of blacks. The increases are linked to the actions of unemployed youth (mostly males) who, while seeking to gain and solidify monetary assets and power in the emerging drug trade, attempted to establish property rights not enforceable through legal means. One result was years of violent turf wars. The domination of neoconservative politics in the 1980s supported enhanced police surveillance and suppression of drug trafficking, which further added to systemic crack-related violence.[41]

Economic displacements in the inner cities also contributed to a significant rise in the percentage of female heads of household. Women began to use crack cocaine in unprecedented numbers in the 1980s, a factor that compounded their vulnerability to violence in distressed neighborhoods. Female crack users who were also sole caregivers of dependent children burdened already strained community resources.[42] Kinship networks that traditionally come to the aid of members in need were economically and emotionally stretched by years of unemployment, divestment, and the ravages of HIV/AIDS, and could offer women only minimal assistance with child care responsibilities.[43] Punitive criminal justice policies, such as the enactment of federal and state mandatory sentencing laws, dealt harshly with cocaine users and African American women in particular; low-level, nonviolent offenders who in other times might have been directed to drug programming became the fastest-growing segment of the prison population. The vast majority of incarcerated women were parents of minors, and the rise in female imprisonment fueled the growth in foster care caseloads; crack use correlated specifically with a doubling of the percentage of black children in foster care.[44] Crack-involved mothers cycled in and out of jails and prisons and, thus hampered in their ability to provide safe and nurturing environments for their children, were often forced to relinquish parental rights.[45]

Neighborhood context affects individuals and families in gendered ways, shaping experiences of violence and choices in behavior. In this historical moment within inner-city neighborhoods during an overwhelming drug epidemic, parent-child and gender roles are pulled and twisted in many directions. When the domestic sphere provides a fragmented and diminished sense of support and protection, street culture often becomes an important socializing factor.[46] The manner in which the girls in this study constituted a femininity that included violence is but one of many possibilities.[47] But community context alone is an inadequate explanator of the girls' behaviors.

Developmental processes and behavioral outcomes are especially sensitive to the dynamics of interpersonal relationships, and few of the interviewed girls had experienced safe and nurturing relationships. At the peak of the era in 1989 the girls were on average only 8 years old and had already suffered extensive losses and victimizations, both in their homes and in their communities. They describe chaotic families where violence is constant, parental figures rotate, and family composition shifts. The girls report being kicked, beaten, stabbed, and sexually coerced by those closest to them; all too often the caregivers responsible for their development and protection failed them. Lacking the support and supervision of loving and attuned adults to help process and psychologically integrate a wide range of potentially traumatic events and the attendant emotional sequelae, the girls were left to contend with an environment devoid of loving attachments and community supports in milieus generally hostile to females.

A Developmental Model

My purpose in this book is to explore manifestations of violence through the lens of significant early relationships and resultant internal conflicts. Drawing from the literature of developmental psychology and applying inductive, theory-generating techniques of grounded theory, I analyze the girls' interview data to identify categories of loss and violence. Through this process I widen the focus from the girls' behaviors to their subjective experiences; the unit of analysis expands from individual girls to girls in the context of dynamic relational processes.[48] I apply a psychosocial understanding of attachment theory to the girls' perspectives and experiences to construct an attachment-based developmental model, or framework, to help explain the processes underlying girls' violent behaviors.

Attachment theorists assume that children require "a quality of care . . . sufficiently responsive to the child's needs to alleviate anxiety and engender a feeling of being understood."[49] A felt sense of safety provides a "secure base" from which to explore the external environment and to which to return in uncertain times. In simple terms, attachment behavior, the formation of an affective bond between children and their caregivers, protects the young from predators in the environment and promotes the development of self-regulatory functioning.[50] Social affiliation is critical to healthy long-term development and behavior; findings on the psychobiology of the attachment system "illustrate only too clearly how important we may well be for one another, not only at a psychological level . . . but also at a physiological level."[51]

Children who have been neglected, abandoned, or abused by primary caregivers may fail to form, or may suffer the disruption or loss of, affective bonds. They may develop a pattern of behavior in which avoidance of the caregiver competes with the desire for care from, and proximity to, that person. In this process, angry behavior is likely to become prominent;[52] society generally finds such behavior intolerable and therefore subject to punishment. As I show in the following chapters, in the aftermath of loss, abuse, and neglect, the girls in this study used various maladaptive strategies to protect against (i.e., avoid) psychic pain. Yet they also expressed a need to stay in connection with others. Though many ran away from seemingly unbearable conditions, at some point they all returned. Girls may often cling to those who abuse and cause them pain because the terror of abandonment exceeds the terror of the abuser; there is comfort in an abusive attachment that is familiar.[53] Some of the girls I interviewed appeared to psychically wall off their attachment needs through excessive drug use, even as they described a longing for close and loving relationships. Acts of violence can also be a form of connection; although maladaptive and destructive, trauma-saturated girls may find it difficult to make the distinction.[54] The girls' efforts to create or recreate attachments to others, while simultaneously attempting to counteract traumagenic effects such as overwhelming feelings of anxiety, rage, and shame, were often the very behaviors that put them in direct conflict with the law. A refined understanding of these behaviors requires a psychodynamically informed analysis that privileges the voice of the outcast child.[55]

Overview of the Book

In Chapter 2, I make explicit a model for exploring the "black box" between experiences of loss, victimization, and other traumatic experiences in childhood, and of violent behaviors in adolescence.[56] The theoretical underpinning of this model relies heavily on attachment theory (which stresses the physical and psychological need for the other) in conjunction with the existent trauma research literature. According to attachment theory, internalized affectional bonds, or working models, are active throughout the life cycle and, for the securely attached individual, provide an internalized model of self as worthy and the world as safe. When the need for one another is thwarted, when the primary relationship is disrupted or abused, the results can be devastating; the meaning given to the trauma and the quality of other interpersonal relationships help to shape the outcome. Absence, malformation, or disruption of psychological attachment may interfere with normal child development and contribute to a range of social problems later in life. When attachment needs are not met, a traumagenic effect may be the interruption of brain development and executive functioning (i.e., judgment, decisionmaking, planning, logical thinking). Such impairment "may produce behaviors perceived as deviant, aggressive, and/or dangerous," but likely serve defensive purposes.[57] Violent behavior becomes an expression of a disrupted attachment system and rage at the psychologically inflicted injury to the self: a "by-product of psychological trauma" and its effects on individuals.[58]

I begin to recount the girls' personal stories in Chapter 3 with an examination of their first and most significant relationship: the affectional tie between the child and her parent or primary caregiver.[59] This bond involves a specific and small number of persons who hold emotional significance and to whom an infant looks for security, comfort, and guidance. This early relationship is instrumental in shaping how we perceive ourselves and how we behave toward one another, not only in infancy but in interpersonal relationships across the life course. Though caregivers within poor and dangerous neighborhoods are subject to severe economic, social, and psychological pressures and conflicts that are likely to affect child rearing, it is how the child perceives the parent-child relationship that is relevant to theories of attachment. The majority of the girls in the current study lived with their mothers most of the time and, thus, the narratives revolve around perceptions of this relationship. The girls reveal a generally weak sense of attachment, feelings of minimal support, and inconsistent monitoring and supervision. Adults unwilling or unable to attend to the girls' innate attachment needs constantly disappoint their expectations of protection and support.

Events and experiences that may be rare in the general population unfortunately are normative among this group of incarcerated girls. In Chapters 4 and 5, I reveal the numerous, varied, and potentially traumatic events that the girls experienced, for the most part, prior to the age of 11 years old. I divide and separately review the girls' extensive exposure to violence in the community and within the home, and the substantial losses they endured. In reality, experiences overlap and seep through these porous boundaries. I begin Chapter 4 by portraying the urban neighborhoods in which the girls and their families lived—neighborhoods that are violent and where drugs and guns are commonplace. Fights, shootings, and killings are the nearly constant background of daily life, with much of the violence directed at women and girls. The girls also talk about the dynamics of violence and victimization perpetrated within the familial setting, and thereby Chapter 4 extends my discussion, begun in Chapter 3, of weak attachments between the girls and their primary caregivers. Violence takes many forms, including physical and sexual abuse, and is often perpetrated by primary caregivers and ignored or inadequately addressed by other adults.

Against the background of community and family violence, in Chapter 5 I reveal the depth and effect of personal losses. The girls reference four major types of loss: death of loved ones; physical absence of caregivers; psychological unavailability of caregivers; and loss of home. The number and extent of such losses is noteworthy, and their traumagenic effects are amplified when considered in the larger context of violence and victimization experiences and the absence of supportive others. The constant and pervasive sense of vulnerability and loss inhibited the girls' ability to manage internal psychological pain.

In Chapter 6, I examine key ways that the girls attempted to cope with the effects of loss, victimization, and violence. In general, the girls made use of avoidant strategies in the form of excessive alcohol and marijuana use and running away while striving to remain attached to abusive or neglectful, but still loved, caregivers. Most of the girls began their drug use in the context of family and home before integrating heavy, regular usage into daily activities and events. Substance use is both a means of connecting with otherwise unavailable caregivers (a relational strategy)[60] and a defense against psychic pain. The girls also left home, some for a night, others for a month or even a year, to avoid seemingly overwhelming problems. Most returned home in the hope of reconnecting with loved ones. To a lesser extent, the girls also engaged in body mutilation or modification and suicide attempts in their efforts to self-soothe and to gain a sense of self-control.

Avoidant strategies failed to alleviate the psychic pain of absent, malformed, or otherwise disrupted attachments, and the girls sought relief and connection in violent behaviors. In Chapter 7, I examine the specific offenses for which the girls were most recently adjudicated and remanded to custody (either a robbery or an assault). Most of the girls did not readily distinguish between the instant offense and any number of other behaviors (violent and nonviolent) in which they had engaged, but these are the labels that defined them. Though each girl's story could be told within the framework of disrupted or malformed attachments, justice systems respond to unacceptable behaviors with labels and legal sanctions, irrespective of the particular nature or meaning of the act(s).[61] Privileging the girls' perspectives, I describe the situational context and characteristics of violent acts as well as the primary motivations for the girls' behaviors: respect, revenge, self-defense, and financial gain.

I reiterate the components of an attachment-based model of female adolescent violence for the purpose of reconsidering those violent behaviors that juvenile authorities formally address. I submit that lack of emotional nurturance disrupted the girls' attachments to others and interfered with the healthy development of a secure sense of self. Isolated and rejected, when confronted with new threats (actual or imagined), the girls responded with aggression—a means of defending and preserving the injured and depleted self through connection with others. Though maladaptive and counterintuitive to mainstream norms and expectations, violence is a means of psychic survival.

In the concluding chapter, I urge practitioners and policymakers, community leaders, and academics to take seriously an attachment-based framework for understanding youth violence. This approach highlights the importance of early relationships with primary caregivers in determining how children perceive themselves and behave toward others, and allows for a deeper analysis of socially disturbing behaviors. Such an approach suggests a reformulation of how we understand girls' behaviors and how we define the purported problem of violence. The chapter considers some of the policy, programmatic, and theoretical implications of addressing juveniles' attachment needs in families, communities, and social institutions, including educational and justice systems.

The voices of young people, specifically young women, are rarely heard and their perspectives on interpersonal violence have been, until quite recently, marginalized; here, their stories are central. Each girl's account is a complicated story, with nuances that statistical data and official labels obscure. The girls speak directly of violence and loss in their young lives, and the pain and rage of having their knowledge and experience ignored or denied. Their statements and circumstances may be shocking, perhaps even unbelievable, and this is exactly why we must not take refuge in safe privilege. Unlike most delinquency studies, the girls in this research are at the deep end of the juvenile justice system: each is adjudicated delinquent and remanded to residential custody for crimes against a person and, as such, constitute a minority among all girls in trouble with the law. The participants cannot be considered typical and may be perceived as, and perhaps even represent, a "tougher," more "damaged" group of girls.[62] They also represent, however, the girls that families discard, and increasingly punitive and intrusive systems of control take in. Their position in relation to the justice system is important, yet relatively unknown. Collectively, the girls' narratives provide a unique entrée into an oft-hidden world; bringing aspects of the private into the public arena, they alert us to the psychological processes that "exacerbate or reduce our need to be destructive."[63]

Notes

1. Official and self-report definitions of violence are not necessarily in agreement and both have been seriously challenged; in feminist criminology, *girls* and *violence* are highly contested terms. See Alder and Worrall, *Girls' Violence;* Leschied et al., "Aggression in Adolescent Girls," p. 8; Messerschmidt, "From Patriarchy to Gender," p. 179; Batacharya, "Racism, 'Girl Violence,' and Murder"; Kadi, *Thinking Class.*
2. Liebson et al., "Counselor Beaten."
3. Rae and Cohen, "Lidia's Story."
4. Kinetz, "School Attack." See also Luke, "Girls' Violence," for a discussion of the emergence of girls' violence as a social problem in the print media.
5. Tyner, *Space, Place and Violence,* pp. 170–171.
6. See, for example, www.greekchat.com, www.stormfront.org; forums.jolt online.com; news.mensactivism.org; and www.freerepublic.com.
7. Rae and Cohen, "Lidia's Story."
8. Foderaro, "Violence Is a Symptom."
9. In this book, I am interested in violence directed against individuals (including the self), not against objects.
10. Finklehor et al., "Violence, Abuse, and Crime Exposure."
11. When sexual victimization and sexual assault are not included, patterns of child maltreatment are similar for girls and boys. Sedlak et al., *Fourth National Incidence Study,* p. 22.
12. Sedlak and McPherson, "Youth's Needs and Services"; Sedlak et al., *Fourth National Incidence Study.* Local studies replicate the national patterns; see Cauffman et al., "Gender Differences in Mental Health Symptoms"; Corrado et al., "Incarceration of Young Female Offenders"; Corrado et al., *Multi-Problem Violent Youth.*
13. See, for example, Davies, "'These Viragoes'"; Godfrey, "Rough Girls"; Alexander, "The 'Girl Problem.'"
14. Rafter, *Partial Justice;* Rose, *Massacre of the Innocents.*
15. Puzzanchera et al., "Supplementary Homicide Reports." See Heide and Solomon, "Female Juvenile Murderers," pp. 245–246. For information on self-

report data, see Steffensmeier et al., "Assessment of Recent Trends." See also Huizinga et al., "Co-occurrence of Delinquency"; J. Miller, *Getting Played;* Chesney-Lind and Belknap, "Trends in Delinquent Girls' Aggression."

16. Violent juvenile crime escalated in the late 1980s, peaked in 1994, and then dramatically dropped in the subsequent decade. Female juvenile arrest rates dropped 11 percent compared to a decrease of 35 percent for male juveniles. Snyder and Sickmund, *Juvenile Offenders and Victims,* p. 8. The number of girls (under the age of 18 years) involved in violent crime remains much smaller than the number of boys. For Violent Crime Index offenses (e.g., murder and non-negligent manslaughter, forcible rape, robbery, and aggravated assault), the 2010 juvenile male arrest rate (358) was more than 4 times the female rate (85). "Juvenile Arrest Rate Trends," OJJDP *Statistical Briefing Book.*

17. In the 1988 election year, stories about the "crack epidemic" appeared regularly in both the print media and on television. See Reeves and Campbell, *Cracked Coverage.*

18. Reinarman and Levine, "The Crack Attack," p. 24.

19. See Lee, "For Gold Earrings and Protection"; Evans, "Young, Female and Turning Deadly"; Chesney-Lind and Eliason, "Invisible to Incorrigible." In their examination of reporting patterns of juvenile homicide in two major Chicago newspapers from 1992 to 2000, Boulahanis and Heltsley ("Perceived Fears") found that the newspapers may have been responsible for socially constructing an atypical image of juvenile homicide by overreporting cases involving girls, Caucasians, and extremely young victims and offenders.

20. Tisdall, "Rising Tide of Female Violence?"; Leslie et al., "Girls Will Be Girls"; Pizarro et al., "Juvenile 'Super-Predators'"; Chesney-Lind, "Jailing 'Bad' Girls."

21. DiIulio, "Coming of the Super-Predators"; Feld, "Violent Girls?"; Benekos and Merlo, "Juvenile Justice."

22. Boulahanis and Heltsley, "Perceived Fears"; Steffensmeier et al., "Assessment of Recent Trends," p. 397. Researchers note the low base rate of girls' offending and the sensitivity of UCR arrest statistics to criminal justice selection bias. When multiple sources such as victimization and self-report data are used to analyze trends in girls' violence, there is no dramatic increase. See also Doob and Sprott, "'Quality' of Youth Violence?"; Stevens et al., "Are Girls Getting Tougher?"; Lauritsen et al., "Trends in the Gender Gap"; Garbarino, *See Jane Hit;* Snyder and Sickmund, *Juvenile Offenders and Victims,* 2006; Carrington, "Does Feminism Spoil Girls?"; Sharpe, *Offending Girls.*

23. See Nanda, "Blind Discretion," for a review of the history and current status of the juvenile justice system as it relates to girls of color.

24. See Fagan, "Gender Cycle of Violence."

25. Robinson, "'Since I Couldn't,'" p. 202; Hyman and Perone, "Other Side of School Violence."

26. Following the lead of Christine Alder and Anne Worrall (*Girls' Violence*), I use the term *girls* to make clear that the participants in this research are young teenagers, not to be confused with young adults. Although at times I substitute the term *young women* for *girls,* it is only to provide variation in my writing and not to distinguish age.

27. For a report on the larger study, see Crimmins et al., *Learning About Violence*.

28. Qualitative data from 27 of the 51 cases were destroyed in the September 11, 2001, attack on the World Trade Center; quantitative data for all 51 cases had been entered and stored off-site and is used here to supplement the narratives. Although this historic event arbitrarily dictated the selection of cases, analyses of demographic characteristics indicate that the surviving group of 24 is similar to the subsample of 51 from which it came.

29. The analysis compared only the robbery and assault offenders (51 female and 209 male offenders) because there were no female sexual assault offenders and the four female homicide offenders were transferred to adult correctional facilities before they could be interviewed.

30. Abbott, "Of Time and Space."

31. Goffman, *Presentation of Self;* Olesen, "Feminisms and Models," p. 300.

32. Pseudonyms are used throughout this book. See Table 1.1 for characteristics of the interviewees. Note that gun use was not common for this sample of girls.

33. Ferraro, *Neither Angels nor Demons,* p. 7.

34. Gadd, "Masculinities," p. 431. Gadd references the Free Association Narrative Interview method piloted by Wendy Hollway and Tony Jefferson ("Eliciting Narrative") in their research on gender, anxiety, and fear of crime.

35. Menon and Bhasin, *Borders and Boundaries,* p. 18.

36. Didion, *White Album,* p. 11.

37. Ryder and Brisgone, "Cracked Perspectives."

38. B. Johnson et al., "Crack Distribution and Abuse"; Hamid, "Developmental Cycle"; Bourgois, *In Search of Respect.*

39. Small and Newman, "Urban Poverty"; W. J. Wilson, *When Work Disappears;* D. Williams, "Employment in Recession and Recovery."

40. Nardone, "Decline in Youth Population."

41. Fryer et al., "Measuring the Impact of Crack Cocaine." See also Goldstein, "Drugs and Violent Crime"; Bourgois, "In Search of Horatio Alger"; Garland, *Culture of Control.*

42. Sampson, "Urban Black Violence"; W. J. Wilson, *Truly Disadvantaged;* Sterk, *Fast Lives;* Goldstein et al., "Frequency of Cocaine Use and Violence."

43. Dunlap et al., "Severely Distressed African-American Family"; Miller-Cribbs and Farber, "Kin Networks and Poverty."

44. Swann and Sylvester, "Foster Care Crisis." Another 15.3 percent is attributed to decreasing Aid to Families and Dependent Children/Temporary Assistance for Needy Families (AFDC/TANF).

45. See Crenshaw, "From Private Violence to Mass Incarceration." Fryer et al. ("Measuring the Impact of Crack Cocaine") also attribute to crack use an increase of more than 25 percent in fetal death rates among African Americans between 1984 and 1994. See Reed and Reed ("Children of Incarcerated Parents") and Schirmer et al. ("Incarcerated Parents and Their Children") for a discussion of the Adoption and Safe Families Act (ASFA) authorizing the ter-

mination of parental rights after a child has been in foster care for 15 of the past 22 months. Because the average prison sentence exceeds 22 months, incarcerated parents dependent on foster care risk losing custody. In June 2010 then New York governor David Paterson signed into law the ASFA Expanded Discretion Act, which allows foster care agencies to refrain from filing for termination if a parent is in prison or residential drug treatment, or if a parent's prior incarceration or program participation is a significant factor in why a child has been placed in foster care.

46. Bourgois, *In Search of Respect,* p. 260.

47. Cain, "Towards Transgression."

48. Daiute and Fine, "Youth Perspectives on Violence."

49. Ansbro, "Using Attachment Theory with Offenders," p. 234.

50. Hofer, "Hidden Regulators."

51. De Zulueta, *From Pain to Violence,* p. 57. Research on neurobiological functions in the brain and the effects of trauma and loss is extensive, and I will only briefly refer to it in subsequent chapters to support an explanation of violent behaviors.

52. Bowlby, *Separation,* pp. 46–47.

53. Shengold, *Soul Murder Revisited.*

54. Fonagy et al., "Morality, Disruptive Behavior"; Herman, *Trauma and Recovery.*

55. Robinson, "'Since I Couldn't.'"

56. Daly, "Women's Pathways to Felony Court," p. 15.

57. Robinson and Ryder, "Psychosocial Perspectives."

58. De Zulueta, *From Pain to Violence,* p. xi.

59. I use *parent* and *parental* to refer to the primary caregiver; the terms do not apply only to a biological parent.

60. Lopez et al., "Drug Use with Parents."

61. Robinson and Ryder, "Psychosocial Perspectives."

62. M. Brown ("Discourses of Choice") and Hussain et al. ("Violence in the Lives of Girls") are among the feminist researchers who do discuss perceptions of girls living outside of conventional family and neighborhood arrangements and their positions on the margins of social life and discourse.

63. De Zulueta, *From Pain to Violence,* p. xi.

2

Understanding Attachment Gone Wrong

I didn't know how to, like, just sit there and really start
a conversation with somebody in my family.
—Elena, 14 years old

Youth violence shatters our image of children as innocent, pure, and in need of protection. Politicians and other decisionmakers offer up the violence as evidence of a "tough new breed" of criminal from a generation of "out of control, disrespectful, anti-establishment and . . . potentially dangerous" youth.[1] New, more punitive legislation generally follows. When girls are the subject of the story, societal responses are especially pointed.[2] Girls who do not quite fit within tightly prescribed gender norms, and by their actions venture beyond hegemonic expectations, become "bad": the focus of professionals, scholars, institutions, and a media seemingly intent on branding girls as "wild" and "mean."[3] The small percentage of young women who use or threaten to use force are vilified as doubly deviant ("as 'not-women' or as masculine, unfeminine women").[4] The normative view is that girls internalize their pain and aggression (e.g., by eating disorders, substance abuse, or suicide); externalized violence is the province of boys. When girls are not compliant in their behavior (i.e., are violent), we confront an "ideological contradiction": girls who are noncompliant with our own understanding of what it means to be a young woman.[5] Physically violent girls present a threat to the established order and make us terribly anxious.[6]

Out of social anxiety and fear whole groups of young women, most notably young women of color, are labeled and punished as *vio-*

21

lent offenders—a deceptively flexible and expanding category that can encompass mean suburban schoolgirls, urban gangstas, and nearly everything in between.[7] This mass labeling process takes place with little sense of how girls define and understand the familial and community contexts of violence in their lives or how those environments shape relationships and behaviors. By these omissions, we separate girls' actions from their meaning and overlook the milieu in which they are based: the "reality that girls experience various forms of violence in their everyday lives."[8] And more important, we fail to see the interconnected and relational quality of violence. Gender essentialism (i.e., the idea that the use of violence is inherently masculine) complicates the discussion and makes it difficult for policymakers, practitioners, researchers, and others to see girls holistically: to acknowledge both the harms girls can and do inflict on others, and the harms that have been done to girls.[9] Policies and praxis instead tend to concentrate on controlling the former, placing thousands of young girls in residential custody[10] with little consideration of—or treatment for—internal relational dynamics that in conjunction with social and cultural forces underlie acts of violence.

Both developmental life-course theories and the feminist pathway perspective have been in the forefront of efforts to bring "the formative period of childhood back into the picture," and link experiences in childhood with later offending.[11] Developmental criminology's emphasis on the continuity of antisocial behaviors and offending from childhood to adolescence to adulthood, and the interest in how transitions (or turning points) reshape life-course trajectories are important to a fuller understanding of violent behavior. But only a few such studies have focused entirely on the pathways of females.[12] On the other hand, over the past 30 years, feminist criminology has generated a significant body of empirical research that documents the prominence of victimization and trauma in the lives of female offenders, with evidence that many of women's so-called senseless and random acts of violence occur after years of abuse and dominance, sexism, and racism. This research demonstrates the potential of gendered life events, such as sexual abuse and assault, to negatively redirect the lives of its victims.[13]

Feminist scholars in both criminology and psychology have continued to expand the discourse, augmenting victimization research with studies of social and cultural factors in the production of violent behavior. Examinations of girls' fights have associated their occurrence with the individual's place in the status hierarchy; trivial altercations may mask symbolic contests of dominance and deference and, in some cases, result in "horizontal" girl-on-girl violence.[14] Research has also exposed the racial and class relationships in girls' aggressive and violent behaviors; in separate ethnographic studies, Nikki Jones and Cindy Ness describe the constrictive worlds of low-income, inner-city girls of color. For girls forced to negotiate potential threats of interpersonal harm in dangerous urban neighborhoods, fighting can be a valuable resource for establishing a sense of security, mastery, status, and self-esteem.[15] Indicative, however, of the need to consider more closely the underlying mechanisms involved in girls' violence, Ness examines girls' "emotional logic" for fighting and, in other work, Susan Batchelor and colleagues attribute imprisoned girls' aggression and negative worldview (in which other people are perceived as being "out to get you") to deep-seated anger related to experiences of family violence and abuse.[16]

If we are to fully acknowledge and seek to explain what much of the prior research suggests—that girls who engage in violence in the context of gendered and racial oppression are often the same who experience extensive violation—it is important to locate girls in the context of their interpersonal relationships. An understanding of emotional connections (or lack thereof) helps to explain individual variation among girls subject to similar social, material, and gendered circumstances. When we explore how internal processes help to shape the meaning of violence, what might these "harmed and harming"[17] girls teach us about links among affectional ties, trauma, and violent behaviors? How might we then reformulate and address the problem that we so easily call "girls' violence"?

A relational model of women's psychology holds that an inner sense of connection with others is a central organizing feature of their developmental path to maturity: "girls' psychological strength derives from their connections with significant others."[18] Turning this around a bit, scholarship working to make sense of recurring themes of disconnection and victimization in female offenders' lives has suggested that the concept of "relationality" may be important to the initiation or acceleration of criminal offending. Citing Jean Baker Miller and Irene Stiver's support of women's "proclivity to nurture and be in relation through biological and cultural imperatives," psychologist Robin Robinson points out that this strength can become problematic and the female psychological self impoverished when women believe that staying in connection requires subjugating their own needs and desires to those of others, particularly those who have power over them.[19] Criminologist Beth Richie elaborates on this development among incarcerated, battered, black women who as youths occupied a privileged status in their families and as adults felt the need to "make good" on the family's investment in their future. With identities linked to meeting the needs of others, the women were vulnerable to abusive adult partners.[20]

Girls in general may be relational and empathic (innately or because of extensive informal and formal social controls, or a combination of both), but girls involved in violence often are enmeshed in nonempathic relationships with histories of loss, neglect, and abuse.[21] Unlike the women in Ritchie's study, the girls interviewed for this book grew up in households characterized by disconnection and violation, conditions that may diminish girls' sense of empathy (for themselves as well as others) and interfere with the development of rational thinking. Relationships as they exist are too often a source of pain, not a resource for girls' strength and power, and relationality is more likely to reference the opposite of an "ethic of care."[22]

Studies of pathways and contexts, and investigations attentive to childhood and gender and underlying mechanisms, are critical research foci that advance the field in multiple and important ways. Yet criminology's answers to questions about how childhood events and experiences influence a young woman to engage in violent behaviors herself remain incomplete. In this book, I draw on both criminological and psychological traditions of developmental theory and examine girls' early relationships in the context of their family and community dynamics.

This analysis is informed, in particular, by the tenets of attachment theory in conjunction with knowledge about the effects of chronic trauma. The result is both a story about the lives of one group of girls imprisoned for a violent offense and a theoretical story—a model for explaining connections between young women's early childhood experiences, internal processes, and violent behaviors. Relying on the words of individual girls, I show how disruptions in early relationships anticipate defensive responses, and how violent behaviors can be understood as what De Zulueta describes as "attachment gone wrong."[23]

In the following section, I summarize major themes. I discuss my findings in greater detail in each of the subsequent chapters using excerpts from the girls' interviews to illustrate theoretical arguments.

Figure 2.1 outlines the elements of an attachment-based model of female adolescent violence, derived from the data, and is presented to assist in understanding those data; as such, the model may not be congruent with studies of other girls in other contexts. This theoretical model illustrates intersecting influences and developments, and provides a framework for making sense of behaviors often measured only in terms of normative and legalistic formulations. It does not suggest causality. I provide a brief overview of attachment theory before discussing how the disruption of relationships may produce traumagenic effects; how the violent behaviors of one group of girls can be understood both as a defensive response and as a distorted attempt to connect with others.

Attachment Theory

Attachment theory addresses "how human beings become attached to their caretakers and subsequently to others." The theory has evolved into a leading developmental and social personality model with varied branches of theoretical and empirical inquiry and a range of applications.[24] At its heart, this theoretical perspective stresses the importance

**Figure 2.1 An Attachment-Based Model
of Female Adolescent Violence**

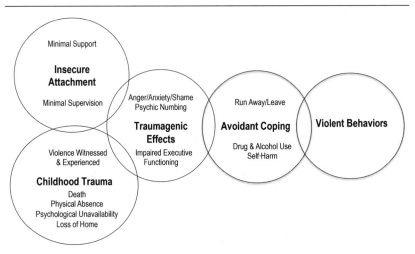

of early childhood relationships with both parents to the child's ability to form affectional bonds; in its various forms, it is key to explaining normative processes of human development.[25]

As with developmental criminology and life-course theories, attachment theories stress the primacy of early childhood as a determinate of later life behavior, but here attachment is conceptualized as the natural bonds of affection between infants and significant others. This is in sharp contrast to theories that assume the absence of attachment to be the natural state wherein socialization, and thereby attachment, is acquired through the imposition of parental monitoring and punishment.[26] Attachment theory asserts that relationships in the earliest stages of life shape basic survival functions and that the ongoing innate need for connection with others is influential throughout the life span: "attachment processes lie at the center of the human experience."[27]

Attachment theory "is the joint work of John Bowlby and Mary Ainsworth,"[28] though Bowlby is perhaps more well known. Originally trained in Kleinian psychoanalysis, Bowlby focused his research on the effects of loss and separation after observing the reactions of British children to the loss of parents in the aftermath of World War II.[29] He incorporated into his work observations of hospitalized and institutionalized children separated from their parents and Ainsworth's empirical studies of children's relationship patterns with their mothers.[30] Bowlby explains that "attachment behavior" refers to various forms of behavior that result in a person "attaining or maintaining proximity to some other clearly defined individual who is conceived as better able to cope with the world."[31] Ainsworth and colleagues used Bowlby's attachment model to develop a procedure (the "Strange Situation") to measure the quality of children's attachment relationships with their parents or primary caregiver, distinguishing between secure and insecure attachment styles.[32]

In the context of the child-parent relationship, attachment is part of an "interactive self-regulatory system" through which newborns develop a repertoire of behaviors directed toward the caregiver under conditions of stress, threat, fatigue, or illness.[33] Signaling behaviors such as babbling, crying, clinging, and the "social smile" gain the caregiver's attention, care, and proximity. Displays of anger also are a natural response of a child when the expectation of safety is jeopardized.[34] All of these behaviors, as well as others, serve to relieve the infant's distress and strengthen the relationship between child and caregiver.[35] The attachment behaviors establish a base to which the child can return when exploring her surroundings; the base promotes a sense of self-reliance and autonomy and enhances a child's resilience when confronted with stress.[36] Eventually, repeated interactions between infant and caregiver form a reciprocal and organized internal strategy, or working model.

Derived from studies of the effects of maternal deprivation on personality development, attachment theory is built on the premise that human beings are social animals. Relationships replace instincts as humans naturally seek attachment and social cooperation.[37] Infants are essentially "preprogrammed to develop in a socially cooperative way; whether they do so or not turns in high degree on how they are treated."[38] Children with sensitive, responsive caregivers develop a secure attachment and a positive working model of themselves and others; they develop a sense of trust, which allows them to tolerate separations, regulate affect, and mature and thrive in future attachments. They are confident that help and comfort will be available when they feel threatened. The early and ongoing experience of having been understood in the context of a secure attachment relationship develops within children a capacity to understand and interpret the behaviors of others in terms of the underlying intentional mental states.[39] This understanding is a developmental achievement, the acquisition of which depends on the quality of attachment relationships.

If attachment is insecure, healthy behaviors (in terms of exploration, play, affect regulation, and social interactions) are impaired. Children whose caregivers are unable to provide a sense of security tend to view themselves and others negatively, and their ability to accurately perceive the mental states of others may be diminished. Some children may come to fear abandonment and seek heightened intimacy in close relationships, or be uncomfortable with closeness and dependency on others.[40] When a caregiver's insensitivity is pervasive, the child's normal anger response may turn to aggression; such aggression, or in Bowlby's terms, dysfunctional anger, further threatens the security of the attachment bond.[41] Whether the working model is secure or insecure, it affects the way children see themselves and how they respond to others. Interactively developed in relation with the caregiver, the template is imposed on future relationships, "distorting the child's perceptions to fit the template, and shaping reactions to the [other] as if to follow the primary attachment pattern."[42]

Weak Parental Efficacy and Childhood Trauma

When interviewed for this study, the girls' average age was 15 years old. Their narratives reveal their struggles to mature in homes characterized by loss, victimization, and neglect.[43] Our inquiries addressed parental attachment, support, and supervision, and each was found lacking. Emotional and instrumental support was rare; the girls rarely spoke with anyone in the household when something was bothering them. In contrast to normative images of the protected female, the girls received little supervision and often rebelled against what existed. Caregivers' limited responsiveness and inconsistent restrictiveness promoted greater autonomy so that the girls were generally on their own to negotiate an inhospitable and difficult world. Adults offered "little to alleviate, and much to aggravate, the anxieties, lonesome vulnerabilities, and bewildering injustice" that many of the girls experienced.[44] The weak parental efficacy that the teenage girls describe is compounded by narratives of extensive childhood trauma within homes and communities where the girls came of age.

Early experiences of attunement with primary caregivers shape children's developing ability to regulate and care for the self, and affect whether they feel that they are deserving or unworthy of good care.[45] When children are neglected, abandoned, or abused, the maltreatment presents a threat and triggers the overactivation of the attachment system "often paradoxically in relation to the abuser who is at once the source of threat and the hope for its containment."[46] They may desperately seek physical closeness while trying to create mental distance because to "recognize the hatred implied by the parent's abuse" is dangerous to their sense of self, forcing these children to see themselves as bad, unlovable, and unwanted by anyone.[47] Such a profound disruption, or lack of formation, of the primary bond implicates attachment processes and can produce traumagenic effects.

Trauma, in a broad sense, encompasses events that are extremely upsetting and substantially change how we think and feel about the world.[48] While many different types of upsetting events and conditions have the potential to be traumatic, whether they become so depends in great measure on the individual's perceptions. Traumatic events contain both objective characteristics and subjective responses of the exposed person.[49] They are those events that the individual cannot assimilate, "events so unfathomable that they fragment the mind."[50] In response, a child may become hypervigilant, constantly on guard for signs of the feared event and physiologically poised to confront the danger. Multiple or intense exposures to danger may activate "the systems contributing to hyperarousal," causing the body to respond to the slightest provocation, even under circumstances that in actuality are nonthreatening.[51] In combination with malformed attachment, proximity of the threat may trigger a defensive violent reaction.

The girls in this study were exposed to community and familial violence, both as subjects and witnesses. The array of their victimizations included physical and sexual assault and severe neglect by caregivers. When the caregiver inflicts harm—the caregiver-turned-predator—the results are especially damaging. The child must confront an impossible situation: "wanting to be comforted by the [caregiver] yet terrified of being annihilated by the [caregiver]."[52] Children in this situation are forced to develop incompatible internal representations (working models) of the self and the other.[53] Maltreated children may mentally "split" off the harming other; Peter Fonagy describes this as the child's mind seeking to compromise by "accepting physical comfort yet creating mental distance."[54] In so doing, children further disrupt their capacity to conceive of and reflect on their own mental states and those of others in the attachment dyad. Other family members, as well as acquaintances and strangers, assaulted the girls in this study, and most girls were witnesses to stabbings and shootings, beatings and killings, and told of awakening to outbursts of nearby gunfire, house fires, and explosions. In describing unsafe, often predatory homes and neighborhoods that conjure up images of war zones, the girls expressed anger, anxiety, and shame at their own vulnerability and the lack of instrumental and expressive support, protection, and guidance from adults. Rather than receive help to internally resolve (work through) these experiences and events, most girls were betrayed, ignored, or punished and left alone to somehow manage traumagenic effects. The absence or disruption of psychological attachments increased their emotional vulnerability and eventually induced what Karen Hayslett-McCall and Thomas Bernard describe as a state of social detachment: "a traumatic failure of the [primary caretaker] to meet the child's attachment needs."[55]

In addition to events commonly thought of as traumatic (e.g., war, torture, and abuse), loss must also be included. The sudden disappearance of a caregiver, for example, may stimulate severe distress and constitute a traumatic experience among children, particularly if there is not another loving and attuned person available. The girls in this study describe multiple losses; grouped into four types, these include *death of a loved one, physical absence, psychological unavailability,* and *loss of home.* On the surface, many of these losses appear ordinary and typical of those in the general population. But a closer inspection reveals an intensity and severity that moves beyond commonplace preconceptions and counters generalizations that overlook the often detrimental effects on children's psychological and emotional development.

The girls spoke of the death of an elderly grandparent—not an infrequent occurrence for their age group. But these deaths were cumulative. Several other relatives and friends also died, frequently under violent and socially stigmatized contexts: the uncle who overdosed in the bathtub, the friend shot in the neck while perched on the curb, the mother who succumbed to AIDS. Similarly, although widespread in US culture, when the girls talked of divorce or marital separation, they typically spoke of fathers who were suddenly and completely absent, frequently replaced by a rotation of strangers. Mass incarceration of poor and African American and Hispanic populations is well documented, and the girls' narratives reflect the personal pain and confusion of recurring parental jail and prison sentences.[56] In other situations, caregivers, though alive and physically present in the girls' lives, were absorbed or otherwise engaged in their own substance use, illness, and activities, unable to emotionally provide for their daughters; some girls were forced to assume responsibility for parents who could not care for themselves. Many girls also suffered the loss of home, having been placed in foster care, residential treatment centers, and group homes, or kicked out, burned out, or evicted from stable family settings.

With her working model of the world impaired, the traumatized child may perceive a lack of meaning, control, or connection in her life and therefore assume there is no place where she is safe.[57] And in an unsafe world, she must be in a constant state of readiness, prepared to act quickly to any perceived hostility.[58] Attachment theory, without using the terminology of object relations (and without a review of that extensive literature and its focus on psychological defenses to preserve the self), suggests a relationship between attachment processes, trauma, and the powerful defense of dissociation.[59]

Dissociation is a protective discontinuity in mental functioning brought on by a perceived threat of danger or annihilation. It allows a child to "maintain the attachment necessary for physical and psychic survival" while, at least temporarily, avoiding pain, feelings of powerlessness, and overwhelming memories (though all may surface in the form of nightmares and flashbacks).[60] Cognition is separated from affect, and the inability to integrate the trauma (a single overwhelming event or a pattern of events) may result in psychic numbing, amnesia, and repetitive reenactments of the event without a sense of its history or purpose. Blocked executive functioning in a trauma-saturated child may produce a range of additional defensive behaviors.[61]

Having endured numerous and varied traumas, and been denied their caregivers' love and attention, support, and supervision, the girls in this study tend to minimize their need for relationships. Many describe feeling emotionally shut down. Psychic numbing may contribute to subsequent defiant, disruptive, and immature behaviors—further complicating relationships with others. Running away from home and substance use (and, for a small number of the girls, attempts at self-harm) seemed reasonable responses to unreasonable conditions: proactive means of resisting abusive treatment and allaying painful emotions. These measures helped the girls psychologically defend against uncontrollable conditions, even as each proved self-injurious and led them into other, sometimes more dangerous, situations.[62] Avoidant coping is ineffective in containing the enormity of the girls' current problems and the emotions associated with earlier traumas. Deciphering the world through the lens of childhood, the girls were caught between internal beliefs fostered by disrupted attachments (i.e., the expectation of hostile others, just as parents and caregivers had treated them) and an external enmeshment in families and communities abundant in perceived and actual threats. Supported by the twin needs of defending the emotional self and seeking attachment and connection, defensive responses become manifest in aggressive and violent behaviors.[63]

Returning to 14-year-old Elena, introduced in Chapter 1, we can see how her history is reflected in the proposed attachment-based model of female adolescent violence (Figure 2.1). Like all the girls in this study, Elena experienced extensive losses and victimizations at an early age. These were not minor stressors, but traumatic events that altered her sense of safety in the world. Having spent her formative years in various foster care placements, Elena's predisposition for closeness is disrupted and her expectations about relationships colored by an early and protracted separation. Within her family of origin, she is physically abused and suffers the loss of several family members to substance abuse, illness, incarceration, and death. Elena describes her neighborhood as violent and, by way of example, tells of witnessing a woman stab a man in her apartment building's elevator in the middle of the afternoon, and of a girlfriend who was raped and left to die on a rooftop. Elena becomes pregnant at 13; her infant son is in another state with the child's father. She has little reflective access to her inner life and psychically walls off emotional needs; she does not tell anyone when something is bothering her "because I didn't know how to, like, just sit there and really start a conversation with somebody in my family." She has come to expect hostility from others and so her internal working model leans toward preemptive aggression.

In the wake of relational disruptions and other traumatic experiences, and lacking attuned others to help process and assimilate traumagenic effects, Elena is overwhelmed by feelings of anger, fear, shame, and guilt. She tries to alleviate her distress and protect herself from unwanted thoughts and memories of those experiences by physical means. She leaves home countless times because "I was really frustrated . . . and I didn't know how to handle myself," and regularly consumes excessive amounts of alcohol and marijuana. She joins an all-girl gang and, due to her violent activities, ascends to the position of "mother." In this context, she attempts to compensate for the support and love that are in short supply from her caregivers. Of her gang activities she says, "I got respect. People trust me."

When faced with new threats to the self, and burdened with years of unresolved trauma, Elena's coping strategies were insufficient in defending against emotional distress. In the incident on the subway train described in Chapter 1, Elena offers a compliment to an older woman that is immediately rejected; the woman insults Elena and her friends as "black Bs" and as "kids" who should be home in bed. Being high on marijuana does not dull Elena's emotional pain or deactivate her state of hyperarousal. The woman's comments provoke in Elena suppressed emotions associated with her long history of rejection, abuse, and loss. Absent rational, reflective thinking, Elena's ability to empathize with the woman and to regulate her own behavior is compromised. Having faced actual abandonment and real threats of annihilation as a younger child, Elena responds to what she considers to be another threat with "extreme and unreasoned defenses of survival."[64] The physicality provides a concrete solution to interpsychic problems. Her behavior, broadly speaking, can be seen as a reaction to her attachment insecurity[65]—a maladaptive, distortive attempt to realize her deep desire for engagement in an emotional interchange.

Disrupted relationships and chronic trauma commenced early in life for all of the girls in this study. In the following chapter, I present their stories as they begin to describe perceptions and recollections of minimal parental attachment, support, and supervision.

Notes

1. Kilty, "Gendering Violence," p. 156; Templeton, "Superscapegoating."
2. See Buzawa and Hirschel, "Criminalizing Assault."
3. Males, "Have 'Girls Gone Wild'?" Girls' participation in street fights, infanticide, and other acts of violence has been indicated for at least the past century, but contemporary fears were heightened in part by discussions in the mid-1990s among some criminologists, politicians, and policy groups of the pending arrival of superpredators (Fox, *Trends in Juvenile Violence;* DiIulio, "Coming of the Super-Predators"; McNulty, "Natural Born Killers?").
4. Heidensohn, *Women and Crime,* p. 96. Gibson ("The 'Female Offender,'" p. 161) quotes Cesare Lombroso's description of the female offender's double deviancy in *La Donne Delinquent* (p. 152): "[a] criminal in civilized society and a woman among criminals" and "as a double exception, the criminal woman is consequently a monster." Two images of an inherent female nature continue to dominate the criminological commentary. One depicts the "bad" woman as dark, hairy, and aggressive (i.e., masculine), a social threat beyond rehabilitation; the alternate image portrays the "good" woman led astray by her own base instincts or by a male consort (Rafter, "Hard Times"; Backhouse, *Petticoats and Prejudice*).
5. M. Brown, "Negotiations," p. 179.
6. Schur (*Labeling Women Deviant,* p. 9) found that attempts of the powerful to define *deviance* are based on perceptions that the object of concern presents "some kind of threat to their specific interests or overall social position." Perspectives on public anxiety associated with violence by girls are discussed in Robinson and Ryder, "Psychosocial Perspectives"; Luke, "Are Girls Really Becoming More Violent?"; Barron and Lacombe, "Moral Panic."
7. The terms *violent* and *violent offender* are used loosely in the public arena to describe a range of actions and behaviors. See, for example, Simmons, *Odd Girl Out;* Scelfo, "Bad Girls Go Wild"; Begum, "Girl 'Gangstas' Siege on Family." In addition to lay terminology, official offense labels have broad definitions that can include behaviors previously addressed outside the justice system. Singer (*Recriminalizing Delinquency*) provides a case study of New York legislation enacted in response to public fears of juvenile violence (in the context of the Willie Boskett subway killings and an upcoming gubernatorial election) that redefined previous acts of delinquency as crimes and delinquents as juvenile offenders. Bartollas ("Little Girls Grow Up") illustrates how relabeling and "bootstrapping" girls' minor offenses (e.g., status offenses such as incorrigibility) to assault and other criminal offenses

34   Girls and Violence

have been particularly pronounced in the official delinquency and confinement of African American girls.

8. Hussain et al., "Violence in Lives of Girls," p. 59.

9. Practitioners have often claimed that girls are more difficult than boys to work with (Belknap et al., "Understanding Incarcerated Girls") and that girls direct aggression and hostility toward workers within the system (Okamoto, "Challenges of Male Practitioners").

10. See Gaarder and Belknap, "Tenuous Borders." The actual number of girls whose lives have been affected by system involvement is substantial. After 1995, girls arrested for a crime against a person faced an increasing likelihood of being formally processed, adjudicated delinquent, and placed in custody. Puzzanchera et al., *Juvenile Court Statistics 2006–2007,* p. 52. In the United States in 1996, approximately 3,400 female juveniles were adjudicated for an offense against a person and placed in residential custody. That number increased every year until 2010, when the number decreased to approximately 3,300. In 2003, the highest number of this category of offenders was 4,500. Puzzanchera and Kang, *Easy Access to Juvenile Court Statistics 1985–2010,* http://www.ojjdp.gov/ojstatbb/ezajcs; Snyder and Sickmund, *Juvenile Offenders and Victims.*

11. Sampson and Laub, *Crime in the Making,* p. 24. Farrington uses the term "developmental and life-course criminology (DLC)" to specify four theories or paradigms that are "essentially concerned with the same interlinked set of issues" associated with the development of offending and antisocial behavior, risk factors at different ages, and the effects of life events on the course of development. It is distinguished from other groups of theories by a particular interest in the relationship between age and criminal behavior across the life span. See Farrington, "Developmental and Life-Course Criminology," p. 222; Farrington, "Explaining the Beginning."

12. Moffitt et al., *Sex Differences in Antisocial Behavior;* Moffitt and Caspi, "Childhood Predictors"; Silverthorn and Frick, "Developmental Pathways." Farrington ("Developmental and Life-Course Criminology," p. 247) states that "generally, DLC findings and theories apply to offending by lower class urban males in Western industrialized societies in the past 80 years or so," and recommends that future DLC research "compare development, risk factors, and life events for males versus females and for different ethnic and racial groups."

13. Reviews include J. Miller and Mullins, "The Status of Feminist Theories"; Siegel and Williams "Child Sexual Abuse and Female Delinquency"; Gaarder and Belknap, "Tenuous Borders"; Holsinger, "Differential Pathways to Violence." See also Arnold, "Processes of Victimization"; Chesney-Lind, "Girls' Crime and Woman's Place"; Gilfus, "From Victims to Survivors"; Goodkind et al., "Impact of Sexual Abuse."

14. Griffiths et al., "Fighting over Trivial Things"; Batacharya, "Racism, 'Girl Violence,' and Murder." Similar to Artz's argument (*Sex, Power and the Violent School Girl*) that as a powerless group, girls mimic the oppressor (males) and attack similarly situated females. L. Brown (*Raising Their Voices,* pp. 4–5) contends that in a sexist society it is easier and safer for girls

to take out anxieties and anger on other girls rather than confront males or the larger society.

15. Jones, *Between Good and Ghetto;* Ness, *Why Girls Fight.*

16. Batchelor et al., "Discussing Violence," p. 3; Batchelor, "Prove Me the Bam!"

17. Daly, "Women's Pathways to Felony Court," p. 28.

18. Debold et al., "Cultivating Hardiness Zones," p. 182. J. B. Miller ("Development of Women's Sense of Self") describes the female developmental paradigm as growth through mutuality by sustaining relations and affiliations with others. L. Brown and Gilligan, *Meeting at the Crossroads;* Debold et al., *Mother Daughter Revolution.* See also Blyth and Traeger, "Adolescent Self-Esteem."

19. Robinson, "It's Not Easy," p. 34; J. B. Miller and Stiver, *Healing Connection.* Failinger ("Lessons Unlearned," p. 497) notes that, for some women, the problem of criminality is specific to "their relationships with men in their lives."

20. Richie, *Compelled to Crime.*

21. Gilligan et al., *Making Connections.* Early research by Konopka (*Adolescent Girl in Conflict*) found that among girls in juvenile court, most of whom were adjudicated delinquent, the need for connection with "real friends" and adults was unusually intense. The girls were lonely and expressed an absence of bonds with adults and peers that would foster a positive self-image. See Artz, *Sex, Power and the Violent School Girl;* Batchelor, "Prove Me the Bam!"

22. Gilligan, *In a Different Voice;* J. B. Miller, *Toward a New Psychology.*

23. De Zulueta, *From Pain to Violence,* p. 64.

24. Farber, "Dissociation, Traumatic Attachments," p. 63. See S. Mitchell, *Relationality;* Bretherton, "Origins of Attachment Theory."

25. Fairchild, "Attachment Theory"; Grossman et al., *Attachment from Infancy to Adulthood.*

26. Hirschi, *Causes of Delinquency;* Sroufe and Fleeson, "Attachment and Construction of Relationships"; Coble et al., "Attachment, Social Competency." Though David Farrington ("Childhood Risk Factors," p. 616) argues that "the sociological equivalent of attachment theory is social bonding theory," sociological/criminological social bond and social control theories (on which DLC theories are based) address childhood bonds only in terms of how effectively caregivers bring under control children's destructive impulses and tendencies toward delinquency.

27. Schore and Schore, "Modern Attachment Theory," p. 9.

28. Bretherton, "Origins of Attachment Theory," p. 759.

29. Newcombe and Lerner, "Britain Between the Wars."

30. See Bretherton, "Origins of Attachment Theory," for a discussion of the theoretical and empirical contributions of Mary Ainsworth and other researchers, including James Robertson.

31. Bowlby, *A Secure Base,* pp. 26–27.

32. Ainsworth and colleagues ("Individual Differences") note three distinct patterns of attachment: secure, avoidant, and resistant/ambivalent. A fourth

36 *Girls and Violence*

pattern, disorganized attachment, was later identified (Main and Solomon, "Procedures for Identifying").

33. According to Sander ("Regulation of Exchange," p. 133), the "infant and the caregiving environment show an organization of their interactions almost from the outset but one which undergoes a process of change in ensuing weeks and months, shifting from a more prominently *biosocial* to a more clearly *psychosocial* level"(emphasis in original).

34. Bowlby, *Separation*.

35. Wenar, *Developmental Psychopathology*, p. 35; Connor, *Aggression and Antisocial Behavior*.

36. Sroufe and Waters, "Heart Rate"; Bowlby, *A Secure Base*.

37. De Zulueta, *From Pain to Violence*; Bowlby, *A Secure Base*.

38. Bowlby, *A Secure Base*, p. 9.

39. Fonagy et al. ("Morality, Disruptive Behavior," pp. 256–257) refer to the capacity to envision the state of mind of the other or to assume the existence of thoughts and feelings in others and in oneself as "mentalization."

40. Ainsworth et al., *Patterns of Attachment*.

41. Bowlby, *Separation*, p. 249.

42. Blizard and Bluhm, "Attachment to the Abuser," p. 384; Shapiro and Levendorsky, "Adolescent Survivors."

43. See Ryder, "'I Wasn't Really Bonded,'" for a detailed listing of traumatic events.

44. Gadd, "Masculinities," p. 443.

45. Farber, "Dissociation, Traumatic Attachments," p. 64.

46. Fonagy ("Male Perpetrators," p. 10) cites Rajecki, Lamb, and Obmascher, "Toward a General Theory of Infantile Attachment."

47. Fonagy, "Male Perpetrators," p. 15. See also Bowlby, *Separation*, p. 238.

48. Herman, *Trauma and Recovery*.

49. American Psychiatric Association, *DSM-IV-TR;* A. Freud, "Comments on Psychic Trauma."

50. Farber, "Dissociation, Traumatic Attachments," p. 64; Howell, *The Dissociative Mind*.

51. Karr-Morse and Wiley, *Ghosts*, p. 162.

52. Farber, "Dissociation," p. 65; Hurvich, "The Place of Annihilation Anxieties." See Robinson's ("Since I Couldn't," p. 199) discussion of Anna Freud's ("Psychic Trauma") three unconscious fears that underlie mechanisms of defense against traumatic stimuli: fear of loss of love object, fear of loss of love from love object, and fear of annihilation.

53. Bowlby, *Separation;* Howell, *Dissociative Mind*.

54. Fonagy, "Male Perpetrators," p. 14.

55. Hayslett-McCall and Bernard, "Attachment, Masculinity, and Self-Control," p. 12.

56. The research on how imprisonment affects both family and community relationships is limited, but see Arditti, *Parental Incarceration;* Siegel, *Disrupted Childhoods;* Johnston, "Effects of Parental Incarceration"; Harris et al., *Children of Incarcerated Parents;* Clear et al., "Incarceration and the Community."

57. Herman, *Trauma and Recovery*.

58. van der Kolk, "Trauma and Memory."

59. Farber, "Dissociation, Traumatic Attachments," p. 64.

60. Blizard and Bluhm, "Attachment to the Abuser," p. 386.

61. Robinson and Ryder, "Psychosocial Perspectives."

62. Mikulincer and Florian, "Coping and Adaptation."

63. M. Erikson et al., "Quality of Attachment and Behavior Problems"; Egeland et al., "Pre-school Behavior Problems"; Sroufe et al., "Implications of Attachment Theory."

64. Robinson and Ryder, "Psychosocial Perspectives."

65. Fonagy et al., "Morality, Disruptive Behavior."

3

The First Relationship: Parental Bonds

I didn't think nobody would listen to me at home.
—*Jackie, 13 years old*

The relationship between a child and her caregiver matters. This may appear obvious, but it is a point generally overlooked by many traditional explanations of adolescent violence. Rarely explored are dynamics of this early relationship and how these dynamics may influence later behavior. We tend to forget "how malleable a child's mind is, how eagerly it absorbs and shapes itself to the notions it is given from sources it has no reason to doubt, no choice but to trust."[1] Nondevelopmental theories applied to the girls in this study might assume that "the behavioral or life-course pathways that eventually lead to these adolescent outcomes also began during adolescence," rather than consider that the violent behaviors that brought the girls into state custody in their teen years were in some measure related to prior relational experiences.[2]

Despite widespread beliefs that adolescence is inherently contentious, this developmental period is not necessarily all storm and stress. Certainly, major realignments in family relations occur during adolescence, but these adjustments alone do not threaten the integrity of the parent-child attachment; most adolescents develop responsible autonomy without emotional detachment.[3] During adolescence the critical parent-child bond may be reconfigured as bonds to social institutions and the adults that represent them (e.g., teachers and employers), but the underlying structures remain the same.[4] Thus, the relational transformation that occurs is moderated by the quality of the parent-

39

child relationship prior to the teenage years.[5] For children with disrupted attachments, then, the transition to adolescence is undermined because psychological structures that reinforce parental bonds have been inadequately developed. Under these conditions, the stresses of adolescence may push some toward violent behaviors.[6]

The First Relationship

Attachment theory assumes the primacy of relationships, and the first and most significant relationship is the affectional tie between a child and her caregiver. By definition, this bond involves a specific person who holds emotional significance and to whom the infant looks for security, comfort, and guidance.[7] The quality of the attachment reflects the quality of care, a finding Mary Ainsworth and colleagues established in both naturalistic home studies and in their Strange Situation research. Replicated multiple times and around the world, the Strange Situation procedure allows researchers to observe behaviors of 1-year-olds in the presence and absence of the primary caregiver.[8] The researchers are then able to demonstrate attachment patterns, grouping the children according to their responses to the separation. Those designated "securely attached" might protest the caregiver's departure and require a moment of comforting on return (a show of irritation or anger signaling the need for proximity), but then the attachment behavior deactivates and the children resume their play. Children in the other two "insecurely attached" groups manifest high anxiety, distress, or ambivalent anger as if uncertain of the caregiver's reliability, or they may show little or no emotion (i.e., presenting a flat affect, averting their gaze, and avoiding the caregiver). In the latter, the 1-year-olds appear to cognitively disconnect feelings from the situation that provoked distress.[9] Children who manifest detached or avoidant behavior after experiences of separation from their caregivers also display high levels of aggression, suggesting a link between loss and deprivation and violent behavior.[10]

As children develop verbal and other capabilities, primary caregivers can assist them with short-term planning and adjustment to separations, and teach them boundaries and new ways to express themselves. When such parenting is provided in the context of a consistent, loving, and supportive environment, children come to understand that their emotions will not overwhelm their caregiver, but rather the caregiver will remain attuned to their needs. Because the children's internal working model of the caregiver (the attachment figure) and the self develops in a "complimentary and mutually confirming" manner, the children acquire an expectancy of safety. They experience the caregiver as available, responsive, and sensitive, and the self as worthy of love and attention. Children whose caregiver's responsiveness helps them to achieve their goals develop "confidence in [their] own ability to control what happens to [them]." As they begin the process of differentiating from the caregiver, a sense of self unfolds.[11]

Conversely, if the relationship between a child and her caregiver is characterized by emotional or behavioral difficulties, the child experiences the caregiver as distant, uncaring, and rejecting, and the self as unworthy of love and attention. When a caregiver judges a child's negative affect (e.g., irritability or anger) intolerable or "bad," without helping her to develop "internalized control or more mature forms of emotional expression," the child may persist in her ways.[12] In time, the behavior can become functional, as a way for the child to engage the attention (attachment behaviors) she needs, but may not otherwise receive from the insensitive caregiver. In her insecurity about the caregiver's love and responsiveness, the child will hold on to even a neglectful, insensitive, or maltreating caregiver and, internalizing the perceptions and expectations of others, cast herself as bad and unlovable. The attachment patterns that ensue may increase the likelihood of behaviors deemed antisocial or deviant.[13]

A caregiver's willingness and readiness to understand a child's needs and mental states is the basis for the development of reflective functioning in the child. What becomes developmentally significant is "the representation of the parent-child relationship in the child's mind."[14] And thus I begin my analysis with the girls' perspectives on that relationship (usually with their mother) in terms of attachment, support, and supervision.[15] But first, it is important to bear in mind the environment in which the girls' perceptions were formed; that is, to ground their observations and evaluations in the context of families and communities. Over 60 years ago, John Bowlby emphasized the necessity of social networks and the importance of economic and health factors in the development of healthy parent-child relationships. He specifies the connection between the well-being of parents and that of their young, and his call to support parents and the work they do is clear, even as it remains contrary to most contemporary public policies and praxis:

Just as children are absolutely dependent on their parents for sustenance, so . . . are parents, especially their mothers, dependent on a greater society for economic provision. If a community values its children it must cherish its parents.[16]

Attachment theorists have continued to identify key environmental influences that can severely undermine the development of secure attachments, including life stress and family adversity, parental psychopathology, and social support satisfaction.[17]

Though the scope of the current study does not include interviews with the girls' parents or other family members, and we cannot know with any certainty the state of the caregivers' mental health or the details of their lives, demographic data and the girls' narratives indicate significant familial stress, social marginalization, and deficient social supports. Much of the described parenting is deplorable, but there exists among these mostly African American and Hispanic parents the real possibility of their own experiences of unresolved loss and violation. In addition, the likelihood is great that the political, economic, and social conditions of the late 1980s interfered with effective parenting in marginalized pockets of the inner city.

The increasing concentration of poverty during the 1970s and 1980s and the "hypersegregration of African Americans" left large numbers unemployed—unqualified for opportunities in emerging technological and service fields and denied access to jobs in far-flung suburban areas or foreign countries.[18] Immigration patterns and economic restructuring, combined with unequal power relations along ethnic and gender lines, dramatically altered traditional family structures.[19] Describing conditions among distressed families in New York City, Eloise Dunlap and colleagues identify a litany of associated negative circumstances: "overcrowded housing, poor physical and mental health, despair, posttraumatic stress disorder, family dissolution, teen pregnancy, school dropout, interpersonal violence, crime, and drug and alcohol abuse, among others."[20]

Young mothers, barely out of childhood themselves, sought to maintain their space in the perceived freedom of (a highly misogynist) street culture while they simultaneously struggled beneath the weight of rigid gender norms that forced on them exclusive responsibility for child rearing. Female drug use was at historically high levels and, when necessary to support their habit, an increasing number of women turned to prostitution—even as the conditions of street-level sex work were rapidly declining.[21] Throughout the 1980s and into the mid-1990s, incidence and mortality rates of AIDS continued to soar, closely intertwined with drug use and sex work. The previously unknown disease terrified the nation, but it was particularly alarming for African Americans.[22] Adjusted rates of AIDS in African American women in 1996 were 17 times higher than that of white women and three times that of Latinas.[23] Though the number of deaths attributed to HIV/AIDS began to decline in 1996, at the end of 1998 in both New York City and the rest of the state AIDS remained the leading cause of death among 30- to 39-year-old black men and women and Hispanic men; it was the second leading cause of death for Hispanic women aged 20 to 39 years old.[24]

In the wake of monumental community dislocation, a generation of young parents living in chaotic, fragmented households and relationships had little time or sentiment for domestic routines supportive of family cohesion. Despite an oft-stated desire to care for their offspring, parents often acted in ways frightening to their children and injurious to strong parent-child bonds and healthy normative development. In adapting to dangerous and violent neighborhoods, caregivers' well-intentioned child-rearing practices may be detrimental in the long run. Prohibiting a girl from playing outdoors in order to protect her from stray bullets, or using punitive physical discipline to prevent her from succumbing to the negative influences of street life, may be sensible, practical strategies, but they may also impede opportunities for social engagement and heighten aggression by promoting the use of violence for social control.[25]

Representations of Attachment, Support, and Supervision

Attachment

Family structures vary by location within racial, religious, and ethnic cultures and geographically specific communities. Regardless of configuration and location, however, it is the family unit that forms the foundation of personality development. It is within the family institution, in the context of human events and interactions, that children develop an understanding of the self and the other. Representation of the attachment relationship is not a picture of the caregiver per se, "but rather the history of the caregiver's responses to the infant's actions or intended actions with/toward the attachment figure."[26] Resultant attachment behaviors are ongoing and open to review and change, especially during adolescence.[27] In this chapter, I offer a glimpse of the interactions within the girls' families in order to gauge how the girls, at the median age of 15 years old, represent the critical parent-child relationship. Their statements reveal how in daily life the pattern and quality of parental attachment, support, and supervision were closely intertwined, often in complex and conflicting ways, as in Adele's appraisal of her relationship with her mother:

> Anything I had to tell her I could tell her. It wasn't like she would beat me for it or anything. So she was open-minded. [Did you ever tell any of the people you lived with?] Nope. 'Cause I didn't want to. It was, I could've talked to her if I wanted to but I didn't want to.

Adele seeks to portray her mother as available and supportive, and begins by contrasting her mother with others who might be worse (she could have beaten her). Despite declaring that she could always talk to her "open-minded" mother, Adele is uncomfortable sharing thoughts and emotions when something is bothering her. This resistance, at least partially, reflects her belief that her confidences will be betrayed: "I guess I wanted to keep it to myself instead of telling her and then her telling, you know, my grandmother and my grandmother telling my aunt, and so on from there."

Adele was not alone in withholding her anxieties and concerns from others: the majority of the girls never spoke to anyone in their home about the things that troubled them. A common statement was: "We just didn't have that kind of relationship." Silence served both to protect the self and to preserve relationships with others. As a result, a sense of loneliness and disconnection was pervasive. The girls keep "their business" to themselves, convinced that there was no one who was available and empathetic. Claiming she has "nobody to talk to," Royale pauses to explain that what she really means is that of the people in her life, "nobody would understand." Jackie makes a similar assertion: "I didn't think nobody would listen to me at home."

In rare instances other adults were available to help relieve girls of their worries. Natalie describes the ease with which she could speak with her father's partner:

> I felt like my stepmother was like my best friend. 'Cause it's not like she's my "mother" mother. She won't yell, like yell, scream, scream. She'll try to understand or whatever. And then she's got a young mind, you know.

Natalie's relationship with her stepmother can be likened to that of *othermothers*—women in African American communities who take a real and persistent interest in the community's children.[28] Akin in some ways to biological mothers, othermothers are distinctive enough to allow girls the room to try out new ideas, speak of their experiences, and develop additional adult relationships uncomplicated by the mother-daughter bond.

Unfortunately, most of the girls in this study did not have the safety valve of an alternate adult with whom they could confide. From early childhood, and continuing into the teen years, the girls were for the most part denied the intrinsic pleasure of "mutuality in relationships" with their caregivers.[29] Internal reflection was not encouraged or practiced, and may have been blocked as a result of chronic trauma. With limited experience in even beginning a conversation about their emotional state, the girls had few incentives to try. Gayle is too "scared or shy" to attempt a discussion with her mother because "I wasn't brought up like, to talk," and Elena is clear: "I can't talk to nobody." The daughter of a crack-using mother and a sporadically present father, Elena laments that there is no time or place to talk to her parents about boys, how to dress, and "how to hold a relationship." Communication in the large and physically dispersed family is impeded "because everybody was just so busy and tired and didn't wanna do anything." Articulating the detached state of many of the girls, Elena describes her emotional isolation: "I wasn't like really bonded with my family 'cause I like to isolate myself from people. I don't like to be around a whole group of people. I hate being around people. That's the thing."

Fearing rejection and sensing emotional danger, girls learned early on to keep quiet ("I just don't, really, talk about my feelings"). Many girls who remained silent believed that, by disclosing their troubles, they would be perceived as a failure or a bad person. Jill describes this dilemma:

> I didn't think my mom would really understand what I was going through and how I felt. . . . I always thought that she's like an old-fashioned mom and that she was, she's different

from everybody else's mom. . . . A lot of things have happened to me that my mom doesn't know about me and I don't want her to think bad things about me, so I just, I didn't bother with it because I didn't want her go around thinking bad things about me.

Girls remain "out of true relationship," but paradoxically hope that in hiding their feelings they will somehow garner the attention they desperately desire.[30] Paula is afraid that her emotional needs will overwhelm or threaten her mother's love, and so she hides behind a defensive stance. She alludes to her yearning for a more loving mother-daughter relationship:

It was both of us. We didn't like each other. Well, I figured she didn't like me so I didn't like her. . . . The way she act, I didn't believe she liked me. 'Cause, it was like, she has a really stink attitude. She has it with everybody but still, I really felt that she shouldn't, 'cause I'm her daughter, you know? I could do nothing to her.

Paula struggles to explain why she never shared her feelings with others in the household, why she "never spoke up for myself." Recalling a simple and poignant example of her silence, she reveals the desire to please her caregivers, and protect the relationship, despite her own humiliation and rage:

I graduated sixth grade and everybody told me to bring in a, wear a white dress. My aunt bought me a blue and white dress, right? I went in the room. I was like, I can't wear this dress—supposed to be a white dress, but then I came out, saw how the dress look on me. She was like, do you like the dress? I was like yeah and everything. Didn't tell her I had to wear the dress to my graduation. The only one not wearing a white dress. I was the last one on line too cause I was the tallest and they was all laughing and stuff. I was mad, but I didn't say nothing.

Paula's perceived need to stay quiet lest she disrupt family relations was played out over and over again among the other girls in various settings. Their statements reflect the wish for emotional proximity and the fear that they will lose their caregiver's love. They discount their own worries and desires because they know that sharing can be dangerous to the self and to their relationships; in defense, they claim they did not "like people to be in my business" and assert they could "handle it or things would work out. I just had the feeling that I could do things myself." In circumstances of unsupportive households and communities, their sense of strength and inner resilience is protective and indeed often admirable, but isolation further undermines their attachments to others.

Just as most of the girls were not willing or able to confide in their caregivers, they generally did not feel emotionally safe and secure with anyone in the household.[31] When asked about emotional security, a number spoke of physical protection. Diane, for example, felt safe with her dad "because he's always taken care of me since I was small, he was always there and make sure I was safe." Lisa states that "my family cares about us, so . . . they're gonna try to protect me the best way they can." One 15-year-old is clear that, despite family infighting, her mother and older sister would protect her: "When we fight its like we hate each other then but when it comes down to it, if something were ever to happen to me they'd go nuts and they'd really be there, they always be there."

For the most part, the girls' sense of emotional security was quite fragile. Talk about the strength of relationships is fraught with contradictions and disconnections. Kathy feels safe with her mother because she trusts her "with everything," including her own daughter, yet she claims her mother "didn't really care, and me and her—we never really got along or anything." Although Jennifer states that her mother is regularly in and out of jail and prison, her mother "would never let nothing happen to me. She was always there if anything happened." Another girl pins her security needs on her 1-year-old daughter because "she was there with me and I can talk to her." She keeps her relationship with her own mother at arm's length, stating only that "I understand her and she understands me." And while Jill acknowledges that her mother is "there to protect me and stuff," she admits that she "never felt safe with her. Maybe because we didn't have a good relationship." Gayle confesses that thinking about who makes her feel safe is "a hard question," and finally decides that there is no one. She lived in a series of state-sponsored homes prior to her incarceration at the time of the interview, and her mother is homeless and a heavy drug user. Yet Gayle assumes blame for her own emotional insecurity and lack of attachments "because I used to always run around and I had no time to get to know people and know what they was about. I used to just run around a lot."

Support

Consistent with developmental studies, criminologists John Paul Wright and Frances Cullen note that adults who "take steps to exercise control *and* to deliver social support" (emphasis added) facilitate children's healthy growth and decreased delinquency.[32] They directly challenge as unnecessarily narrow one of the most prominent criminological conceptions of parenting—that which asserts that children's delinquency can be constrained through the use of controls alone. In contrast, they propose a broad model of parental efficacy that, in addition to monitoring and discipline, includes emotional and instrumental social support.[33] Research has indicated that social supports and nurturance have direct effects on juvenile delinquency and are positively associated with child-parent attachment, while exposure to harsh or inconsistent punishment increases the risk of delinquent behavior.[34] Carter Hay and Walter Forrest further demonstrate that youths' levels of self-control are related to early parent-child bonds based on both warmth and control, and thereby affirm that "parenting still matters . . . beyond childhood."[35] A developmental and relational conceptualization of parenting helps to explain how loss of, or abuse by, caregivers might adversely shape early social (attachment) bonds and contribute to subsequent violent offending.

Parental support comes in many forms, including the provision of material goods (e.g., food, housing, and clothing) and emotional and instrumental aid (e.g., declarations of love, praise and encouragement, and participation in joint activities). All are essential to children's healthy development; all were in short supply for the girls in this study. Their families were generally among the working poor who survived on low-paying jobs and the neighborhood underground economy. Though basic necessities were usually provided ("I ate regularly, lived in a regular house, like my mother would cook us dinner"), the contexts in which provisions were offered did not feel particularly supportive. Valerie's account makes the point: "My grandmother gave me a couple of dollars every day. Went shopping like every month. I ate sometimes. Yeah, we don't sit down to eat at the table, but we just eat, you know." The few outright compliments and statements of love were recalled with pleasure, in sharp contrast with the girls' customary experiences. Gayle, who blames herself for not having anyone to keep her safe, was thrilled on those rare occasions when she was the center of her mother's attention:

> When I come around she'd like brag about me, be like "this is my daughter, the person I been talkin' about, remember?" And then everybody wanna hang with me and that's when they find out everything I do. 'Cause my mother used to brag, like tell them about me.

Gayle relishes her infrequent visits with her mother and stepfather (both heavy drug users) despite the disparity between her portrayal of a loving and supportive relationship and the mother's absence and her own history of rotating through the foster care system.

The girls described aspects of *childhood adultification,* a process in which young people are regularly, and often inappropriately, exposed to adult knowledge and are required to assume adult responsibilities within the family—circumstances that reflect the opposite of parental support. In her examination of adultified behavior, Linda Burton notes that children growing up in long-term, sustained poverty are more likely than others to be called on to contribute labor (i.e., child care and housework), capital (legal or illegal), and emotional support in stressed family contexts. The inconsistency between what social institutions expect of children and what poor families require of them can send "mixed messages about what constitutes contextually appropriate child behaviors" and places adultified children in conflict with established legal, educational, and social welfare systems. Adultified children receive little guidance in performing the tasks prematurely imposed on them and may face "considerable developmental challenges and lost opportunities" throughout their lives.[36] Burton identified successive levels of adultification, from the most basic and tenuous to highly complex forms in which the parent-child hierarchy dissolves and there is blurring of generational boundaries; for the purpose of meeting specific family needs, a child's duties and responsibilities may model those of a spouse or a parent. Gender typing suggests that, while the eldest boy may become a family breadwinner or a mother's confidant, the eldest girl in a family is somewhat more likely than others to step into homemaking and caregiving roles.[37] Cultural understandings and expectations of childhood are additionally confounded by parental status factors such as employment, physical and mental health, and substance dependency and abuse.

In the current study, the girls were often called on to fill the void, "parenting" their parents and siblings in efforts to keep the family unit emotionally and physically viable. Natalie and Marcella are representative exemplar cases. Stating that she "practically raised" her little sister because of her parent's work schedule, Natalie, an African American 16-year-old, is frustrated by the time- and labor-intensive caregiving obligations placed on her:

> I'd be the only one there so I had to get her dressed, take her to the babysitter, and then go to school and then pick her up, if they [parents] had to do overtime, which they was doing most of the time, then I had to, like, take care of her.

Demonstrating greater enmeshment in the parental role is Marcella, a 15-year-old of Puerto Rican descent, who states repeatedly that she "had a lot of responsibilities" and "it was very stressful for me." She has no recollection of her father, and her only sister, 5 years her senior, moves out of the household when Marcella is 10 years old. Her mother is confined to a wheelchair, paralyzed by a random gunshot when Marcella was an infant. Marcella stops attending school after the 6th grade and, with little family support or access to professional services, assumes much of the responsibility for her mother's physical and emotional needs:

> When she got shot, it messed up her insides, so she had to urinate in a catheter. I help her with that . . . it's hard for her to get to the toilet as well; I had to put diapers on her, clean her hair, help her bathe, help her move from place to place, had to cook for her.

Alcohol- and drug-infused fights are common in the home, both between the girl and her mother and among the mother's friends.

> Bein' that she was drunk, she was real hard to deal with, she would like want to go outside, she always tried to commit suicide a lot, too. So, I would try and stop her from doing that—grabbing pills outta her hand, knives and stuff. . . . A couple of times, she'd punch windows and get her fists sliced up.

Marcella fends off her mother's drunken male visitors who sexually attack both the mother and daughter. Despite her own troubles with her mother, Marcella remains highly protective: "Since she's in a wheelchair, a lot of people from around try to take advantage of her."

Supervision

Effective parenting includes supervision, a form of direct control that requires a caregiver to be aware of children's whereabouts and activities, to be responsive to their needs, and to be appropriately restrictive of their behaviors.[38] When asked, the majority of girls state that their parents and other caregivers had only a general sense about where their children were when not at home, who they were with, or what they were doing.[39] Although three-fourths of the girls note that the adults in their lives did not usually know when they would be home, nearly all of the girls knew how to contact the adults if they needed to do so.

A small number of girls speak of being closely supervised—in a way that they describe as gendered and almost suffocating. One protests that her mother was quite strict and "always wanted me to be in the house, around her like underneath her . . . I wanted to be outside. I didn't want to be in the house. I just didn't like staying in the house, babysitting all the time and whatever." Michelle says she "really didn't get a chance to go places by myself" and so remains mostly at her grandparents' apartment. Sent north to New York by her mother who remained in Barbados, Michelle feels disconnected in the large, strange city. Her loss and loneliness are exacerbated by her grandmother's admonitions to stay indoors and to "be religious." She complains that her grandmother:

> didn't want me outside most of the time; I was always in the house. If we're like just sitting around and I was like "I'm tired, I'm bored" or something, she'll be like "go read a Bible." I don't want to read the Bible. . . . If I did something bad, my grandmother would hit me.

Caregivers may have set boundaries to protect their charges from the dangers of the street and raise the girls to be "decent," but the girls clearly chafe under the restrictions.[40] Lisa describes her parents as intent on insulating their children from the violence of the neighborhood. She and her nine siblings "used to always stay in the house . . .

just sitting in the house watching TV, probably eating." Occasionally, she ventures "straight to the store and back home, and school," avoiding the nearby park.

> I know what was in the park, that's how come I used to stay in my house. [On weekends] I could ask for permission, 10 o'clock [curfew], to like play in the hallway or something, or out in front of the building. 'Cause any later, [pause] uh-uh, it's real dangerous.

Despite the acknowledged dangers of their urban neighborhoods, the girls describe social lives centered on "hanging out" with peers in the community:

> We'd mostly just hang out on corners in front of the school. We never did anything that was worthwhile, I'd say, . . . staying at friends, while we were out all night. And then we just hang out. We never did anything like go to the movies. We just hung out.

Often they congregate close to their apartments and houses and, even if their parents do not know exactly where they were, many girls believe they could be quickly located because, "I won't really be nowhere. I just be on the same street," or "down the block, outside and they could drop by and see me." A few girls note that "sometimes I called [parents] and told them" their location. However, most of the girls contend that their parents did not know where they were.

Supervision was difficult not only because of an individual girl's actions, but because of the tremendous amount of residential instability and a shifting configuration of caregivers. At some time in their lives, nearly three-fourths of the girls lived with adults other than their parents, residing in kin or nonrelative foster care, residential treatment centers, or group homes. Locations changed when caregivers were imprisoned or admitted to drug treatment, or families were evicted or forced to leave unsafe conditions. The household composition changed when a parent's new partner arrived or girls moved in with extended family or friends. Parental separations could be brief or last for months—even years—when parents could not or would not care for their children. Natalie lived mostly with her mother, but describes a residential fluidity that is fairly typical:

I was in a group home before that because I had ran away [and] then they had to put me there but most the time I was with my mother, . . . her boyfriend, my brother, and my little sister and my stepsister. Well, her boyfriend now was like, for four or five years, but my little sister's father, I was brought up with him when I was real little. . . . But, 'cause, my sister's father and me we didn't get along, so I be at my father's house a lot too. But I didn't live there, I was just visiting over there. . . . And then I went to live him for like a year. . . . While I was living with him, he had got arrested for murder. And then my stepmother brung me to my mother. Well, she's not my step-mother, she's my father's girlfriend, but she got kids by him so she brung me to my mother.

With changing caregivers and residences, reformulating families, and the struggles of living in disadvantaged communities, the supervision and monitoring of the girls is difficult at best. Arguments flare over curfews, with girls strongly resisting parental supervising efforts: "My mother, she was all the time she would tell me to come in early, come in early, and I wasn't trying to hear it." Diane states what many others suggest: "I didn't want nobody telling me what to do, I just wanted to do what I wanted to do. Nobody could tell me anything." Paula is matter-of-fact in describing how she "ran over" her father:

He said be in the house at 11:00. I'm leaving at 9:00. There's no way in the world I'll be in at 11:00. He's lucky if I come in the next week. We outside 2, 3, 4 o'clock in the morning. I'll come back, . . . get a change of clothes and shower and stuff and I'm gone again.

Paula does make a minimal effort to stay in relationship with her father, perhaps hoping to be missed: "Sometimes I would call him so at least he'll know I'm still living." Similarly, 16-year-old Rose claims she "would just run around the streets and not listen to my parents." The core of the problem for her was "all because my stepmother was in the house," and she resents her father's wife trying to "be my mother."

Generally, the girls ignore curfews and other rules, despite the worry they know this causes their caregivers. Valerie confesses:

I made it bad, 'cause I would, I didn't want to follow no rules.
I want everything to go my way and came in the house any-
time I wanted to, that's when I wanted to. I worried my grandmother a lot and sometime I never come in.

Maria belittles her mother's ineffective attempts at setting a curfew and controlling her activities:

My mother just used to tell me that you could be home at
9:30, she was like when you be with your friends, what that
get you? And I just laugh, I be outside, doing bad stuff, breaking bottles, doing bad stuff to people. And she be like you
could be home looking at TV, she was like, doing something
positive, rather than doing something negative.

Her mother is inconsistent, telling Maria that if she is late she will
not be allowed out the next day, but then retracts the statement with:
"I'll probably let you go outside but you be home at like 6 o'clock, 7
o'clock, I'm not trying to let you lie to me." Eventually, the mother
stops trying:

My mother's like, look there's nothing I could do, she was
out, I try my best to keep you home, keep you safe, keep you
out of that community, keep you from doing bad stuff, but you
don't understand—you don't want to.

Like Paula, Elena usually does not bother to tell her mother where
she is going:

I be, all right bye, I'll see you later. If she wants, like I had a
pager so she could just page me and find out where I was but
I wouldn't tell her where I was going 'cause I just felt that was
not her concern. Most of the time she wouldn't really know
where I was, but once in a blue moon she would.

Elena's mother expresses little interest in or responsibility for her
daughter's activities, which, like nearly two-thirds of the girls in this
study, involved drug sales. Elena describes an instance when she
planned to rent a skating rink. The rental agreement required an adult's
signature and Elena asked her mother to sign, assuring her that she
could pay the purported fee of $5,000. Apparently knowing, but not

wishing to acknowledge how her young daughter had acquired such a large amount of capital, Elena's mother signed the agreement: "I had my mother. She was like 'where did you get all this money from?' I was like, don't worry about it. She didn't even ask me no more 'cause there was no more need to ask."

In a very different context, the supervisory skills of Elena's mother were equally limited. Alerted of a rapist's reported presence in the apartment complex, her mother suggested that Elena walk home with a girlfriend who had been visiting. Sending the two 14-year-old girls out alone, Elena's mother offered the protection of a cell phone: "Anything happens, you just call me real fast." Elena returned home safely, but later learned that her friend was sexually assaulted that night.

The caregivers who relinquished the most parental authority and control were those who used substances with or in the presence of their daughters, or who included the girls in drug trafficking.[41] Drug-using parents' erratic lifestyles also distanced them from their children. Gayle describes visits, while she was in foster care, that were punctuated by her mother's need to acquire or use substances: "Once every while I used to meet my mother over there, and she used to go across the street and get the drugs and then go in the bathroom." At her mother's home, drug use and sales were a regular occurrence:

> Sometimes, it be like 10, 15 men in there or young boys in there having a party. My mother just let them in the house and they spends the night while my mother be out helping them sell the drugs . . . my stepfather, he used to be a big-time drug dealer too.

Joanne and her siblings sold drugs out of the family apartment, and there were "a lot of people coming in and out of my house so, a lot of—police were at my house a lot." The youths' drug activity "stressed my mother out," but parental efforts at control had little effect:

> My mother used to get all paranoid and stuff and she used to lock me out because she didn't want me to get in trouble, and if she locked me out she wouldn't, she thought I wouldn't do it again 'cause I'd want to come home.

Eventually, Joanne's mother also began to deal and to use drugs in their home. At first claiming this was "fun," Joanne came to acknowledge its negative effects, including having to be responsible for maintaining some routine such as getting herself to school in the morning:

> Because my mother used to have people in and out of the house, she used to have, she used to just have parties and stuff and it'd be on a school night, and then I'd be up to like 3, 4 o'clock in the morning and I'd have to get up at 6 o'clock and get ready for school.

The late night parties and constant visitors kept Joanne up and her mother estranged: "When I got older, it bothered me because it started to take more of the relationship out of all of us."

A different approach to supervision was to call on the power of the state. One-fourth of the girls' parents attempted extreme measures of direct control by signing Persons in Need of Supervision (PINS) warrants against their daughters. Typical offenses included running away from home and fighting with a caregiver. Describing her "very strict" mother with a "stink attitude," Paula claims she rarely was allowed out to play with friends when she was little and instead had to clean the house and do other chores. Clearly angry with her mother, she blurts out: "You know, and she wonder why I was like 8, 9 years old she had to keep putting PINS on me." As a child Paula was shuffled between foster care and group homes, her "patient" aunt who "knows I'm a sick person," and her fighting parents. She'd leave these places and go to her grandmother's house, perhaps seeking her love and support, while also gaining attention (albeit negative) from her mother. This resulted in only heightened punitive actions: "The only reason I stayed in the house was 'cause the judge kept saying he was gonna send me, he gonna lock me up, and I was scared back then so I listened."

For several years Marcella served as caregiver to her wheelchair-bound mother, but acknowledges that the two also physically fought. The mother's method of exerting parental control is to call the police:

> Since I used to hit my mother and stuff, she would, like, call the police and things, and every time the police came, they would tell her they couldn't do anything about it 'cause they didn't have evidence of this, so they would just tell her, go to court and fill out a PINS warrant out on me.

This scenario is repeated numerous times until Marcella resists a police officer who is summoned by her mother. The ensuing struggle lands Marcella in the psychiatric unit of a hospital for 2 months before she is eventually placed with child services.

Many girls began their interview with an idealized description that portrayed their parents as more loving and supportive than the oral narrative could sustain. While some girls recalled instances when parents were demonstrative in their love and support, these tended to be singular occasions, not normative behaviors. Parenting styles varied but overall, in the girls' assessments, the caregivers who were responsible for their growth and healthy development were deficient in nurturing the parent-child relationship: attachment behaviors were weak, support was minimal, and monitoring and supervision were inconsistent.[42] Most girls were uncomfortable confiding in their caregivers; did not feel emotionally safe; and expressed feeling distant, misunderstood, isolated, and angry. Furthermore, other attuned adults were rarely available to fill in the gaps.

Though normal adolescent development can be a period of conflict, the girls in this study experienced highly stressful family relations born of circumstances that predated their teenage years. Persistent poverty and compromised parenting forced many girls to assume adult roles and responsibilities at an early age; with parents and adultified children playing egalitarian roles in the household, girls came to resent inconsistent and arbitrary implementation of rules and regulations, and often responded as if adults were incidental to their lives.[43] Expectations of help and support from others were constantly thwarted, and attachment was strained as children grew into adolescents with caregivers who remained rejecting and even hostile. In this environment emotional bonds with parents, rather than serving as "relational" or indirect control mechanisms, became a source of pain and generated anxiety and rage among the girls.[44] Frustrated in their desire to connect with caregivers, they sought to control the conflict between activated attachment needs and anger. By outwardly rejecting close relations and psychically blocking their vulnerability and dependency needs, the girls could maintain some form of relationship without experiencing anger.[45] Internal stress remained high and contributed to manifestations of defiant, disruptive, and immature behaviors—defenses that enable a girl to stay in relationship when she "both needs her [caregiver] and fears her rejection."[46] Without caregivers who were willing and able to address their need for love, support, and guidance, these young women stood at a great disadvantage when confronted with communal and interpersonal violence, victimization, and loss.

Notes

1. Griffin, *Season of the Witch,* p. 34.
2. Thornberry, "Some Advantages," p. 3. Thornberry emphasizes that the relationship between age and crime may be one of the most stable empirical research findings (e.g., delinquent and criminal behaviors begin and quickly escalate in late childhood and early adolescence before tapering off, for most offenders, by the late twenties), and argues for the utility of a developmental perspective. Yet most sociologically based theoretical perspectives pay little attention to the age-crime curve and provide static explanations for criminal behavior.
3. Across socioeconomic, racial, and ethnic groups, teens who reported feeling relatively close to their parents scored higher than their peers on measures of psychosocial development, behavioral competence, and psychological well-being, and lower on measures of psychological and social problems including drug use, depression, and deviant behavior. Steinburg, "Autonomy, Conflict, and Harmony," pp. 359–360.
4. Fonagy et al., "Morality, Disruptive Behavior" p. 241.
5. Greenberg et al., "Role of Attachment Processes."
6. See Salzinger et al., "Physical Child Abuse"; Herrenkohl et al., "Child Abuse and Youth Violence"; Thornberry et al., "The Importance of Timing."
7. Bowlby (*Attachment,* p. 303) does not claim that an infant can become attached to only the mother, or even only one person. The "mother figure" can be anyone in the role of principal caregiver. Ainsworth ("Infant-Mother Attachment," p. 935) notes that, in her research, "infants are highly selective in their choices of attachment figures from among the various persons familiar to them . . . and no infant has been observed to have many attachment figures."
8. Ainsworth et al., *Patterns of Attachment.* Mother and child are observed together in a room filled with toys. A stranger is introduced and the mother quietly slips out the door, leaving the child alone with the stranger. The mother returns, greeting and comforting the infant, and encouraging play. She leaves again, this time saying "bye-bye." The child is briefly alone with the stranger before the stranger also leaves. The stranger returns first, followed shortly thereafter by the mother. How the child responds to the mother's return is revealing.
9. Ainsworth, "Infant-Mother Attachment"; Main, "Avoidance." Avoidant behavior with the mother in the Strange Situation is linked with high heart rates, indicative of strongly activated attachment behaviors despite appearances of disinterest (Sroufe and Waters, "Heart Rate").
10. Ainsworth, "Infant-Mother Attachment"; Main, "Avoidance."
11. Bell and Ainsworth, "Infant Crying," p. 1188. See Bowlby, *A Secure Base.*
12. Greenberg et al., "Role of Attachment Processes," pp. 200–201.
13. Sroufe et al., "Implications of Attachment Theory."
14. Fonagy et al., "Morality, Disruptive Behavior" p. 243.
15. Sixty-three percent of the girls reported living mostly with their moth-

ers prior to being remanded to custody and, thus, most of the following statements pertain to mothers.

16. Bretherton ("The Origins," p. 766) cites John Bowlby, *Maternal Care and Mental Health,* World Health Organization Monograph (Geneva: WHO, 1951).

17. Fonagy et al., "Morality, Disruptive Behavior" p. 242.

18. Small and Newman, "Urban Poverty"; Massey and Denton, *American Apartheid,* p. 74.

19. Bourgois, *In Search of Respect.*

20. Dunlap et al., "Severely Distressed African-American Family," p. 118.

21. Maher and Daly, "Women in the Street-Level Economy."

22. Gamble, "Under the Shadow of Tuskegee."

23. Wohl et al., "Sociodemographic and Behavior Characteristics," p. 413.

24. New York State Department of Health, *AIDS in New York State,* p. 193.

25. Burton, "Childhood Adultification"; Ryder and Brisgone, "Cracked Perspectives"; Garbarino et al., "What Children Can Tell Us."

26. Main et al., "Security in Infancy," p. 75.

27. At this stage, adolescents' capacity for abstract thinking enables them to think about their relationships and, perhaps, change their internal working models. De Zulueta, *From Pain to Violence,* pp. 87–88.

28. Collins, "Meaning of Motherhood"; Sampson et al., "Neighborhoods and Violent Crime"; Debold et al., *Mother Daughter Revolution.*

29. Jordon, "Meaning of Mutuality," p. 87.

30. Stern, "Disavowing the Self," p. 112.

31. While most claimed "no one," an assortment of identified family members included mothers, a father, an aunt, a foster mother, a sibling, grandmothers, and "the whole family."

32. Wright and Cullen, "Parental Efficacy," p. 697.

33. See Gottfredson and Hirschi, *General Theory of Crime;* Wright and Cullen, "Parental Efficacy," pp. 696–697; Cullen et al., "Parenting and Self-Control," p. 73.

34. Colvin, *Crime and Coercion;* Farrington, "Explaining the Beginning."

35. Hay and Forrest, "Development of Self-Control," p. 757. See also Simons et al., "Identifying the Psychological Factors."

36. Burton, "Childhood Adultification," pp. 331–332.

37. Ibid., p. 336.

38. Baumrind, "Influence of Parenting Style."

39. During a portion of the time when the girls in this study would have been living in their neighborhoods, national juvenile arrests for curfew and loitering violations increased dramatically: 113 percent between 1990 and 1999. In 1995, the year prior to the interviews, girls represented 30 percent of all curfew and loitering violation arrests. Snyder, "Juvenile Arrests 1995"; Snyder, "Juvenile Arrests 1999."

40. Anderson, *Code of the Street;* Jones, *Between Good and Ghetto.*

41. Unlike drug usage in prior eras, crack cocaine attracted nearly as many women as men in the late 1980s, often with debilitating consequences for their children. See Sterk, *Fast Lives;* Dunlap et al., "Normalization of Violence";

Dunlap et al., "Mothers and Daughters." Ryder and Brisgone ("Cracked Perspectives") examine the effects of the crack cocaine era on the lives of poor, minority women and their children, particularly their daughters.

42. E. Erikson, *Youth and Society.*

43. Glenwick and Mowrey, "When Parent Becomes Peer."

44. Hirschi, *Causes of Delinquency;* Hagan, *Structural Criminology.*

45. Main, "Peculiar Form of Reunion Behavior."

46. De Zulueta, *From Pain to Violence,* p. 85.

4

Traumatic Childhood Experiences of Violence

People selling a lot of drugs, smoking a lot of weed, always
shooting each other. They were always doing stupid stuff
like that. A lot of people killing each other. We used to
come from school and we see my friend's aunt, somebody
raped her, pushed her off the building naked.
—Natalie, 16 years old

Victimization, maltreatment, abuse, trauma—the words have become
so much a part of our vocabulary that they often sound jaded and
abstract, separate from the flesh and blood of real people and disconnected from the experiences of actual girls. Though widespread media
coverage of catastrophic and terrible incidents has increased public
familiarity with the language of trauma, for most of us the reality of
such events remains distant and apart from the business of daily life.[1]
For the two dozen girls whose stories I present here, community and
interpersonal violence and loss were personal and deeply painful, and
their weakened, disrupted, or nonexistent attachment bonds left them
vulnerable to traumagenic effects. Though urban girls of color "live
with some kind of trauma every day," little is known about their perceptions of such events and effects.[2] Likewise, the underlying mechanisms linking experiences of childhood trauma to violent behaviors in
adolescence have rarely been investigated. Such knowing will require
intense and extensive additional study, but the first step is to overcome
our deep reluctance to listen to stories of hurt and sorrow. To begin to
understand trauma in the context of urban girls' lives, we must replace
resistance with a willingness to bear witness to and "share the burden
of pain."[3] This is not an easy undertaking.

Leonard Shengold notes that "some amount of lack of care and even torment is inevitable in the course of everyone's growing up."[4] Experiencing any individual, particular event, or even a couple of events, is not necessarily indicative of trauma. Rather, *trauma* is an extreme subset of stressful life events that breaks through internal protective defenses and overwhelms normal coping mechanisms;[5] in traumatic experience, "external and internal, real and instinctual dangers converge."[6] Sociologist Kai Erickson describes a state of mind in which individuals are disconnected from their relationship to the world:

> Something alien breaks in on you, smashing through whatever barriers your mind has set up as a line of defense. It invades you, possesses you, takes you over, becomes a dominant feature of your interior landscape.[7]

Trauma challenges basic assumptions of safety and predictability, and fairness and justice. It is "the story of a wound that cries out, that addresses us in an attempt to tell us of a reality that is not otherwise available."[8] While trauma often indicates a dramatic change in the environment, it is just as likely to point to ongoing threatening or harmful conditions.

Whether a particular upsetting event or condition is perceived and processed as traumatic depends on a variety of factors. Hence, the American Psychiatric Association states that a traumatic event contains both objective characteristics (i.e., "actual or threatened death, or serious injury, or a threat to the physical integrity of self or others") and the subjective response of the exposed person (i.e., "fear, helplessness or horror").[9] Subjective responses or perceptions also are shaped by the context in which the event was experienced, and the availability and effectiveness of social supports.[10] How children experience internal and external threats depends on their maturation level and degree of reliance on parents and other adult caregivers, which in turn determine the developmental impact of the experiences.

Children with insecure attachments and exposure to other forms of maltreatment, community violence, or loss are particularly vulnerable to psychological trauma, the effects of which can alter the course of normative biological, psychological, and moral development.[11] Negative and highly stressful experiences affect changes in the brain, and consequently change physiological responses in the rest of the body.

Chronic fear and pain, for example, may cause children to be on high alert for signs of the feared event, generating constant anxiety, rapid heartbeat, and high blood pressure.[12] Children's brains continue to grow and mature throughout adolescence and, because executive functions (i.e., cognitive processes that involve higher-level organization and the execution of complex thoughts and behavior) may be the last to mature, they are more susceptible to environmental influences.[13] As a result of psychological trauma in childhood or adolescence, faculties such as planning and social judgment, abstract reasoning, moral development, and impulse control may become impaired.

Experiencing multiple types or the repeated experience of a single type of trauma can worsen effects.[14] Victimization may not occur as a single incident, but may be "part of a pattern of on-going, multiple victimizations" more akin to a condition than an event. Such polyvictimization is a "powerful predictor of trauma symptoms."[15] The repetition of trauma has an exponential, rather than additive, effect on adverse consequences, wearing down a child's ability to successfully address and cope with psychological challenges that arise in daily functioning. After multiple or intense exposures to danger, "the systems contributing to hyperarousal will become sensitized, ready to flip on at the least provocation" even in a nonthreatening situation; in a constant state of readiness, a traumatized child is prepared to respond quickly to any perceived hostility.[16]

Gender and age at the time of an incident may be instrumental in how children adjust to disruptions in loving and secure attachments as well as other traumas, and how these affect their developing sense of self. Several studies have found that girls and young children report more posttraumatic stress disorder (PTSD) symptoms, anxiety and depression, and a higher amount of family conflict than boys and older children.[17] Race also may play a role, but research is extremely limited. The majority of the existent trauma-related research that has examined racial variation among adult females found that "African Americans do not differ from Caucasians in prevalence, severity, or manifestation of PTSD symptoms despite greater exposure to certain types of traumas."[18] In victimization research with adult African American women, Sarah Hood and Michele Carter thus argue that theories based on experiences of whites do not necessarily apply to those of blacks. They suggest the possibility that pervasive exposure to discrimination may develop resiliency, or that the manner in which African American women are socialized may assist in the formation of protective factors that hinder the development of additional PTSD symptoms.[19] Matthew Makarios also found no racial differences in the effects of childhood abuse on violent criminal arrests among young adult women. He submits that, because of concentrated sexual exploitation and victimization, "minority females may be socialized to expect victimization and perhaps learn mechanisms to internally cope with abuse."[20]

Rates of mental and emotional disorders may be more common among incarcerated youth than community samples and among incarcerated girls than incarcerated boys.[21] Different types of traumatic experiences can produce different outcomes, and these may vary by gender.[22] In general, trauma-exposed girls have been more likely than their male counterparts to develop PTSD, to develop substance abuse problems, and to become involved in drug-related and serious delinquent activity.[23] In the first study of PTSD among incarcerated female delinquents, the racially diverse sample of girls was 50 percent more likely than a comparison sample of incarcerated boys to exhibit symptoms of PTSD. Girls were more likely to report being the victim of violent abuse whereas boys were more likely to report having witnessed a violent event, causing the researchers to suggest that the variation in type of traumatic experience explains female delinquents' greater susceptibility to PTSD.[24] In another study specific to justice-involved adolescent girls, both chronicity and the variety of traumas experienced predicted criminal offending and risky sexual behavior.[25]

The intersection of trauma, abuse, and interpersonal violence is a relatively new and interdisciplinary area of study,[26] and as a result little is known of victims' perceptions, particularly those of minority girls from distressed communities who are deeply involved in the juvenile justice system.[27] What we do know is that traumatic experiences can extract a heavy toll and that childhood occurrences potentially contribute to the development of antisocial, delinquent, and violent behaviors in adolescence and beyond.[28] Citing Pynoos and Nader, Victor Balaban notes that untreated, PTSD symptoms in young children may affect "cognitive functioning, initiative, personality style, self-esteem, outlook, and impulse control."[29] It is likely too that violence, victimization, and loss contribute to girls' antisocial and maladaptive behaviors and "psychological problems ranging from depression to suicide, to problems with the criminal justice system resulting in incarceration."[30]

In this and the following chapter, I explore the girls' narrative data to learn how they describe and understand disruptive and extremely stressful events in their lives. In contrast to research that has examined maltreatment generally, or physical or sexual abuse specifically, the current study is expansive in its investigation of trauma, incorporating a range of witnessed incidents, direct victimizations, and losses.[31] The quantitative data reveal an average of nine traumatic events in each girl's lifetime, nearly half of which occurred prior to the age of 11, and the qualitative data provide details of these incidents.

Compounding the girls' difficulties arising from disrupted and malformed attachments is a litany of victimizations and losses to which they were exposed in their neighborhoods and homes. It is in these stories that we confront the lived experiences of trauma. All interpretations are "essentially determined by the social context in which we live," and I consider the girls' statements meaningful constructions of events significant to them that served to shape their interpretation of the world.[32] This is important because "how we interpret our experiences has a direct effect on how we respond to trauma."[33] Initially experienced by the girls at young ages, the accumulation of events can be likened to a chronic traumatic condition. Or perhaps, as Shengold dramatically described childhood abuse, a form of "soul murder."[34]

I have roughly divided the rest of this chapter between violence in the larger community among peers and strangers, and violence in domestic settings and among loved ones. This, however, is a somewhat artificial dichotomy as incidents often crossed the boundary between public and private spheres: young women fended off abusive strangers in their homes and witnessed family members being attacked or attacking others on the streets. The girls were both witnesses to and subjects of varied and multiple victimizations by peers and strangers, caregivers, and other known adults. Incidents occurred at developmentally vulnerable ages, and in contexts lacking adult guidance and support.[35] The picture is further complicated by the interactional nature of violence in which the girls were both targets of and participants in family violence. Either having sustained abuse themselves or witnessed someone else being harmed, the girls described their own actions as defensive or protective and thus blurred any presumed boundaries between victim and offender. Regardless of the context and players, pervasive violence gnawed at already frayed bonds of attachment.

Exposure to Violence in the Community

The National Survey of Children's Exposure to Violence confirmed that "most of our society's children are exposed to violence in their daily lives," either directly or indirectly. In a nationally representative sample of 4,549 children, more than 60 percent had been exposed to violence within the past year, and reports of lifetime exposure were approximately one-third to one-half higher.[36] Of particular concern is that more than 10.0 percent of children reported 5 or more direct exposures to violence, and 1.4 percent reported 10 or more direct victimizations. Although not stated, it is likely that the higher rates were located within historically marginalized populations and communities that are structurally damaged and thus more susceptible to the many emotional and behavioral problems that exposure to violence may cause. According to the survey, "these children [with multiple and cumulative exposures] are the most likely to suffer serious long-term physical, emotional and mental harm." It emphasized that "exposure to one form may make a child more vulnerable to other forms."[37] Exposure to violence has damaging consequences for children's physical and mental health that may be expressed internally in the form of anxiety and depression; externally as in delinquency, aggression, and violence toward others; or both. The damage also may be long term, affecting adult functioning and well-being.[38]

People in the United States tend to live in neighborhoods that are both racially and economically homogeneous. As a result of residential segregation, poverty and its multitude of associated problems are clustered in particular areas and a selection of neighborhoods: generally, communities of color with constrained social, political, and economic opportunities. Without stable and effective familial, educational, religious, and cultural institutions to intercede, violence is a common strategy for advancement. The effects of exposure to violence on youth in such neighborhoods is comparable in many ways to those of young people growing up in war zones. The pervasiveness and accessibility of guns is a major characteristic of this world, and it contributes to a pessimistic future orientation wherein children may believe they will not reach adulthood; thus, they hesitate to establish bonds that they fear will likely be broken. Children living under the chronic threat of unpredictable, lethal violence find various ways to adapt to the danger, but many of these strategies are also dysfunctional and socially maladaptive.[39]

Between 1984 and 1994, the availability of guns accounted for an increase in violent crimes generally, and in every category of homicide particularly. Adolescents 14 to 17 years old constituted the largest proportional increase in homicide victimization and commission, with guns playing a prominent role.[40] The girls in this study describe their neighborhoods as urban and generally well-maintained places, but also violent ones with an entrenched drug trade; nearly three-fourths of the girls reported witnessing at least one killing, primarily as the result of gunfire and frequently by other teens.[41] When asked to describe the area where she lived, Marcella says it is a "typical neighborhood in Brooklyn [with] a lot of drug spots and bums and stuff . . . a lot of violence, shooting—a lot of people are killed there a lot." Jennifer, a 9th grader, claims violence is "all over" so that, even if a person is not directly involved, they cannot help but be affected:

> You hear a lot of gunshots, um, you see the aftereffects when somebody get shot, like you could see . . . you could be driving by and you see somebody laying there, what happened? They just got shot, or they just stabbed, they just got in a fight.

All of the narratives recount a violence that is just beneath the surface or around the corner. Violence is not an abstract concept "out there," but a very real presence that can instantly alter lives. In this world children are vulnerable, perhaps even expendable. One girl describes watching as a "big boy probably like 15, playing with a M80, put it in the little boy's pocket, and the little boy just blew up. He started bleeding, an ambulance came, he was like on fire." Guns are integral to much of the indiscriminate neighborhood violence, and Christine states it succinctly: "You can get shot over the stupidest things. If you take somebody's bike, you're putting your life in jeopardy 'cause they will shoot you over a bike or a dollar." The girls distinguish between certain blocks and buildings that are more dangerous than others and describe at length the safety precautions that they employ. They know not to look out the window from a low floor and explain that plexiglass is installed "because they shoot there." They know to call up to the apartment for someone to meet them at the elevator, and they know to stay inside after 10 P.M. to avoid serious gunfights.

Though the community violence was widespread and touched all residents, the girls explicitly include that which is directed at females:

"They be shooting in the park, shooting off the roof. Shooting in the staircases, shooting in the elevator. Fighting in the park and in the staircases, men beating their girlfriends up." As preoccupied with survival as any of the young men in the neighborhood, the girls know that their distressed neighborhoods "do not come with a special girls-only pass"[42] that will protect them; rather, because of their devalued female status, the danger and fear is heightened. Natalie quietly describes finding a woman's body on the street: "We come from school and we see my friend's aunt, somebody raped her, pushed her off the building naked." The violence is systemic, well beyond the efforts of individual girls "to be safe." After walking her best friend home one night and parting ways at the door of her apartment building, one girl learned "two days later they found her body on a roof. She was raped but she wasn't . . . she ain't die. She was just on a roof."

The young women's descriptions of their neighborhoods usually began with a general overview, but quickly shifted to significant personal experiences. Natalie, for example, portrays her neighborhood as "the projects, people selling a lot of drugs, smoking a lot of weed, always shooting each other. A lot of people killing each other." She fills in this picture a bit more, adding that she often accompanied her father on drug dealing rounds and "used to see him shoot people and kill them." She was with him when he killed a man, an offense that sent him to prison.

> First we were in the car, then they was calling him, he didn't come, they went upstairs, and they came back down, got his stuff, he [father] went back up and then I know. When Earl [his friend] came down he was, you know, had blood all over him and then I seen a guy fall from the window. I was like 7.

Not only was the community dangerous in the general sense, but Natalie's caregiver directly involved her in his trafficking activities, including killings. The boundary between home and community was porous: violence was instigated both by and against loved ones.

The girls described witnessing and being directly victimized by adults and peers with guns. In communities where ties with law enforcement were tenuous at best, petty theft could trigger an extreme response, as in the case of Paula and her boyfriend stealing from a local bodega:

> It was my 14th birthday . . . I was at a club, right? Went out
> the thing and stole a beer. . . . My man stole something out of
> the store. They came out of the store [and] chased him . . . I
> got shot at 'cause I went there and just ran with it. I hope to
> God those was blanks, it was either blanks or he just really did
> not want to shoot me, 'cause I was running and he was shoot-
> ing behind me and I was screaming. . . . But I wouldn't let go
> of the thing or drop it or nothing. You know, you scared, you
> like ah! I'm not gonna stop now.

Though she conveyed youthful excitement and exhilaration at having
escaped without harm and scoring a free beer, Paula also expressed
fear and a sense of the fragility of life. Where violence is public and
random, the threat of danger or even annihilation is intensified.

Gun violence was perhaps most discussed as a characteristic of the
drug trade, an arena in which most of the girls were active. Disputes
over turf, quality of product, or money suddenly turned ugly when
guns were present, and even being in proximity to the drug spots that
proliferated throughout the community could be very dangerous: "My
friend got shot in his face because he was there, just because he was
watching." A misinterpreted movement (Joanne was shot in the leg
when "something went wrong with a deal she [her cousin] was making
and I got out of the car") or an argument over payment can quickly
instigate gunfire:

> The guy pulled out a gun. He shot my brother. My brother
> shot him, then his friend shot my brother, and then my brother
> shot him and then I got shot, but I didn't really get shot, it just
> skimmed right off me. It was a really bugged-out day.

Drug money was appealing, but the trade was dangerous. Several
girls manipulated gender identities to better protect themselves on the
streets. Fourteen-year-old Elena at first assumes an exaggerated femininity to improve drug sales:

> People are always talking about they make more money than
> me, and I would sit there and I would be like, take this block
> and I'll take that block. And I swear to God, I would dress so
> nice and they would see how many guys would come to me,

how many would come and they be like, "Oh yeah, Shorty, I'll be back," let me go get some more . . . come right back to me.

Elena becomes increasingly aware, however, of the dangers that the street trade holds for young women and switches to a tough masculine persona ("'Cause guys used to try to gyp me and stuff . . . and now I act real tough and I'll act like a guy"). Yet she continues to rely on an older, male "manager" for safety and direction ("He makes sure that I'm safe and secure. . . . He don't even like me dressing all nice and stuff like that"). Another 16-year-old crack seller took herself off the streets, making her connections in a restaurant dressed like a young man. That presentation of self provides protection from both males on the streets and the police; even though she perceives that she might receive a harsher penalty for selling inside a business ("store mean more time"), it is a risk she is willing to take in exchange for immediate safety.

[I'd] go inside a Chinese restaurant, buy a egg roll or something and I was dressing like a boy just in case I did get caught (store mean more time) 'cause DT cop [the undercover detective] cannot search me. Right? All I gotta do is, like, no sorry, but I'm a female, you can't do that. You know, then, they couldn't search me. I would look just like a guy.

The girls complained that, while selling drugs, they were shot at, physically threatened, and sexually assaulted. Thus, despite some success on their own, most eventually came to rely on male managers for protection, precisely because of their gender and age. The power inequity of the arrangement also placed the girls in a vulnerable position, often replicating prior experiences of victimization and loss.

Adolescent heterosexual romantic relationships were an additional arena in which the girls were subjected to violence or the threat of violence. Disputes between girls in this context centered around the threat to status, in relation to any particular boy (i.e., a girl's fear of losing her identity as a boy's girlfriend). According to Elizabeth Griffiths and colleagues, violence often erupts over seemingly trivial things when the relationship between opponents is apparently equal: there is no socially recognized dominance hierarchy. In symmetric social roles, competitors become "locked in a battle for social rank."[43] Kathy describes being threatened with a gun and then beaten up by her boyfriend's new girlfriend: "one time [it was] over my baby's father. It was a girl saying she would blow my brains out if I ever messed with him again." Donna describes a similar scenario in which a girl challenged her with a gun: "This person think I like the boy. She said she was gonna shoot me for that. She said she was going to shoot me, so I told her to bring her motherfucking ass over here and shoot me then." Donna and her challenger are on equal footing though her relationship to the boy is unclear ("This person think I like the boy"). She responds defensively and with little forethought; beyond a concern with status, psychically Donna cannot afford to back down. Donna's history of childhood trauma and her thwarted desire to stay in relationship interferes with her reasoning and anticipation of consequences. Her defiant stance is likely to contribute to a greater involvement in violence.

Though the girls might fight other girls to maintain their position as the primary girlfriend, boys regularly attempted to force girls into submission. The girls were constantly reminded of their devalued position in the hypermasculine street culture and were well aware of the power differential. When guns were introduced to the situation, which they often were, the stakes were raised. But girls could also be bold. Alona says she "used to mess around with" a boy who, in an attempt to control her behavior, put a gun to her head after he saw her talking to other boys. Despite his threats to kill her, Alona dismissively demanded his compliance: "He thought I was scared and that I suppose to cry, like please, don't kill me, please, please." He put the gun away. Most of the girls' efforts to assert themselves in similar situations had a more brutal ending.

The girls' safety was especially at risk in the context of dating relationships and local parties where sexual experimentation could turn into sexual assault. Valerie describes being with a neighborhood boy she knew when they argued over having sex: "I didn't get raped, he was just tryin' to force me." Rose's story is fairly typical. She describes meeting a boy through friends and, when they were all gathered at the apartment of one of the friends, "he did . . . one of them guy things: 'let's go into the room so we can talk.'" The boy put a 9-millimeter handgun to her head. He told her:

> "If you don't have sex with me, I'm going to shoot you." First I told him go ahead and shoot me, do what he gotta do. Then I just gave in 'cause I thought about my little brother [with whom she was very close].

Disrupted attachments with primary caregivers negatively influence one's internal representation of the self and contribute to a sense of helplessness in affecting the actions of others. Traumagenic dynamics also may compromise judgment in social interactions. This is a potentially dangerous combination for young girls in an already violent environment.

Like others living in war zones and areas of long-term conflict, some of the girls demonstrated bravado in threatening circumstances, or expressed a sense of acclimation and detachment that may have been indicative of psychic numbing in the face of danger in overwhelmingly violent, disorganized neighborhoods: "I'm used to it 'cause I've been around that all my life, so I still feel safe even though all them things are going on." The girls projected a boldness ("I'm my own person, I'm my own leader") that only partially masked vulnerable emotions; many also expressed fear and powerlessness against the onslaught. Paula recalls the pain of her younger self when, as a 2nd grader, she was regularly jumped by 6th graders. Her childish efforts to emulate Popeye, the cartoon character, were not successful.

> You see how he eat a little vegetables and he was strong, he could beat everybody up. That's what I tried to do. It used to never work. I used to get beat up every time. I used to be crying 'cause I used to be in pain.

After a couple of girls threatened to kill her and her cousin, Kathy acknowledges:

> I used to think nothin' could happen, people used to threaten me all the time and I was like, OK. No, until I seen it, until I got jumped one time and I got scared, and until that happened I thought nothing could happen.

Chronically violent environments can arouse fear and foster a well-founded preoccupation with danger, particularly among children with weakened attachment bonds and minimal social supports.[44] The girls' exposure to community violence contributed toward beliefs that life is short and violence inevitable; defensive responses, including antisocial behavior and, for some, fatalistic violence, were compounded by experiences of violence within the home.[45]

Exposure to Violence in the Home

Rather than shielding children from the perils of the outside world, the family itself is often a significant site of danger. This is particularly true for both white girls and girls of color.[46] For the girls in this study, home was the site of pervasive victimization, a significant portion of which was associated with parental friction and discord. As a result, the girls witnessed violence against their mothers and other loved ones, and also experienced direct physical and sexual abuse at the hands of caregivers, siblings, and others.

The girls describe numerous fights in the home that began as simple verbal quarrels and quickly escalated to physical contact: "My mother was cooking and she had a step . . . a boyfriend, or whatever . . . and they got into an argument and she went to throw a pot and he kind of smacked it, and it fell all over her hand." Other conflicts were long-standing, simmering until the moment they erupted into violence. Paula claims her parents "can't stand—they try to kill each other. Literally tried to kill each other." Sounding emotionally detached and as though she had told the story many times before, Paula describes a vicious fight between her parents. She was very young at the time and only recalls fragments of what occurred in this particular instance, but brutality and animosity are integral to the family narrative.

> She [her mother] put glass and roaches and bottle tops in his food and he tried to strangle her [laughing]. I was little. I remember the glass and stuff in my father's food, but he told me after that he was choking her and stuff and she laid there like she was dead. He got scared so he took me over to a neighbor's house, packed up his stuff, and then he saw her move, he was so happy, he ain't know what to do—all he just said was "you dirty bitch." He was so mad, but he was happy 'cause she ain't dead so, you know, they was like—"we won't work out."

Defending against the reality of a violent home and the disruption of parental attachments, Paula laughs at the viciousness displayed. She later reveals that she was the target of parental physical and sexual violence.

Many of the girls witnessed fighting between parents, but the preponderance of violence was inflicted on their mothers by husbands and boyfriends. In these often complex situations, the girls' own safety was at risk. Gayle describes the actions of her stepfather:

> When he get drunk, he like threatens me and my mother with a gun telling us to get out of his house 'cause my mother used to wreck his house, 'cause he gots money hiding in his house so my mother used to wreck his house to find the money. My stepfather used to abuse my mother and me.

Even as young children, the girls attempted to defend or protect their mothers, actions that could be physically and, potentially, legally dangerous.[47] Sixteen-year-old Natalie describes seeing her father beat up her mother from the time she was a toddler and then, when her mother remarried, witnessing her stepfather do the same. When Natalie was in elementary school, her mother threatened divorce after the stepfather had impregnated another woman. A physical fight broke out and Natalie tried to protect her mother and herself: "He tried to hit her and then I came out you know, I was screaming on him or whatever and then I was telling him to leave and he ain't leave . . . he tried to hit her, he tried to beat her up." The stepfather eventually moved out, but continued to terrorize the household: "He left and he used to like come in the middle of the night, banging on the door and stuff like that." Subsequently, the stepfather claimed the mother had hired someone to kill him and succeeded in having her arrested and jailed for several months.

Marcella also tried to protect her mother. One night her mother and a boyfriend were "sitting there in the kitchen drinking" just before Marcella went to bed. In the middle of the night, she is suddenly awakened by her mother's cries for help:

> I went to sleep, and I wake up and she's screaming, "get away from me, get off me." My instinct was to beat him off—that's what I did. She was calling me and I came and I fought the guy off with a broomstick.

The violent attack is confusing, not only because the attacker is a known boyfriend, but also because of the mother's reaction:

> She didn't . . . she didn't want to tell the police, though. I wanted to call the police, but she didn't, so I wonder to this

day, like, did she really want it? I mean, I asked her to call the police, she said no.

Regardless of the mother's reason for not wanting to bring the police into the situation, the message she conveys to her 11-year-old daughter is that the girl is responsible for her own safety as well as that of her mother. Marcella illustrates how this message was consistently reinforced when she segues into a similar story of victimization:

I don't know if [he] was going for me or my mother, but one day I was in the house by myself and my, my nephew, and some other girl I was babysitting. We was sleeping, and I woke up to this guy named [Joe], he just came from jail. He was one of my mother's friends, and he was butt naked on top of me!

After fighting off her assailant, Marcella calls the police. She says she was scheduled to go to court to testify, but "I didn't go 'cause I didn't have nobody to take me." As a child Marcella had no protection (she had to defend herself against her mother's "friend" while babysitting other small children), no emotional support in the home, and no police or legal recourse in the public arena.

The mothers' varied responses to their own abuse (e.g., wrecking a house, divorce, police involvement, and resignation) caused suffering among their daughters who witnessed the violence. Dissension and violence in the home deprived the young women of parental time and attention—resources necessary for guiding healthy development. Exposure to the violence of one parent against another created a frightening and confusing world: when the very person to whom one looks for protection is beating or being beaten, children's sense of their own physical and psychic security is threatened.[48]

Physical Abuse

Child victimization, particularly that perpetrated by a child's caregiver, is a gross disruption of attachment—a failure to meet the child's natural needs. In addition to witnessing violence perpetrated between and against parental figures, the girls in this study spoke of their own direct victimization and of witnessing physical violence against siblings. The girls describe parents and other adults hitting them with fists, shoes, and baseball bats, and cutting them with razor blades, knives, and bottles, but tend to minimize these familial assaults. Fighting was common ("so many times I can't count") and began early. Asked about the first time she was hit, kicked, or bitten by a family member, Joanne responds, "when I was old enough to fight back, like 6 years old." She portrays violence as a way of connecting and engaging with her otherwise emotionally unavailable parent. With a sense of camaraderie, she recalls fighting with her drug-abusing mother:

> Me and my mom, [chuckles] we got into it a lot. We had our fights. We've stabbed each other before; we've done a lot of stuff to each other. I put her in the hospital, she put me in the hospital; it's just like that all the time.

Alcohol and drugs were often part of the mix. Elena claims that she and her mother "used to not fight, but we used to verbally go at it." But then, when asked about her mother's substance use, she answers:

> [Her drinking affected me] because she used to beat me real bad. And she used to like take, when she was high, she used to like take the hangers and beat me with it and I remember one time she broke a glass on my leg and she, um, took a baseball bat and hit my leg. She used to really abuse me.

She describes how she first tried to avoid and then endured physical blows from her mother as well as her brothers:

> Like, she used to hit me and she used to hit me with her bare fist and I couldn't, I couldn't hit her back, but now if she was to hit me, I still wouldn't hit her back but I would block her from hitting me—but all my brothers do that to me, they like hit me with their hands . . .

Dismissing the pain she might have felt and focusing on her "triumphs," she states, "But it don't hurt me no more 'cause I build strength in myself. I don't even cry. I laugh. That gets them angry." In an oppositional twist of empowerment, she learned to be tough and to defy others by shutting down her own physical impulses and emotional responses—at least within the home and among family members.

Jennifer similarly believed her mother's crack smoking was a factor in physical attacks, but unlike Elena, she sometimes fought back.

I didn't like it and me and her was always fighting. 'Cause, like, she'd come in the house, she'd be cranky, she'd be yelling at me for no reason. Sometimes I'd just ignore her and then sometimes, she'd make me mad, we'd get into an argument. She'll . . . I don't know, she'll pull me and things, and just by reflex I'd swing back, and we'd start fighting.

Others noted caregivers' maltreatment, but directed their anger elsewhere. Jackie complains about living with her aunt and relates her own delinquent behavior to the family's behaviors:

They used to treat me wrong, different. They used to treat me like I was a dog. That's why I think I was doing stuff I was doing 'cause they didn't treat me right, and I didn't like that and I was getting older and I didn't like being treated like that.

The girls tend to believe they deserve harsh discipline and to absolve adults' use of violence against them. Gina, for example, explains that she frequently "caught an attitude," and so her grandmother would chase her and hit her with a large wooden stick: "She beat me, but I deserved it. She wouldn't do it just to beat me." Self-blame is congruent with the normal thought patterns of children and, of particular importance here, with the thought patterns of those who have been traumatized.[49] Children look for faults in their own behavior to explain or make sense out of what has happened to them; if they believe their innate badness is the cause of abusive behavior, then their caregivers (who they need) are good. Children can always try to be good, and they can always try to earn their caregivers' forgiveness to gain their protection and care. In this belief, they have the power to change things if they just keep trying.

Traumatized children may rationalize the acts of abusers as appropriate or the best means of addressing a problem. Gayle describes beatings by her foster mother and makes the assumption that the woman resorted to violence because she did not know any better:

The foster parent used to beat me and stuff 'cause I never used to go to school and she was trying to discipline me. I never used to go to school. That's the only way she knew how to take care of me 'cause she didn't have no kids, she couldn't have no kids.

Valerie's father died when she was 5 years old and her mother is incarcerated so she lived with her aunt, cousin, and grandmother. She knows her relatives "loved her deep down inside," but they hit her because "I was messing up . . . at the time it was for my own good, though." Paula also contends that she was hit because she did "stupid" things:

> Oh, okay . . . just, I don't know 'cause she would get mad, you know how you do stuff—well, I was one of them kids you had to . . . 'cause, I used to do very stupid things. No reason for it, but I did it so I would get beat up for stuff.

She explains that her father could tolerate only so much and then would get to a point where he'd "have to" hit her, eventually nearly strangling her:

> And the last time that happened, he ain't hit me, he just picked—he just had me by my neck like this—he was like, "you staying and listening" and I was just steady fighting, fighting and stuff trying to pull away and stuff . . . I wouldn't hit him and give him a reason to hit me back.

Sexual Abuse

The girls in this study were vulnerable to the sexual harassment and assaults of male peers in neighborhood settings. So too, they were subjected to unwanted advances of male adults, many of whom were acquaintances of the girls' caregivers and included family friends and relations. Michelle is typical in that she is quick to list the adult men who had made sexual advances toward her: "My friend's mother's boyfriend. This [other] guy, he used to DJ with my uncle . . . there was my aunt's boyfriend tried to kiss me one time" and the building superintendent who would "make me kiss him on the lips."

There has been much research to demonstrate that girls are especially vulnerable to sexual abuse. Because assailants often live within the same household, sexual abuse begins at an early age and stretches over a long period of time.[50] The intimate context in which sexual abuse generally occurs and the close relationship between abuser and the abused tends to undermine the possibility that other adults will be available to protect and comfort the girlchild. The abuser seeks to ensure secrecy by whatever steps necessary, including verbal and physical threats against the child and those who she loves. The girl's shame, depression, and, perhaps, PTSD symptomatology may persist throughout childhood; in adolescence, they may place her at risk for delinquent behavior.[51]

David Finkelhor and Angela Browne conceptualize child sexual abuse as a process, not a singular event, and identify four traumagenic dynamics—traumatic sexualization, stigmatization, betrayal, and powerlessness—as the core of the psychological injury inflicted by child sexual abuse.[52] *Traumatic sexualization* is "an acceleration of a girl's identity as a sexual being, often coming long before a cognitive ability to understand sexuality in the context of relationship."[53] The abuser may use rewards for inappropriate sexual behavior, and as a result a girl may adopt sexual behaviors to manipulate others, involving herself in precocious sexual activity and aggression. The second traumagenic dynamic is *stigmatization*—the received negative messages (e.g., badness, worthlessness, shamefulness, or guilt) that may be overtly communicated as a way of blaming or labeling, or covertly communicated through the secrecy of the abuse. Stigma can attach to a child when others (perhaps family members) discuss and morally judge her. A sense of otherness may compel defensive moves including substance abuse, self-harm, and delinquency (as a means of affiliating with others or displaced rage). A third dynamic comes into play when a child realizes that someone she trusts and depends on wishes or causes her harm; the *betrayal* is powerful and compromises not only her relationship with the abuser, but places all relationships under suspicion. Finally, *powerlessness* results from a girl's body space being "invaded," generating feelings of intense vulnerability and fear as her desires and wishes are overruled. A girl's self-efficacy is damaged when her efforts to stop the abuser fail and her attempts to convince others to intercede and stop the violation also fail. In the girl's struggle to regain some control and power, she may run away; drop out of school; develop eating, sleeping, or substance abuse disorders; or act aggressively.

The girls in this study spoke of their own experiences of sexual abuse, and of witnessing the sexual abuse of siblings and others by fathers, stepfathers, and other male relatives. A particularly gendered offense, the sexual abuse and the disbelief and inaction of other trusted adults ("she just said it was probably an accident") generated anger and shame in the young women. As a result, their retelling was often hesitant and scattered.[54] Sexual abuse makes them "feel disgusting" and they are horrified ("he was my father, I didn't think he was capable of that") and humiliated ("just being disrespected by my own father"). Kathy was 9 years old when she was raped in her home, by "one of the boys in the neighborhood." She claims she was not at all upset about it because: "It's that I talked about it before. My mother took me to counseling sessions." She did not tell her mother, however, that in the previous year her uncle, the husband of her mother's sister, began sexually assaulting her. The abuse continued for a total of 3 years, "whenever we went to visit, holidays, I'd say in a year, about 12, 13 times." Kathy did not tell her mother because she is fearful that she will not be believed and instead will be judged.

> I told my sister. I didn't tell my mother. The only thing she knew about was when I was raped [by the neighborhood boy]. 'Cause that was in my home when she was at work and then she came home. Uh-huh, 'cause it was her sister's husband and I didn't want to have her think that I'm lying or have her not believe me, so only my sister knew.

Jennifer also remained silent about her uncle's sexual advances. Her uncle molested and exposed himself to her "a lot," for 6 years, beginning when she was 7 years old. It was not until she learned that the uncle was also molesting her younger sister ("she told me that and I believe her") that she said anything. Jennifer had not named the abuse—even to herself—and had tried not to think about it.

> It wasn't anything, I really believe. I didn't really, I didn't really think, think [nervous laugh] of it until I was like 13, I didn't really think of it. I didn't really think of it as nothing, I didn't tell nobody until I was 13. I told my mother because, um, my little sister she told me the same thing and she was only 4, and I flipped.

Protective of her younger sister in a way she had not been for herself, Jennifer courageously reveals the abuse and confronts her uncle: "I told that person, I was like 'I'll kill you if I ever' . . . you know." She is uncertain, however, whether her mother and grandmother will believe her or her sister and becomes defensive. Jennifer says: "After a while I think she started believing me, but I don't know though, but

. . . I don't know if they believed me, but I had the feeling that they didn't, so I was like I don't care." She is enraged, perhaps with her mother, but clearly with the uncle who she contends she "disowned." Crying, she has thoughts of violent retaliation:

> I be thinking about this and I believe I'm gonna kill him. I do. 'Cause I don't know where he at. No, I'm serious. I know but, um, because I don't know where he at and I don't know if he be going back to my room in the house where my little sister at.

The dismay at not being believed is nearly as devastating as the abuse; Jennifer is powerless in convincing her family to intercede. She remains fearful of her uncle and his whereabouts and is frustrated in her desire to protect her sister, especially because she is in custody hours away from home.

Michelle's father began molesting her on his release from prison when she was 8 years old, and continued to do so for 5 years. She struggled to tell her mother about the assaults but, when her credibility is questioned, she blames herself:

> She didn't believe me. I was trying to get along with her, but every time I tried to talk about it, she be like, "nah, I don't believe you." . . . I can't tell nobody 'cause I knew nobody was going to believe me. Nobody trusted me, 'cause when I was living with my grandmother here, before I moved back— remember I told you I did bad things?—I used to steal and stuff and lie about it when I was little. So, nobody believe me.

The abuse began when Michelle was living in Barbados with her grandmother and father while her mother worked in the United States. After 2 years, the girl and her father joined her mother in New York, but the abuse continued. Unprotected in two households, Michelle had no expectation that anyone would believe her or save her because of her own previous "bad" actions. She, like most of the other girls, also fear "causing" additional disruptions to already tenuous relationships.

The lesson the girls learn is that speaking the truth and trusting adults can further humiliate and endanger them. As witness to her stepfather's nightly abuse of her older sister, Joanne knows the terror of not finding safety in either parent. After her mother left for work at the local hospital, he used to come in my room and he used to drag her out by her hair, he used to smack her up and just jack her up against the wall and started kissing her and stuff, . . . and he, he just molest her on the walls, in the closet, in my mom's room, on my mother's bed, in front of my younger brother and sister and in front of me and my older brother.

When Joanne finally tells her mother, she is shocked to learn that "my mother knew, but she didn't know what to do." The stepfather had threatened to kill her mother and so she ignores the ongoing abuse of her daughter. Instead, her mother told him of Joanne's "betrayal"; both adults beat Joanne with a switch and demand that she too adhere to the code of family silence. In an act of bravery and defiance a year later, Joanne goes to the police who finally convince the mother to leave with her children. They arrest the stepfather. The nightmare is not over, however. Upon his release, the stepfather stalks the family and harasses relatives while looking for Joanne. The girl is spared only because of a mistaken identity:

My cousin Nicky, she was just like me, that he thought she was me and he beat her. He beat her. . . . He cut her from her ear to her mouth with a razor and she had to get stitches on both sides so it looks like she got. . . . He, he, just did something to my cousin. He almost killed my little cousin. In the schoolyard, I mean that's just how he is.

In a flat affect, she concludes her story: "He's dead now, I don't know what happened to him, but from my understanding somebody shot him and killed him."

The girls' appraisals of events provide context and complexity and illustrate what quantitative studies suggest: in both their neighborhoods and their homes, these young women were witness to significant trauma, the nature of which was "markedly violent."[55] Their families struggled in distressed communities with limited political voice and economic opportunity, and all of the accompanying social ills fell hard on girls unprotected and lacking in loving relational attachments. The girls were provided no safe place. Traditional constructs of home and family that assume the safety and protection of children are of limited application here. Caregivers who cannot protect their daughters from the dangers of the street, often allow, even invite, predators into the home. Caregivers may themselves be fearful, angry, ill equipped, or unsupported in their parental responsibilities; entrusted with the well-being of young girls, they violate that trust and inflict emotional, physical, and sexual harm and abuse.

With expectations of their safety destroyed, the girls' felt sense of attachment with their caregivers was severely damaged. Traumagenic dynamics negatively affected the internalized sense of self and, without the loving support of adults to address the vestiges of victimizations and other forms of violence, contributed to the girls' perceptions of powerlessness and vulnerability. The message, both implicit and explicit, was that they were alone, disposable, and unworthy of love and protection. Girls struggled in silence to contain overwhelming emotions of shame, guilt, and anger. Elena tries to explain:

> I always was blaming myself. . . . If you was to see me in the community, everybody used to be like "oh, she's happy and smiley." But if you was my boyfriend or something like that, you knock on my door, you know that I'm having family problems and I was really going at it.

Efforts to regain some power and control may drive defensive (and often self-injurious) behaviors that manifest in ways that come to the attention of agencies of the state, including the juvenile justice system. Elena concludes: "I just started flipping and going wild, doing things I wasn't supposed to be doing—then got locked up and that was it."

For these girls who endured polyvictimization and recurring trauma in the home, the menace and brutality of a structurally violent community may have intensified distress reactions, reinforced perceptions of the world as relentlessly dangerous, and contributed to problem behaviors, including aggression toward others.[56] Adding to this volatile mix of disrupted attachments and exposure to violence in the community and in the home were extensive histories of loss. In the next chapter, I review these losses and their traumagenic effects.

Notes

1. Rogers et al., *Trauma: Life Stories,* pp. 5–6.
2. Frazier et al., *Placing Black Girls at Promise,* p. 5.

3. Herman, *Trauma and Recovery,* p. 7.

4. Shengold, *Soul Murder Revisited,* p.1.

5. Herman, *Trauma and Recovery;* Dise-Lewis, "Life Events and Coping Inventory"; A. Freud, "Comments on Psychic Trauma."

6. Pynoos et al. ("Traumatic Stress in Childhood," p. 338) cites Sigmund Freud, "Inhibitions, Symptoms and Anxiety" (1926/1959).

7. K. Erikson, *A New Species of Trouble,* p. 228.

8. Caruth, *Unclaimed Experience,* p. 4.

9. American Psychiatric Association, *DSM-IV-TR,* p. 467. Though the criteria for posttraumatic stress syndrome draw heavily on aspects of terror, Becker-Blease and Freyd ("Beyond PTSD," p. 405) note that "few traumatic events that cause long-lasting harm involve solely or even mostly terror." In cases of sexual abuse in which a child is groomed to view the behavior as acceptable, for example, there may be no immediate fear for life but the sense of betrayal and isolation may be as predictive of negative symptoms as the amount of terror. Loss, too, is often experienced as traumatic. Abused children, for example, may suffer traumatic grief at the loss of relationship when the abuser is removed.

10. Pynoos et al., "Traumatic Stress in Childhood," p. 338. Age, developmental stage, and life course, as well as duration and severity of the event, can all moderate associations between maltreatment, trauma, and delinquency. See Kendall-Tackett et al., "Impact of Sexual Abuse on Children"; Luthar and Zigler, "Vulnerability and Competence"; McLeod and Kessler, "Socioeconomic Status Differences"; Crimmins et al., "Convicted Women."

11. Bowlby, *Attachment;* Bowlby, *Separation;* Bowlby, *Loss, Sadness and Depression.* See also Garbarino et al., "What Children Can Tell Us"; Eth and Pynoos, "Developmental Perspective on Psychic Trauma."

12. Perry et al., "Childhood Trauma." Robinson and Ryder, "Psychosocial Perspectives."

13. Casey et al., "Structural and Functional Brain Development"; Alverez and Emory, "Executive Function."

14. Herman (*Trauma and Recovery*) argues that the study of a single traumatic incident is inadequate for understanding trauma among victims of violence. Solomon and Heide ("Type III Trauma") propose a typology of trauma survivors that accounts for those who have experienced a single event, multiple events, or multiple and pervasive events beginning at an early age and continuing for years.

15. Finkelhor et al. ("Poly-victimization," p. 8) examined a variety of victimization exposures in a general population study of children ages 2 to 17 years old. They define "poly-victimization" as a large number of different kinds of victimization in a single year.

16. Karr-Morse and Wiley, *Ghosts from the Nursery,* p. 162. See also van der Kolk, "Trauma and Memory."

17. Stoppelbein and Greening ("Posttraumatic Stress Symptoms") compared parentally bereaved children (7–17 years old) with a disaster comparison group and a nontrauma control group and found that the parentally bereaved group reported significantly more PTSD symptoms than did the dis-

aster and nontrauma control groups. Also, among the bereaved, girls and younger children reported more symptoms. Allison and Furstenberg ("Marital Dissolution") reported the effects of a marital dissolution to be larger for girls than boys and larger for children who were very young at the time of the dissolution. Black and Pedro-Carroll ("Role of Parent-Child Relationships") found the effects of interparental conflict on psychological well-being to be mediated by parent-child relationships. For women, parental divorce also was found to affect adjustment indirectly (via disrupted father-daughter relationships), although no such path emerged for men.

18. Hood and Carter, "A Preliminary Examination of Trauma History," p. 182.

19. Ibid., p. 188.

20. Makarios, "Race, Abuse," p. 112. See also Baskin and Sommers, *Casualties of Community Disorder.*

21. Sedlak and McPherson, "Youth's Needs and Services," p. 6. Cauffman et al. ("Gender Differences in Mental Health Symptoms") used demographically matched samples to quantify the higher levels of externalizing problems among detained populations compared to community populations and to demonstrate that detained versus community differences are larger among girls than among boys. Detained girls exhibited greater levels of symptomatology than would be predicted on the basis of gender or setting alone. See also Hennessey et al., *Trauma Among Girls.*

22. Boney-McCoy and Finkelhor ("Psychosocial Sequelae") found that violent victimization is more likely than witnessing violence to lead to mental health problems. Arguably, girls have a distinct profile of familial risk factors, and there may be significant differences in how criminality and mental health are manifested in male versus female adolescents. See Silverthorn and Frick, "Developmental Pathways"; Alemagno et al., "Juveniles in Detention"; Hoyt and Scherer, "Female Juvenile Delinquency." Also Abram et al., "Posttraumatic Stress Disorder and Trauma"; Blackburn et al., "The Next Generation."

23. Breslau et al., "Traumatic Events"; Breslau et al., "Sex Differences"; Horowitz et al., "PTSD Symptoms." See also Widom et al., "Alcohol Abuse"; Harlow, *Prior Abuse;* Wood et al., "Violence Exposure and PTSD"; Rivera and Widom, "Childhood Victimization."

24. Cauffman et al., "Posttraumatic Stress Disorder." Most trauma history studies of adolescent offenders are either of exclusively male samples (e.g., Steiner et al., "Posttraumatic Stress Disorder"; Ruchkin et al., "Violence Exposure, Posttraumatic Stress"; Wasserman et al., "Assessing Mental Health Needs of Youth") or primarily male samples that include a small number of females (e.g., Crimmins et al., "Trauma, Drugs and Violence"; Abrantes et al., "Prevalence of Co-occurring Disorders"). Exceptions include Siegel and Williams, "Child Sexual Abuse and Female Delinquency"; Heide and Solomon, "Female Juvenile Murderers."

25. D. Smith et al., "Adolescent Girls' Offending."

26. Gold, *Not Trauma Alone;* Strand et al., "Assessment and Screening Tools."

27. For a review of studies that seek to measure traumatic events among female juvenile offenders, see Ryder et al., "I've Been Around and Around."

28. Elliott et al., *Multiple Problem Youth;* Briere, "Methodological Issues"; Finkelhor, "Victimization of Children"; Loeber and Stouthamer-Loeber, "The Development of Offending"; Kelley et al., "Developmental Pathways." In a longitudinal community study of maltreatment, for example, Lansford and colleagues ("Early Physical Abuse") found that youths who had been physically abused in the first 5 years of life were more likely than those who had not been physically abused to be arrested for both violent and nonviolent offenses as juveniles.

29. Balaban, "Assessment of Children," p. 62, citing Pynoos and Nader, "Prevention of Psychiatric Morbidity in Children After Disasters," in *Prevention of Mental Health Disturbances in Children,* edited by S. Goldston, J. Yager, C. M. Heinicke, and Richard Pynoos (Washington DC: American Psychiatric Press, 1990). Many studies have found evidence that PTSD symptoms occur in young children. See Lieberman et al., "Preschooler Witnesses"; Scheeringa et al., "Toward Establishing Validity for PTSD"; Scheeringa and Zeanah, "Reconsideration of Harm's Way"; Terr, *Too Scared to Cry;* Stover and Berkowitz, "Assessing Violence Exposure."

30. Browne and Finkelhor, "Impact of Child Sexual Abuse"; Dembo et al., "Physical Abuse"; C. Smith and Thornberry, "Childhood Maltreatment and Adolescent Involvement"; Schaffner, "Violence Against Girls," p. 1233.

31. In an effort to determine the breadth and depth of experiences in the lives of youths adjudicated for a violent offense, the original LAVIDA project developed a population-specific trauma inventory to inquire about potentially traumatic events, including items that may be rare in the general population but normative among incarcerated juveniles. Events were then investigated more deeply through open-ended questioning. See Ryder, "I Wasn't Really Bonded"; Ryder et al., "I've Been Around and Around."

32. Naples, *Feminism and Method,* p. 90.

33. De Zulueta, *From Pain to Violence,* p. 3.

34. Shengold (*Soul Murder Revisited,* pp. 1–2) explains that the term "soul murder" was probably coined in the nineteenth century. He uses it to describe the effects of willful abuse and neglect of children by adults to the extent that children's "emotional development has been profoundly and predominately negatively affected; what has happened to them has dominated their motivating unconscious fantasies; and they have become subject to the compulsion to repeat the cruelty, violence, neglect, hatred, seduction, and rape of their injurious past."

35. Exposure to violence reflects the broader range of experiences of child witnesses. Some may not have directly seen violent acts, but they may have heard the abuse as it was happening, seen the physical and emotional effects, or heard about the violence from others. Levendosky and Graham-Berman, "Parenting in Battered Women"; Groves et al., "Silent Victims."

36. Finkelhor et al., "Violence, Abuse, and Crime Exposure," p. 1. The National Survey of Children's Exposure to Violence investigated 48 types of victimization within seven categories (conventional crime; child maltreatment;

peer and sibling victimization; sexual victimization; witnessing and indirect victimization; school violence and threat; and Internet violence and victimization). The findings corroborated prior research indicating that girls were more likely than boys to be sexually victimized and to report slightly higher incidence rates of psychological and emotional abuse.

37. Finkelhor et al., "Children's Exposure to Violence," p. 8. Research has shown that prior exposure to trauma also signals a greater risk of PTSD from subsequent trauma. See, for example, Breslau et al., "Previous Exposure to Trauma."

38. Fantuzzo et al., "Effects of Interparental Violence"; Fantuzzo and Lindquist, "Effects of Observing Conjugal Violence"; Margolin, "Effects of Domestic Violence"; Osofsky, "The Effects of Exposure to Violence"; Marans and Cohen, "Children and Inner-City Violence"; Langhinrichsen-Rohling and Neidig, "Violent Backgrounds"; Hughes, "Psychological and Behavioral Correlates"; Elliott, "Serious Violent Offenders"; Rouse, "College Students"; Mangold and Koski, "Gender Comparisons"; Fergusson et al., "Childhood Sexual and Physical Abuse"; Kendall-Tackett, *Treating Lifetime Health Effects*.

39. Garbarino et al., "What Children Can Tell Us," p. 378. See also Bell and Jenkins, "Traumatic Stress"; Lauritsen, "Families and Communities."

40. Cook and Laub, "Unprecedented Epidemic," pp. 57, 60; Cook and Laub, "After the Epidemic," p. 26. According to Fox (*Trends in Juvenile Violence,* p. 2) before youth gun violence in the United States reached its peak in 1993, juvenile homicides committed with handguns quadrupled.

41. Fifteen girls said that they had witnessed at least one killing. One girl answered "no" when asked directly if she had witnessed a killing, but later disclosed that she saw her father accidentally shoot and kill her aunt. Another declined to answer the question, but responded to the follow-up questions (age at the time; number of killings she had witnessed; and how upset she felt at the time).

42. Jones, *Between Good and Ghetto,* p. 5.

43. Griffiths et al., "Fighting over Trivial Things," p. 88.

44. Garbarino et al., "What Children Can Tell Us."

45. Garbarino, "An Ecological Perspective."

46. K. Mitchell and Finkelhor, "Risk of Crime Victimization," p. 958. Research by the US Department of Health and Human Services (*Child Maltreatment 2010,* table 3-13, p. 47) indicated that, among all black children (not delineated by gender), child maltreatment victimization rates were nearly double those of white children (14.6 percent vs. 7.8 percent).

47. Pro-arrest domestic violence statutes have brought more girls into the justice system, criminalizing, for example, girls defending a mother against a batterer or children fighting with parents (American Bar Association and National Bar Association, *Justice by Gender*). Buzawa and Hotaling ("Impact of Relationship Status," p. 352) reported that daughters were arrested in 92 percent of the cases they reviewed, "whereas arrest occurred in 75 percent of incidents in which a son assaulted a parent."

48. Margolin and John, "Children's Exposure."

49. Herman, *Trauma and Recovery,* p. 103.

50. DeJong et al., "Epidemiologic Variations"; Browne and Finklehor, "Impact of Child Sexual Abuse"; Finkelhor et al., "Violence, Abuse, and Crime Exposure."

51. Feiring et al., "Potential Pathways."

52. Finkelhor and Browne, "Traumatic Impact."

53. See Robinson, "Crystal Virtues," p. 65, for a summary of David Finkelhor and Angela Browne's framework and the relationship to female delinquency.

54. In describing women's experiences of violence, Das and Nandy ("Violence, Victimhood," p. 55) state that women "retained the memory of loot, rape and plunder" in their bodies and so remembered it differently than men.

55. Lederman et al., "Characteristics of Adolescent Females," p. 325.

56. Duckworth et al., "Influences of Interpersonal Violence."

5

Traumatic Childhood Experiences of Loss

It upset me 'cause I seen him on the floor bleeding,
but I didn't really, I didn't really know about death then
'cause I was only 5 or 6 years old.
—*Christine, 14 years old*

All of the girls in this study have extensive histories of loss. In some respects, this is not unusual. In the general youth population, familial injuries and illnesses are common, and most adolescents have experienced the death of a loved one. In the United States, approximately one-half of all marriages end in divorce. For a variety of reasons, a large percentage of children in New York State and New York City live in single-parent families (approximately 36 percent and 43 percent, respectively).[1] Among minority and low-income communities, escalating incarceration rates since the late 1970s have been an additional and significant factor contributing to family disruptions.

Though the girls' experiences may be common, they become alarming when we consider the significant role of attachment and the overlay of extensive loss among children already exposed to community and family violence. Furthermore, many of the girls' losses were experienced in violent or socially stigmatized contexts (e.g., homicide, AIDS, drug overdose, incarceration, or homelessness). In assessing these experiences, I derived four broad types of loss from the narrative data. Sixteen-year-old Gayle's history, however, demonstrates how complicated life situations belie simple categorization. Her father died before she was born (death of a loved one) and her mother often left her alone while adults drank and used drugs inside the home (psycho-

89

logical unavailability). Eventually, her mother was "busted" for selling drugs: "She went to jail for like 2 years (physical absence), and they put me in the foster home and I couldn't get no contact with my mother" (loss of home). The four types of loss are closely intertwined, but a separate examination of each provides context and insight to the girls' responses.

Death of a Loved One:
"I Didn't Get a Chance to Say Good-Bye"

Eighty-three percent of the girls had experienced the death of at least one person they loved and with whom they were emotionally close. They reported the deaths of parents and grandparents as well as siblings, relatives, and friends. Deaths occurred in a variety of ways—after a long struggle with an illness, accidentally, and by homicide. Many girls reported in graphic detail what they experienced while others retained only partial memories and associations. The death of grandparents was relatively common, most of whom had died of diseases or complications of age. Because they were young children when their grandparents passed, the girls were uncertain of the causes and unfamiliar with medical terminology. Few mentioned any adult assistance or support in comprehending the death. Describing her response to her grandmother's death, Diane explains that, at 5 years old, "I was very upset and I was confused too, because I was younger then and I didn't know what was going on." Fifteen-year-old Lauren asserts that her grandfather died "just laying in bed" and Lisa believes her 97-year-old grandmother "caught a heart attack" after being frightened by loud noises. When asked what happened to four family members who had died, 16-year-old Rose responds: "I don't know, they just died. One of my uncles he died of AIDS. I think the other ones died of cancer or something like that."

Parental deaths also occurred during the girls' early developmental years, with lasting effects. Valerie, now 15 years old, remains extremely upset by the death of her father when she was 5 years old. She recalls with sadness that he was shot and paralyzed, and died while still a young man. Elena's father died from an unnamed disease when she was 11 years old. His passing preceded by months the fatal stabbing of Elena's younger brother and the imprisonment of her older brother. The family had multiple, long-standing problems, but for Elena the loss of her father signified the demise of family cohesiveness.

Before I came to DFY,[2] we had so many family problems because I had just lost a little brother, just lost my father; I was really out of control. My family was really slipping away, oh God. It was just breaking off in pieces.

When a parent's death is abrupt or unexpected, the loss can be particularly difficult. Alona was 9 years old when her father died. She emphasizes the unexpectedness of his passing when asked what bothers her most: "AYAHH, because I missed him. AYAHH, I loved him and he was my father. I didn't get a chance to say 'goodbye, I love you.' No hug or nothing." Even after controlling for other vulnerability factors, children who experience a sudden loss of attachment are more likely to develop depression and are at higher risk for PTSD than children who do not face such an unexpected loss.[3]

Adults were rarely available to help the girls understand what was happening or how to adjust to life without the deceased. Sadness and fear is a toxic mix that often fuels anger. Combined with the loss of numerous family members and friends, several girls worried about additional disruptions in their close relationships and the potentiality of death. The girls were angry at doctors because "they wasn't really doing nothing to help" ailing relatives; angry at adults who tried to shield the loss ("I was really upset because nobody told me until 5 days later"); and angry when elders survived their children ("I was real mad, I was upset, 'cause I didn't know or understand why he died and my grandmother didn't die. 'Cause she was always getting sick. She was older than him too").

Lisa explains how, when her grandparent died, it was "sad for me," but the loss also angers her and makes her anxious about the future. Two years after her grandparents died, Lisa's baby sister "had to go to the hospital to get surgery 'cause she had cancer and a tumor in her head," and her brother was born premature and "almost died, so he had to stay in the hospital, and get fed through a tube." Struggling to explain her feelings, Lisa says she

> didn't want to go through an experience like that, [and] I couldn't hurt myself 'cause somebody else was hurt. So, I was mad. I was real mad. You know, 'cause I had to go through all that, and I didn't wanna to go through all of that. It just made me mad. Because, it made me mad that . . . my grandmother and grandfather had to die, and it made me mad because my baby sister and brother could've died.

Distressed by the actual loss of her grandparents and without the help of adult support, Lisa is unable to access the psychological space wherein she can allow herself to feel emotional or physical pain. Unconsciously, she defends against other potential losses and uses anger to express her annihilation anxiety and fear.[4]

Many girls began to talk about their grief over a loved one's death, but then quickly turned to their current situation. Marcella, for example, relays the story of an aunt who recently died of AIDS and, in the telling, switches to a description of her young cousin: "He has seizures. That's scary 'cause he had a seizure in front of me, we thought he was gonna die." Speaking first of her grandfather, Kathy segues to her mother's illness: "Yeah, he had cancer. It was like eating the skin and, . . . like my mother right now, she's having, um, I don't know if it's cancer, but they had to open her throat and put a box in it." In a similar narrative pattern, Lauren states that the death of two grandparents, each from a stroke, was extremely upsetting for her. In the course of this revelation, she shifts to her mother's current illness before adjusting her language to speak of her mother in the past tense: "My mother . . . she got HIV. One of these days she can go, you never know. She can pass away. [She] was somebody that was really, really close to me and the other one is my grandparents." In a number of cases, not only did a family member's illness and subsequent death cause immediate distress, but the experience generated additional fears about the impending death of other loved ones: if disease can kill one person, it is likely that others will also be lost.

Guilt can contribute to survivors' traumatic stress and children are vulnerable to the fear that a death was somehow caused by something they did or failed to do, or by something they thought.[5] Joanne believes she is partially responsible for her grandfather's death, which occurred while she was on the telephone with her grandmother:

> He was screaming in the background, "I want to see my granddaughter before I die" and I was like 12 hours away and didn't know what to do. If he wouldn't have gotten so upset about that he probably would have lived longer. They would have gotten him to a hospital, but he was spas'ing out.

Christine offers that her uncle "took too many different kinds of drugs and his heart exploded," and yet she felt guilty watching him die of an overdose:

It made me feel like it was my fault because it's—I know in my, in my mind that it wasn't nothing I could do because his heart was, 'cause the hospital told us his heart was gonna explode even if we would have called right away, his heart still was gonna explode. But in my heart, I just feel like maybe if we would have called the ambulance right away when we seen him, he probably would still be alive today. . . . He was in the bathtub and he was just shaking, and we was like, 'cause, my, my, um, friends and they mother—they was like no, just leave him 'cause he's gonna be alright.

The sense of guilt may be even more pronounced in the case of homicide. Rose, who witnessed gang members murder her brother, blamed herself for "not being able to do nothing about" the attack.

The homicide death of a loved one is a unique loss, a juncture where "personal reactions to trauma clash with grief and mourning."[6] Emotional responses are heightened and the homicide creates for co-victims (i.e., family and close friends) a very different experience "than deaths caused by acute causes, terminal illness, suicide or accidental death."[7] Covictims must live with the knowledge that their loss is the direct and willful consequence of another person's actions,[8] an act of volition that is often sudden and violent. Homicide covictims are likely to experience intrusive thoughts and grotesque imagery, feelings of sadness and longing that may vacillate with guilt and anger, and a general numbness. The closer the emotional attachment between victim and covictims, the more amplified are the traumagenic effects. Compounding the trauma in this study, many of the girls (covictims) knew both the victim and the perpetrator.

Joanne was reluctant to talk about her experience of witnessing a killing until, in another context, she began to talk about a boyfriend. In the discussion of dating relationships, she disclosed the murder of her boyfriend and that of the friend who killed him. She says:

So, he [boyfriend] was a little over protective, and this boy that I grew up with . . . he shot him [the boyfriend] 'cause he was getting all in his face and he was saying "oh, you touch my girl and I'm gonna shoot you," and he was like "yeah, fine, I'm gonna shoot you first." Then they both pulled a gun out at the same time and they both fired. But the other guy shot my man. He's dead. He died on my birthday.

Later, a member of Joanne's family killed the friend. Joanne annually marks the loss of these relationships.

In another account, Donna tells of an incident at a family picnic. She describes the shooting death of a beloved aunt (that may have been an accident) and illustrates how quickly an argument can turn fatal with the introduction of a gun:

> My father told her to stop playing and she kept on playing, playing. So, my father pulled the .38 out and her husband tried to grab my father. The gun went up in the air. It went out of control and shot her in her stomach. My father knocked the hell out of her husband and he fell out.

Donna is haunted by the gory imagery ("see[ing] it with your own eyes") and she struggles with the knowledge that "if it wasn't for my father, she would still be alive."

The girls' stories of homicide were frequently associated with gang activities and the flourishing drug trade in local neighborhoods. Though specific circumstances of the drug deal were often unclear, when something went wrong the results were devastating.[9] Christine believes that the fatal shooting of her uncle (brother to the man she watched die of an overdose) "had something to do with drugs." A young child at the time, she vividly recalls the details of his murder:

> Seeing that he was running down the block, and somebody was chasing him with a gun and they shot him in his head and he fell to the ground. It upset me 'cause I seen him on the floor bleeding, but I didn't really, I didn't really know about death then 'cause I was only 5 or 6 years old and I didn't really understand it.

Others also reported grisly memories of friends and family being killed. Kathy witnessed drug-related, neighborhood violence on a regular basis, but suffered a horrible shock when her best friend and the friend's brother were killed by a drive-by shooter:

> We were sitting on the corner and she got shot in the back of the neck. I didn't move, I didn't know what to do. I just stood there. And I didn't realize she got shot until she fell and she was bleeding on me, and I had blood all over me and stuff too.

. . . They killed her and her brother, just went crazy, tried to
kill everybody. To see her get shot. To see the blood come out
of her head. To see her eyes roll back. Started turnin' colors
and see her brother screamin', goin' crazy.

The girls' reactions parallel suggestions in the literature that covictims of homicide are often more traumatized than bereaved and that
trauma reactions may interrupt and impede mourning. Efforts to block
recurrent imagery associated with the homicide make it difficult for
covictims to acknowledge and adjust to the loss, thereby delaying
recovery.[10] For some, homicide has a chronic quality that cannot be
integrated; the death destroys the covictim's entire meaning system.[11]
Recovery from the trauma can be particularly difficult for children,
who require adult guidance in navigating through the introspective
process of adjustment. One of the few studies specific to child covictims indicates that bereaved siblings manifest depressive, PTSD, and
anxiety disorders, and have difficulty with peer relationships.[12] They
may become hypervigilant in their awareness of their surroundings and
fearful of perpetrators still at large. In describing the particular and
complicated emotional responses to having witnessed the killing of a
loved one, many of the girls in this study spoke of crumbling relationships and the feeling that life was less meaningful and manageable.[13]
One admits that, in the aftermath of a family member's killing, "my
family, ever since then, we just been separated. We just all go our separate ways." Isolated and left to their own devices, many of the girls
rendered homicide another loss for which there was little emotional
space or time for reflection, grief, and integration.

For others, knowing the identity of the killer spurred thoughts of
vengeance. Noreen Stuckless suggests that among mourners, survivor-
victims of homicide who attributed culpability to a particular person
were angrier, had more vengeful emotions, and felt the world was less
comprehensible than mourners whose loved ones died from illness or
accidents and did not attribute responsibility to a specific perpetrator.[14]
Holding a specific person or persons responsible also is a way of
focusing painful emotions. Maria was awakened by gunshots one
morning and then saw from her window that "somebody was bleeding
out of their head." It was a friend, a local drug dealer. Two weeks later,
Maria derived some satisfaction from the fact that local crews (i.e.,
gangs) including her own, joined together to avenge her friend's death:
"I guess they [the killers] just wanted to have his money. But we got

them back!" Likewise, Kathy, whose friend was killed in a drive-by shooting, recognized some of the shooters and predicted that at least "one of them's a dead man" because her own gang had plans to retaliate. After Elena learned that the person who killed her brother was likely to be released, she hints at her desire to attack the boy regardless of the legal ramifications:

> He was only locked up for 2 years! What's going on? Everybody was like, he gonna be coming out on probation [*sic*]. I was like, if he come out on probation and I come back home, I'm coming right back upstate [to a correctional facility] 'cause, what's going on?

In chronically dangerous environments, children not only experience the death of loved ones from aging, illness, and substance abuse, but are forced to confront death caused by willful acts of carnage. The accumulation of such losses can reinforce beliefs that life is short and violence inevitable; defensive responses may include antisocial behavior and, for some, fatalistic violence.[15]

Physical Absence: "Never Seen Her, Really"

Death, as devastating and complete as it is, unfortunately was only one type of loss common to the girls in this study. They also suffered the loss of loved ones who, though alive, were physically absent. Physical absences generally were associated with separation or divorce, imprisonment, or hospitalization of parents or primary caregivers. As with other types of losses, children's adjustment to their caregivers' separation or divorce is determined by several factors, including the child's age at the time of the event, the prior parent-child relationship, and the frequency and type of contact with the nonresident parent.[16] Most of the girls' parents (88 percent) were divorced, separated, or never together, and separations occurred when the girls were on average only 3 years old. Several girls had numerous stepparents and parental figures in addition to their biological parents, and it was not always clear if it was the biological parents or others who were divorcing or separating—or both. Some couples separated more than once. As Adele explains, "I was like 3 and 7. It [parent's relationship] was off and on, on and off." Royale's parents divorced when she was a newborn. She lived with her mother, and although her father lived in the neighborhood, he generally was not part of her life. This was particularly upsetting to her because, for a time, she had enjoyed visits with him: "When I was younger my father used to take me to his house and we'd stay like a weekend over there, but after awhile that stopped." After the visits ended, she saw him only occasionally: "I see him walking down the street sometimes. I'd just say hi and bye. . . . " His close physical proximity and Royale's memories of the time spent together underscore her sense of abandonment.

Elena's parents separated when she was just a year old. She primarily lived with her mother, and though she references her father's frequent visits, it is unclear as to the amount of time either parent was actually present. Elena speaks explicitly of her desire to be the center of two parents' loving attention, but her expression of loss reflects a more general yearning among all of the girls for close attachment and models of "how to hold a relationship":

> I wanted to be different from everybody else. My whole gang, they don't have both of them, don't have mothers and fathers and . . . I just, I wanted to be different. I wanted to have both. I didn't want to have one or the other. . . . I wanted both so when I need to talk about boys, I wanna talk to my daddy. When I need to talk about girls, I wanna talk to my mother. When I wanna know how to dress, I wanna talk to my mother. When I wanna know how to hold a relationship, I wanna talk to my father.

Unfortunately, parental figures moved in and out of the girls' lives, even as the girls themselves were shuttled among relatives, social services, and the juvenile justice system.

In many situations, both parents were physically gone for long periods of time. Gina, who does not know her father, has little contact with her mother because "she used to have a problem with drugs and alcohol and so she gave me to my grandmother" when she was only a year old. "She [mother] was in one of them rehabilitation centers" before reclaiming her daughter 4 years later. Paula mentions that the adults in her life "just tell me little bits and pieces of the story and stuff," but she does know her parents separated when she was less than a year old and that, several times thereafter, "they got back together and broke up again." She assumes the separations were somehow her fault.

They kept trying, in that time, they kept trying, went back together, but it wasn't working out . . . for some reason, after me, they just couldn't take each other no more. Before I was born, everything was fine and after I was born, they started arguing and fighting and stuff. Then she would leave or he would leave and they kept doing that.

Paula lived with an aunt because her mother left and "my father don't know how to take care of a child by himself." When she was 3 years old, "I came back to live with my mother . . . I don't know where she went, then she came back and got me later." Years later when Paula's mother was admitted to the hospital ("she had to get the lining around her heart removed"), the experience was reminiscent of Paula's earlier abandonment when she was left with relatives for her first, developmentally critical years without knowledge of her mother's whereabouts.

Imprisonment was yet another cause of parental absences. The girls were not shielded from the effects of mass incarceration, including its disparate racial consequences.[17] In many of their families incarceration was tied to both existing and subsequent difficulties and losses, and was itself, perhaps, a form of death.

My brother got a life sentence. But most likely he be getting probation [*sic*], but I don't look at him like that. He 19, by the time he come out, what's gonna be the use? So there's no point for him to come out. I don't even look at it like that no more.

Though men make up the bulk of the US prison population in terms of numbers, the annual growth rate of female imprisonment has outpaced that of male imprisonment, and many of the girls in this study reported the incarceration of mothers.[18] Jennifer's parents divorced when she was 6 years old, and she first claims that "me and my mother, we were like sisters" and that her mother let her do "anything I wanted to do." Then, in a striking contradiction to this idealized vision of attachment, she adds "my mother, she was alright, she wasn't never really ever there 'cause she was either locked up or I was locked up." At the time she was interviewed, Jackie was 13 years old and her parents had "never been together." She does not remember how old she was when her parents abandoned her, only that her mother was incarcerated and she has "never seen her, really." Jackie had lived most of her life with her aunt:

> 'Cause my mom couldn't take care of me. My mom went to jail so they didn't have nowhere to put me, and I had to go to court and they gave me to my aunt 'cause my mom said she didn't want me—that I should live with somebody else. At that time, my father wasn't available. I don't really know. I just hear little parts of it, but I don't really know why he couldn't get me—but they gave me to my aunt—no, yeah, my father choose for me to go with my aunt.

Jackie's childhood losses are significant and her feelings of abandonment, resentment, and unworthiness are prominent. Despite the passage of years, no one has dispelled Jackie's belief that her mother "didn't want me." Neither has anyone offered a satisfactory reason as to why her father "couldn't get me," but chose to let her aunt care for her.

In a complicated story of separations and incarcerations, rejections, and revolving caregivers, Natalie says she was somewhat "used to" her biological father "getting locked up" off and on from the time she was a baby. Her mother left her father because "he used to beat her up sometimes," and eventually remarried. Natalie did not get along with her stepfather and, against her mother's wishes, went to live with her father and his new family. The girl's desire to be with her previously absent father, and her parents' ongoing conflict and inability to resolve their own differences, precipitated the loss of her mother's physical and emotional presence: while Natalie is living with her father, her mother refuses to see or talk to her young daughter. The scenario changes again because "while I was living with him [father], he had got arrested for murder" and Natalie returns to live with her mother. Several years later, her mother is accused of hiring someone to kill Natalie's stepfather and is jailed.

Fourteen-year-old Christine describes the physical loss of her father who is imprisoned, and acknowledges that from the time of her birth until she was 11 years old, one or both of her parents were gone. Her parents never married, but she remains hopeful that "when he come home, they gonna be back together."

> He, my father, he's been in jail off and on, so, I'll say he lived with us for a good 1 year straight. My mother was still preg-

nant with me when my father first went to jail. And he came home when I was like, 3. [And went back] when I was like, 5.

Her father's incarcerations are extremely upsetting to her, made worse by the loss of her mother "when I was like 8 or 10 or 9, that's when she went to the drug program and she came out, like, 18 months later." Christine was placed in kinship care (foster care with relatives)[19] and lived with her grandmother and uncles.

In another example of the extensive effects of incarceration on family structure, Michelle explains that her father was incarcerated in the family's native Barbados when she was 2 years old. His imprisonment and the resultant economic instability caused her mother to send Michelle to live with maternal grandparents in New York. Though not an uncommon solution among island residents, the practice is not without emotional consequences. Michelle expresses great sadness at the loss of both parents and the notion that (from her perspective) her mother came to the United States only because of Michele's misbehavior:

I was being bad and my grandmother was like "I'm not going to take care of her if she keeps on being bad. You are going to have to come and take care of your responsibilities." That's what she used to tell my mother.

At the age of 8, Michelle is sent back to Barbados where she stays with her paternal grandmother for another 2 years until her father's release from prison. Finally, after her mother sends for Michelle's father, she (at the age of 11 years) and a younger brother join both parents in New York.

Psychological Unavailability: "We Didn't Hardly Talk"

In contrast to losses where the loved one is dead or physically absent are those circumstances in which children's parents or primary caregivers are physically present but emotionally unavailable: the result is "the atrophy of the [attachment] bond."[20] The unavailability may develop because of substantial drug use or addiction, serious illness, injury or disability, or the distractions of attending to other children, work, or personal problems. The girls in this study frequently spoke of feeling detached from parents and primary caregivers and described situations where adults appeared incapable or unwilling to nurture their emotional needs. Adolescents often feel an emotional gap between themselves and their caregivers, but what stood out for these girls was the pervasiveness and extent to which the adults were emotionally unavailable at critical points in their psychological and social development.

Even when parents who were physically absent left daughters in the care of relatives or friends, the secondary caregivers often were not present emotionally. Gina's mother was not around much of her life because of a substance abuse problem, and her grandmother and aunt with whom Gina had lived since she was a year old were emotionally disengaged toward the girl. Gina describes a typical scenario:

> I would want to go outside and do something that like a mother would do with you, but my grandmother wouldn't want to go outside or play cards with me. Or, you wanna go to the mall, but my grandma don't drive. [My aunt] worked at night so she sleeps in the daytime. So, sometimes she was tired. My grandmother watched soap operas and my aunt slept and I be outside, running the streets.

On the surface, this is a simple story of a lonely girl looking for companionship; examined closely and placed in context, it represents a childhood wrought with loss and a yearning for love and attachment.

Marcella has no recollection of her father, and her only sister, 5 years her senior, moves out of the household when Marcella is 10 years old. Her mother is confined to a wheelchair, paralyzed by a random gunshot when Marcella was an infant. Marcella stops attending school after the 6th grade and assumes much of the responsibility for her mother's physical and emotional needs. She bathes, diapers, and cooks for her mother, and tries to control her mother's drinking and attempts at self-harm.

> She became an alcoholic. . . . And bein' that she was drunk, she was real hard to deal with, she would like want to go outside, she always tried to commit suicide a lot, too. So, I could try and stop her from doing that, grabbing pills outta her hand, knives and stuff. . . . A couple of times, she'd punch windows and get her fists sliced up.

Marcella says that the two of them "had a lot of problems" and "didn't have a lot of communication . . . there was like nobody I could really talk to." Marcella's mother is unable to nurture, protect, or provide for her daughter; thus, with their caregiver roles reversed, Marcella becomes the physical and emotional support for her mother.

Absorbed in their own world of drug use, many parents and caregivers had little time or energy for, or were oblivious to, the basic emotional needs of their adolescent girls. Rose, commenting on her father's daily use of alcohol and cocaine, admits that "I thought my father depended more on that and cared more about that than he did about me." Exemplifying the frustration and anger of many young women whose substance-using parents were psychologically unavailable, Royale complains that her drug-using mother provides physical necessities but that an emotional void exists between them: "I ate regularly, lived in a regular house, like my mother would cook us dinner." But when asked about her relationship with her mother, she says only that "it was OK, we, never, we didn't hardly talk." Sounding disgusted, she adds, "'cause my mother was on drugs so my brother had to take care of us." Even calling home is a frustrating experience. Annoyed, she states that "sometimes, I don't even know where my mother's at sometimes. Like sometimes she be home [but] she just don't answer the phone, she just sleeping." Royale has not witnessed her mother's drug use, but she perceives the change and notes the disingenuousness of her mother's demeanor: "[I] never seen her do it, I could just tell . . . 'cause she act nice. My mother's nice but she act nicer." Royale clearly is upset by the changes in her mother and adds: "I didn't like it when she was drunk . . . or when she was high. I didn't like the way it made her look and I didn't like the way it made her act."

Describing her mother as a "Buddha-head" and "a chronic for crack," Elena is angry when she discovers that "long, long, long walks" with her father and trips to her grandfather's house are ruses designed to get her and her siblings out of the house so her mother can get high. When the children remain in the house and the mother is high, she can be punitive. As Elena explains, her mother's inconsistent disciplinary actions appear to be linked to the mother's drug use:

> She would put me on punishment for like 6 months and the next day I would be off punishment. And she be like you can't go outside and the next day I could go outside, and I knew

there was really something wrong with her. I don't know, it was just the crack just really getting to her.

Elena describes her mother as "like antisocial. She don't like speaking to nobody. So she just keeps her problems in." After Elena's father and brother die, her mother's isolation worsens and the emotional withdrawal intensifies Elena's feelings of rejection, loss, and detachment.[21]

Loss of Home: "I'm Not Living with Nobody"

Losing one's home can be devastating. A person's home is their "personal and familiar environment," an object of attachment that plays a significant role in "determining [their] emotional state."[22] Without a place to call "home," it is difficult to maintain one's sense of self and one's social role.[23] As is the case with so many girls caught up in the justice system,[24] the young women in this study had little residential stability in their lives, either in terms of parental figures or in physical settings. They spoke of being evicted by landlords, or forced to move because their buildings were unlivable. State agencies removed girls from their primary caregivers and placed them in foster care, mental health treatment programs, and juvenile justice facilities—actions that replicated prior disruptions. In many of these cases, the loss of home was preceded by a parent's death, absence, or unavailability, thereby compounding the girls' losses. In addition to state actions, the young women told of ongoing family arguments over curfews and other "stuff with my mother" that resulted in being thrown out of the home or placed in institutions.

In a few cases, the girls told of voluntary moves made to improve the family's situation. Describing the extensive drug use and related violence in her Bronx neighborhood, Lisa explains "that's how come we be moving. We be moving from place to place, place to place in the Bronx . . . 'cause you know over there, they's like bad, they is real bad, . . . I don't like that place."

More common were evictions and, for two young women, house fires were the cause. When she was 9 years old, Marcella and her sister temporarily lived with an aunt. One morning as the girls lay in bed, "there was a fire, and we evacuated and the building ended up burning down." Fires occurred many times in Paula's apartment building, so often that in her description of the structure she states "that building stayed on fire" because "every crackhead that had a lighter came to that building to shoot up—to smoke and they kept dropping lighters and stuff." Eventually, someone burned a hole in her apartment's ceiling and they had to move out.

> I used to be crying 'cause my building on fire. Where we gonna live at? Also . . . every time we had a fire, I could never find that darn cat I had 'cause my mother bought me a Siamese for my birthday when I was like 7, and every time there was a fire, he . . . he go hide. . . . Last time, after they had the fire, we couldn't live there anymore, we didn't find him till like 4 days later under my high-rise.

The trauma extended to the loss of Paula's close friend because the fire forced all occupants to move out and settle elsewhere. Her home was gone, as was her cat (temporarily) and most of her possessions: "We came in the house, get some stuff, see what could we save."

In addition to situations where their families had to move, a majority of the girls lost their homes and the company of relatives because of state interventions; 71 percent had spent some time in an out-of-home placement such as foster care or a group home, with the length of placement ranging from a few days to over a decade. Alona describes how she came to be involved with various child welfare systems. Her parents separate when she is 2 years old and her father dies when she is 9. She lives with her mother until she is 12 years old, when (for reasons she does not recall, or perhaps even know) she is placed in nonrelative foster care. There Alona describes ongoing arguments until, after a year, she loses that "second" home as well:

> My [foster] mother kicked me out . . . 'cause, for her boyfriend. . . . We had this fight and she had took his side. He asked her, that if I don't leave, he gonna leave. You know she love him and stuff like that so she like "get out!"

She is not "asked to leave"; neither have arrangements been made for her departure. Rather, the foster mother chooses the love of a boyfriend, and 13-year-old Alona is again on her own.

Other girls had no memory or understanding as to how or why they had been removed from their home. Ruptured attachments may be so difficult to bear that memories are suppressed or denied, and there is no verbal narrative or context.[25] Elena states simply that she was in foster care "age 1 to 7—then I came home." Lisa, who was placed in foster care at the age of 10 for "no longer than probably a year," cannot remember why she was removed from her home: "That's one thing I don't remember. I can't remember all the way back. . . . I try, but I can't."

The disturbance of the child-parent attachment can be traumatic even when the home setting is not supportive and protective, and the child's relationship with the parent is strained. Marcella's mother has her arrested for hitting her, enabling the Bureau of Child Welfare (BCW) to remove the girl from her home. Despite the emotional and physical danger of living with a violent and drug-abusing mother, Marcella is distraught and resistant when the two are separated. She threatens suicide and is placed in a hospital for observation. After her mother comes to visit and is preparing to leave, Marcella becomes frantic. Terrified of being abandoned, she follows her mother down the hospital hallway and announces: "You leavin', I'm leavin'!" Prevented from doing so, Marcella hurls a scissors at the staff, promptly alerting security guards who converge on her with leather restraints.

> They grabbed me and they straightened me and put me in my hospital bed, stuck me with a needle and I fell asleep, and I woke up in the psychiatric floor, with the adults, and I was there for 2 months.

The BCW has made several attempts to remove Marcella from her home and, on her release from the hospital, the separation is accomplished:

> So, this social worker was trying to take me away from my mother for the longest, and so, now was his chance, so when I left the hospital, he came and got me and put me in a car and we went straight to the group home in Staten Island.

Marcella is furious with her mother for her abusive and neglectful behaviors, but turns her rage toward the actions of the social worker. In the face of separation, she fights to preserve her connection and faith with her primary caregiver by pardoning her mother of any blame or responsibility. Despite Marcella's clearly stated desire to stay connected with her mother, social services focus on removing her from her home and do little to attend to the physical and psychological needs of mother and daughter. Suffering the loss of her mother's love and bereft of her sister's companionship, Marcella's attachments are further disrupted by systems personnel intent on punishing her behaviors rather than understanding their meaning.

Children placed in kinship care may experience an aggravated and more complicated sense of loss than those who are placed in foster care with nonrelatives.[26] Placement with relatives has the potential to buffer feelings of abandonment, depending on the circumstances in the home of origin. The reconfiguration of the household composition, however, can also generate adjustment difficulties and add to feelings of loss. Placed with relatives, Jackie feels unjustly treated, believing her aunt spends money designated for her care on others while she goes without:

> She get money for me 'cause she had custody of me from my mom and she get the money for me, but they never gave it to me and she just bought, the money that they gave me, I never seen it. She bought her daughter stuff and herself with it, and it made me feel bad 'cause I was going [to] school with the same clothes on.

It is difficult to ascertain the household environments, and we cannot assume that extended families are able to automatically or completely offset children's sense of emotional loss and detachment from their primary caretaker. The girls in this study may (or may not) have been provided for in terms of basic necessities, but the loss of their home had more extensive ramifications. Not only did they have to adjust to their parents' absence, but they had to move from their home base into that of another, exchanging familiarity of one location and their own life story of events with that of a new "other" place, as Mindy Fullilove describes.[27] In this other place, it was likely that the hosting relatives were also financially and emotionally stretched and, more important, there was no assurance that the girls would be made to feel significant, special, and loved.

The girls describe a pattern of being in and out of foster care, group homes, and detention centers several times. Gayle is first placed in foster care when she is a toddler because her mother was selling drugs in their house. She remembers being taken away:

It was, like, hard to leave her. The BCW they came to pick me up and it's like I didn't cry or nothing. It's like I knew, I was young, and I knew that I was gonna get taken away because my aunt used to talk to me about it, like someday they're gonna catch your mother.

At the age of 16, she has already spent a dozen years in "9, 10" places including foster care, group homes, and detention centers.

Many of the other girls could not remember where their placements had been, only barely distinguishing between foster families and institutional care such as group homes, psychiatric evaluation centers, and juvenile justice facilities. The differences seemed unimportant. What the girls did describe was being without a home base and the disorienting process of moving among facilities or alternating between a home and various locations. Some girls, like Jackie, were not sure where "home" was:

Mostly, I was back and forth because I was in—it depends—I would be in foster care, then I would be in group homes, then I would go AWOL, go to my house, then leave. Go to, go back into it, and I would just go back and forth so I really can't say. I don't know where my house—I would, me saying my house—that meant I would go to my father's house and just he lived there. Other times, I would go to my boyfriend's house or my sister-in-law's house.

Jackie struggles to recount years of various out-of-home placements. Frustrated and tired, she finally concedes:

I haven't been home since, I don't—it's been a while, I think it was since '94. That's been happening since '94, . . . I don't know, but I guess it's for a long time now. I'm saying that, I been around and around and around. I went back and forth and back and forth.

She identifies home as with her previously "unavailable" father and his new wife, yet she also refers to time spent with her aunt prior to more recent institutional placements. The loss of her parents, her aunt, and the drift between institutions leaves her sounding drained, confused, and helpless: "I lived with her [aunt] for a long time—up until now but I don't think I'm living with her. I'm not living with nobody. I'm in DFY. So, I guess I'm up to the custody, up to DFY."

The girls' narratives describe the pervasiveness and meaning of the often multilayered losses associated with the death of a loved one, prolonged separations from their mother or mothering figure, psychological unavailability, and loss of home. In addition to these four major categories, a small number of the young women talked of health-related losses, including the loss of hearing and sight. When Kathy was 7 years old, she was told that she was 50 percent deaf: "I had to have an operation with a tube through my ear drum. I was upset about that for like a month. I was so scared—that was my first operation, and they put tubes in my ears." Paula was shot in the eye when the gun her friend was playing with accidentally fired. She reflects on her future:

Because now, I gotta go through that for life. The other things, you know, I can cover up. But that, I can't cover because I can't see on the other side of my face. Somebody stand over me, I can't see them. . . . I can't do like, some jobs I can't do 'cause you need your eyesight. All of a sudden, I've gotta wear thick glasses. My eye is getting weak. People be like writing and stuff, I don't see it. You ain't making a noise, I don't know you in that room with me.

Saddened and frustrated by her receding eyesight, she was also fearful of a future where she might not be able to work or protect herself from, literally, unseen danger.

While many of the types of loss the girls describe are not uncommon among adolescents in the general population, this group of young women had experience with a great many of each, and often in violent and socially stigmatized contexts. For example, the separation or divorce of parents often meant the total disappearance (usually) of the father, a loss that was often compounded by the marital conflict and physical violence that preceded it.[28] In cases of parental incarceration, the girls had to contend with sudden departures and prolonged absences. Identification with the arrested parent, feelings of survivor guilt, and forced silence about imprisonment may increase their vulnerability to traumatic effects.[29] The girls also described parents who, though alive and physically present, were too involved in their own substance abuse or illness to provide anything but the barest of necessities. Such psychological unavailability is evident in ineffective, inconsistent, and irresponsible parenting. Finally, many girls depicted the loss of their home by parental rejection, city eviction, or child welfare intervention. These significant and cumulative losses and separations were painful and upsetting, and inhibited healthy relationships. When combined with previously disrupted attachments, loss can generate overwhelming feelings of grief, anxiety, guilt, and anger, and may contribute to depression, aggression,[30] delinquency, and violence toward others.[31]

Adapting to the loss of a significant person or object is a process, often with lifelong consequences that may not be recognized or acknowledged until years after the event, if ever. As such, loss requires an investment in coping strategies. Without the support and guidance of adults to assist in the bereavement and adjustment processes, the girls in this study sought to "deal" with their feelings by avoiding or discounting them. Their attempts at defending against physical and emotional distress incorporated a variety of maladaptive behavioral strategies that are the focus of the next chapter.

Notes

1. Annie E. Casey Foundation, "Kids Count."
2. The former New York State Division for Youth (DFY). In 1998, DFY merged with the former Department of Social Services to form the Office of Children and Family Services.
3. Melhem et al., "Sudden Parental Death."
4. A. Freud, "Comments on Psychic Trauma," pp. 226, 228–229.
5. Pynoos et al. ("Traumatic Stress in Childhood," p. 337) reviewed childhood traumatic stress studies and the contribution of children's subjective perceptions of threat to the severity of posttraumatic stress. They state that "guilt over acts of omission or commission perceived to have endangered others has also been found to predict distress." Also see Doka, *Children Mourning*.
6. Bell and Jenkins, "Traumatic Stress," p. 178.
7. Armour ("Experiences of Covictims," p. 109) cites Therese A. Rando, "Complications in Mourning Traumatic Death," in *Living with Grief After Sudden Loss: Suicide, Homicide, Accident, Heart Attack, Stroke,* edited by Kenneth Doka (Bristol, PA: Taylor and Francis, 1996).
8. In addition, covictims' privacy rights are often trampled and how they are portrayed in the media is out of their control. Spungen, *Homicide,* p. 217. Because murder is a crime against the state, the needs of covictims are secondary to the needs of the criminal justice system. Thus, bereavement is not private, but a process very much controlled by the social milieu. Redmond, "Sudden Violent Death," pp. 65–66.

9. For an in-depth analysis differentiating between nonviolent and violent outcomes in drug business disputes, see Taylor, *How Drug Dealers Settle Disputes.*

10. Armour, "Experiences of Covictims"; Rynearson and McCreery, "Bereavement After Homicide."

11. See Masters et al., "Helping Families."

12. Freeman et al., "Neglected Victims."

13. Armour, "Experiences of Covictims," p. 111.

14. Stuckless, *Influence of Anger.* Many of the girls in this study whose loved ones died from an illness or accident directed their anger at particular persons who they held responsible.

15. Garbarino, "An Ecological Perspective."

16. Allison and Furstenberg, "Marital Dissolution"; Black and Pedro-Carroll, "Role of Parent-Child Relationships"; Kelly, "Children's Adjustment."

17. See Western and Wildeman, "Black Family"; Wildeman et al., "Despair by Association?"; Irwin and Austin, *It's About Time.* Much of the current research demonstrates the "normalness" of jail and prison time among non–college educated black men. Pettit and Western ("Mass Imprisonment," p. 164) estimate that in 1999 the risks of imprisonment for young black men were three times higher than 20 years earlier and risks were greatest for high school drop-outs. At the end of 2009, among offender age groups, about 3.1 percent of the nation's black men were in state or federal prison, compared to just under 0.5 percent of white men and 1.3 percent of Hispanic men. See also Glaze, *Correctional Populations.*

18. The Sentencing Project ("Incarcerated Women Fact Sheet," p. 1) states that between 1980 and 2010, the number of women in prison increased at nearly 1.5 times the rate of men (646 percent vs. 419 percent). In 2010, 112,822 women were under the jurisdiction of federal or state prison authorities (Guerino et al., *Prisoners in 2010,* appendix table 3, p. 16). At the end of 1996 (when the girls were interviewed) the number of adult women in state and federal prisons was approximately 75,000 (Gilliard and Beck, *Prisoners in 1997,* p. 5), with an additional 55,800 women in local jails (Bureau of Justice Statistics, *Correctional Populations,* p. 20, table 2.3).

19. See Simpson and Lawrence-Webb, "Responsibility Without Community Resources."

20. Wenar, *Developmental Psychopathology,* p. 35.

21. See Ryder and Brisgone, "Cracked Perspectives," for a more detailed discussion of the effects of the crack era on women's and girls' drug involvement and familial relations.

22. Bowlby, *Separation,* p. 148.

23. K. Erikson, *Everything in Its Path;* Fullilove, *House of Joshua.*

24. Corrado et al., "The Incarceration of Young Female Offenders."

25. Herman, *Trauma and Recovery.*

26. English et al.'s longitudinal study (*Childhood Victimization and Delinquency*) suggests that children who initially stay with their primary caregivers and are later placed in nonrelative foster care have the highest risk for juvenile, adult, any, or violent arrest. This may be because public welfare systems

generally seek to preserve the family composition, removing children only after establishing that the abuse or neglect is serious and the child cannot be protected in the home. Coming from more chaotic and abusive homes, the children are then placed in nonrelative foster care, where they exhibit more behavioral problems.

27. Fullilove, *House of Joshua.*

28. Rebellion, "Broken Homes/Delinquency Relationship"; Kelly, "Children's Adjustment."

29. Johnston, "Effects of Parental Incarceration"; Siegel, *Disrupted Childhoods.*

30. Ainsworth, "Infant-Mother Attachment"; Hughes, "Psychological and Behavioral Correlates"; Mangold and Koski, "Gender Comparisons."

31. M. Erikson et al., "Quality of Attachment and Behavior Problems"; Egeland et al., "Pre-school Behavior Problems"; Elliott, "Serious Violent Offenders"; Fantuzzo and Lindquist, "Effects of Observing Conjugal Violence"; Rouse, "College Students"; Crimmins, "Early Childhood Loss."

6

Coping Strategies: Running, Drugging, and Self-Harm

I just finished smoking marijuana. I think, I guess I wasn't thinking right. It's like whatever came to my mind, I did it.
—*Gayle, 16 years old*

The girls in this study tended to keep "their business" to themselves. Knowing the scarcity of emotional and physical supports and resources, they sought their own means of survival in a threatening and dangerous world. Their psychologically adaptive efforts at self-preservation produced defenses that, for those on the outside looking in, often appeared maladaptive and self-destructive. Yet, their self-reliance helped them navigate nearly impossible family and community situations and environments and, at least temporarily, meet their attachment needs. In this chapter I examine three primary behavioral strategies that the girls used to cope with their histories of extensive violence, victimization, and loss: running away, substance abuse, and self-harm. These avoidant measures led to additional problems and pain, and were effective in alleviating distress only in the short term.

Richard Lazarus and Susan Folkman's transactional theory of stress and coping defines "coping" as the effort to "manage specific external and/or internal demands that are appraised as taxing or exceeding the resources of the person."[1] Some methods are more effective than others in the long run, but all are attempts to regulate emotions and solve a problem (i.e., how to feel better, or how to stabilize the self in a stressful or unstable environment). When broadly categorized in terms of function, such strategies can be thought of as either emotion or problem focused.[2] *Emotion-focused coping* attempts to regulate the distress that the problem or stressor has generated by changing how the situation is attended to, or the meaning of what is happening.[3] Examples include avoidance, withdrawal, minimization, and denial, wherein one tries to avoid thinking about or dealing with the problem directly. *Problem-focused coping,* on the other hand, attempts to change the stressful situation by acting on the environment or the self. Strategies may include formulating a plan and seeking social supports. Though the appropriateness of any particular method depends on the situation, problem-focused coping generally is considered effective or positive whereas emotion-focused coping is often related to negative psychological outcomes. Research has consistently found, for example, that the use of avoidant strategies has the highest risk for psychological dysfunction, while the existence and use of social supports mitigate negative effects of stressful and traumatic experiences and serve as a "source of coping assistance."[4] No single coping strategy is helpful in all situations. Thus, individuals who tend to cope well in the world are inclined to employ a variety of methods and are flexible in their choices, selecting those that are best suited to the particular context.[5] Little extant research, however, has focused specifically on the coping strategies of adolescent females who have endured traumatic experiences.[6]

Coping is a process of adapting to stressful events, a process of "constantly changing cognitive and behavioral efforts" that evolve over time.[7] This evolution allows us to adjust our responses to life's stressors as we gain some emotional distance from events, and as we develop in age and maturity. For the adolescent girls in this study, the distance between them and recent harms was negligible. They were enmeshed in violence and loss; much more than stressful events, their experiences constituted extensive histories of psychological trauma. Evidence from the family violence literature has suggested that children growing up in families with disrupted relationships (i.e., lacking in warmth and closeness and fostering hostility and fighting) tend to demonstrate "increased levels . . . of dysfunctional coping strategies."[8] The violence within the family unit corrodes norms, trust, and the predictability of relationships, and so contributes to the production of emotional alienation. Children feel powerless and may doubt their ability to handle their lives. In such environs,

> instead of developing flexible boundaries between self and others and experiencing competence in shaping their lives,

adolescents might need to invest energies in defending themselves from violence and in concealing family secrets from the outer world.[9]

Certainly, not all adolescents exposed to violence and other traumatic events suffer to the same degree or react in the same manner. It is not the objective threat alone, but how individuals interpret the threat that influences how they will respond. Fear, for example, is "central to theories of maladjustment in violent settings" and linked to elevated rates of aggressive behavior.[10] Generalized family and community violence may induce greater fear than any specific violent event that is believed to be manageable or contained. Accordingly, when the threat is perceived as uncontrollable, problem solving or "making a plan" may seem pointless, even a waste of limited resources. Taking action, if irrational or impulsive, may make the situation worse. Those already surrounded by threat are susceptible to traumagenic dynamics, including impaired executive functioning. This may help to explain why survivors of traumatic events often develop a limited, rigid, or detrimental repertoire of coping strategies that are employed repetitively, even after the original situation has changed.[11] The efforts to prevent additional harm may seem counterproductive and even detrimental but, in the context of lives inundated with violence, victimization, and loss, such strategies might in fact be (at least) "pseudoeffective."[12]

"I Just Run Away When I Don't Like Stuff"

Girls represent the majority of juveniles arrested for running away from home[13] and, between 1995 and 2005, "the increase in runaway and ungovernability case rates for black youth outpaced that for juveniles in any other racial category."[14] Among juvenile detainees, girls reported staying away for two nights or longer because they were fearful of a situation at home; compared to male detainees, females were less likely to report having a supportive family and more likely to report violence within their homes.[15] The American Correctional Association conducted a national survey of girls held in juvenile correctional facilities, which indicated that 81 percent had run away from home; of these, 39 percent had run away 10 or more times.[16] Similarly, 88 percent of the girls in the current study reported running away from home overnight at least once; the median frequency was nine times, beginning at the median age of 12 years old.

In the interviews, we specifically asked girls if they had ever run away from home overnight. Their responses often made a distinction between adult perceptions' of the labeled offense and their decision to just not come home: "I went to a friend's house and I went to my cousin's house, but I never thought that I was running away but everybody else did." Though gone for days at a time, Royale explains, "It wasn't really running away, I just left." Another acknowledges staying out overnight but, when specifically queried about running away, retorts "of course not, no. I don't call it that. I was with my friends." Similarly, Kathy says she ran away "at least once a week," but clarifies that "it wasn't that we were running away. It's just that we were hanging out and we couldn't come home overnight. We never really packed our bags and left . . . we just stayed out." Clearly distinguishing between home and state institutions, Christine discusses her months "on the run" from a group home even as she insists that she has never run away.

Whether the girls define their actions as running away or just staying out, leaving home offers an outlet and escape, the space to soothe anxieties: "Just for like a day or something, because I was, I was really frustrated 'cause I couldn't get my way and I didn't know how to handle myself." Running away also opens up opportunities for socializing and a taste of the excitement of the streets ("I wanted to for the fun of it. To hang out with the boys and play with my friends"). Not coming home at night was "like daring almost, 'cause in the neighborhood where I live, there's a curfew." It could also be a strategy for avoiding the consequences of breaking curfew in the first place, and it could extend for a while. Adele, who "was running away with my sister and I wasn't . . . mainly I wasn't never home," explains that "I had a early curfew so . . . when I go out I would stay out, past my curfew and didn't wanna come home and get on punishment or anything. So I stay out like for 2 weeks or whatever."

Many of the stated reasons for leaving home were typical adolescent complaints (e.g., "I didn't get to go shopping," or "I couldn't get my way"). When we consider, however, the multiple and significant relational disruptions and past hurts, the trivial can become momentous and may represent a breaking point: the instant when shame, anxiety, frustration, and particularly anger can no longer be contained, and the girls searched for a way out. The first time Gayle ever ran away was when her best friend left their group home, a common occurrence in institutional settings. But the loss is significant for Gayle because the group home where the two girls met is the place she has lived the longest. Gayle's relationship with her mother and other caregivers was disrupted long ago and now, with her one close friend gone, she suddenly feels completely unmoored. With her friend's departure, Gayle begins a pattern of running away from foster care and group homes; these institutions are poor substitutes for the internal attachment she craves. Her actions eventually lead to residential confinement in a state juvenile facility.

Most of the girls also referenced a desire to avoid difficult and violent situations at home. The introduction of a new man into the household was often part of the problem; referring to their mothers' romantic partners, Jennifer says, "I didn't like her husband," and Rose complains, "Me and her boyfriend didn't get along." In need of close and loving attachment bonds with their caregivers, the girls found themselves further displaced by these newcomers. Other girls cited the actions of both male and female adults currently in the household. Michelle explicitly states that she ran away because of her father's ongoing sexual molestation and abuse and her failed attempts to secure her mother's protection ("Every time I tried to talk about it, she be like, nah, I don't believe you"). Royale justifies leaving "because I hated my mother, 'cause she told me, she used to always yell at me for no reason," and Alona says her foster parents "get me sick . . . they get me mad [because] they be all up in my business." Jill complains that she and her mother "just argued all the time," the two of them yelling and cursing and then not speaking for days. Jill left home with a fatalistic perspective on what the future held:

> 'Cause my mom, we just had an argument and I didn't feel like staying with her anymore. 'Cause I thought it was always going to be like this and I [would] never get along with her. Sooner or later I was going to leave anyways, probably because I always thought of moving out soon as I turned 16, so I never thought that I was going to be able to make it in that house.

Burdened with the responsibility of caring for their abusive, disabled mother who drank excessively, Marcella and her sister ran away after relatives berated the girls.

> The family [grandmother and uncles], they would come to the house once in a blue moon. . . . And since we had problems with my mother, they would all, like, lecture us. . . . Being that she [my mother] used to abuse us, we used to, not run away from her, but when she got a hold of us, she used to really beat on, uh, so, like, we used to get tired of it. We used to hit her back, and then she'd tell the family we hit her, and so they'd come down on us: that we don't listen to her, and that we run away. One day my sister got real upset with them lecturing us and she was leaving and I followed behind her. . . . We just walked around; we didn't know where to go. So, we were just walkin' around. We wasn't gonna go home.

The sisters ran away not only from their mother, but also from other adult family members who provided no support and offered only reprimands.

Like Marcella, most girls who leave home overnight do not travel far and many seek temporary refuge with another parent, extended family, or friends. Girls may not stay away long, and often find similar difficulties in the household they run to, but the change provides a respite from the immediate difficulties at home.[17] The new location, however, may not provide what most are also seeking: the loving support of known others. Jackie was taken from her imprisoned mother and given to her aunt to raise, before being placed in foster care and group homes. She describes running "from my aunt's house to my father's" where she stayed for weeks at a time. Sixteen-year-old Paula also alternated between households, seeking a change and attachment:

> This woman [my mother] don't love me. I don't wanna be with her. That was mostly it. I went to my father. . . . I wanted to be with my father—you know, you think the grass is greener on the other side, so I used to always do that. That's the reason why I always ran away.

Running to others within a trusted social network is quite different from turning to the streets and, thus, has different consequences. Research has demonstrated the danger of the street context for young girls, linking running away with enhanced risk for physical and sexual victimization and exploitation, sometimes leading to drug use and criminal activity.[18]

Only two girls in this study discuss lengthy periods of being away from home and living, generally, on the streets. Joanne recalls first running away during an explosive family fight; she was only 6 years old when she "got mad at my mom because she and her boyfriend were arguing and she threw a bottle at him." The girl "went a couple blocks down to my grandmother's house," and ended up staying for 3 months. She tells of running away "plenty of times," packing a suitcase and going down the street, usually to stay with her mother's best friend. Joanne continues her pattern of leaving as she grows older, and her absences last longer as her troubles escalate. She explains that "if it was something really serious, I used to go away for like weeks, months, I don't know, it was a really long time." Discussing her troubled relationship with her mother, Joanne describes how she resolves problems by avoiding conflict:

> I used to like go away for like a month, I'd go downstate, I'd go to Manhattan and stuff, and I'd stay there for like a month, and I used to go to Phoenix for the summer. If she didn't, if she kept bothering me, I used to just go away for a long time, and when I'd come back and stuff, it'd be different.

Maria also spent long periods of time away from home and on the streets. She claims she was only 10 years old when she ran away the first time, stating her mother "just got on my nerves one day."

> She be like, "Look, if you want"—I know she don't mean it—"you just leave out my house if you have to." And then I was, "Fine with me, I'll leave" . . . and I was like, "Bye." And my mother was like "You ain't going nowhere, I ain't meant to say that." She was, "I was just thinking about something." And I just left her.

Maria is gone for 2 years. Sometimes extended family and friends provide temporary shelter, but she frequently is homeless. She sleeps in abandoned buildings rather than face the possibility of placement in a state institution:

> I used to be there by myself sometimes at 12 o'clock, 3 o'clock in the morning. Sometimes I stayed there, just awake, but I used to be scared, I used to be scared, I use to hear noises

and there used to be birds flying through. . . . I was scared and I was not trying to get locked up, I'd rather be there than locked up.

On occasion, she bumps into her older brother who brings her home—until she runs away again. Despite the obvious estrangement, Maria stays in contact and calls home regularly. Displacing her own loneliness and fears of abandonment, she worries about her mother:

I know when my mother is worried, 'cause I would, I feel when my mother's worried. I be thinking, "God, I left my mother home worried, crying about me." Then I just think and like something's telling me, I hear her telling me come home, come home, she's crying, and . . . I got to call home, see what's up with my mother.

At the age of 12, "that's when I start calling back home. When she seen me after 2 years, she was like where you been? Oh my God, it was just a surprise, I felt like I never met my mother before!" Maria's chronology varied somewhat throughout her interview but, when asked with whom she mostly lived before being remanded to OCFS, she says she visited her mother, "but didn't really live with her—I used to run away a lot."

Leaving home seemed to offer a viable solution, at least temporarily, but this course of action also placed the girls at risk for assault, disease, and additional loss and victimization. And for some, it had immediate legal consequences. Natalie, for example, begins running away after her parents move to Long Island: "I didn't want to move to Long Island . . . it was boring, it's dead out there." She returns to her old neighborhood in New York and stays with a friend. This occurs so often that, "my mother knew, she knew I was going over there because every time I just don't come home, she know I'm over there." In response, Natalie's mother solicits the power of the state and has her daughter placed in a group home for 7 months.

Girls whose primary attachments have been severally disrupted and who are already under the care of state agencies are perhaps even more likely to run away from institutions that cannot provide the required supportive attachment. Gina, whose drug-dependent mother had left her with her grandmother, ran away on a regular basis and was subsequently ordered to various foster and group homes, which she also left. She attributes her current placement in OCFS to her running behavior and because she "was too bad."

> Alright, when I was 13, I ran away a lot so they placed me and he [judge] kept giving me chances and chances. And then I got into selling drugs so he placed me and he kept giving me chances. And then I ran away one time, I sold drugs, then this woman set me up to come to that place and said we have a warrant for your arrest, you have to go to Tryon [a secure OCFS facility]. I said where? I tried to leave and I assaulted the probation officer and that's why I'm here. [Why did they want to send you to Tryon?] Because I had ran away—running away and selling drugs—so when I tried to leave, they sent me here.

Michelle's attempts to flee her father's sexual abuse also resulted in state custody.

> When I turned 13, my mother had signed a PINS against me. Me and my mother had our own problems, she didn't know what was going on. I use to run away from home; they was like, either you go back home or you go to a group home. I was like I'll try a group home 'cause I didn't want to go back there.

Faced with having to confront her abusive father and an "unknowing" mother, Michelle "chose" to enter the juvenile system through a group home. She did not stay in the group facility and was subsequently remanded to custody in a secure residential facility.

The outcomes of the girls' actions differed somewhat, but the underlying motivations for leaving home—regardless of how they defined their actions, the length of their absences, or the places they went—were along a continuum. The act of leaving may be a way of taking a breather from stressful situations or an attempt to escape the horror of abuse. Running may be a test of the primary relationship, or a precursor to eventually cutting off that relationship. Each of the girls had a narrative replete with victimization within their homes and pervasive violence in the surrounding community. Each recalled major and often violent losses. What is both significant and paradoxical is that, at least at this stage of their young lives, all who left eventually returned. The girls ran away but came back, demonstrating the need each had to be in relationship; even when the relationship was not a healthy or supportive one, it was where the girl felt some connection.

"Every Teenager Used Marijuana and Alcohol— That Was Like Normal"

Childhood maltreatment increases the likelihood of adolescent alcohol and drug use, and female maltreatment victims are more likely than males to develop drug problems and to become involved in drug-related crime.[19] Substance use in this context may be "an attempt at self help," a psychological escape from the trauma of abuse, and a common strategy for self-medicating feelings of anxiety, depression, and anger.[20] In the midst of traumatic experiences of violence and loss that began early and were ongoing, the girls in this study began using alcohol and marijuana at the median ages of 10 and 12 years old, respectively. One-third of the girls reported drinking alcohol on a regular basis (at least 3 to 4 days a week), and nearly three-fourths smoked marijuana regularly. Often marijuana was smoked as a blunt, wrapped inside a cigar shell. Over a third regularly used both alcohol and marijuana, so much so that they generally did not differentiate between the substances: "I use to smoke weed and nothing else, you know, and drink, nothing else." Two girls had tried powder cocaine, but none reported ever using crack and emphatically renounced that form. Jennifer claims that "the older people smoke crack, it's not . . . you don't see no younger kids that smoke crack." Indeed, the girls were contemptuous of those (usually adults) who did use crack cocaine: "Crackheads are crazy. They'll do anything."[21] Though none reported trying heroin or injecting any drug, four girls had tried hallucinogens and three girls had experimented with phencyclidine (PCP).

Typically, the girls' alcohol and marijuana use began at home among family members, and none considered their initiation into substance use a significant event; they portrayed it as a natural progression. Nearly 80 percent of the girls reported that someone in the household drank alcohol or used drugs, with mothers mentioned most often (approximately two-thirds of the girls lived mostly with their mothers for at least a part of their lives). As we have seen, caregivers' drug use can compromise the quality of the parent-child relationship and cause children "to internalize a representational model of others as more dismissive, rejecting, and inconsistent, and the self as unworthy and unlovable.[22] A number of girls used drugs with their parents and other caregivers as a way to gain the attention of those adults. Exposed to a drug-use lifestyle in their homes and feeling rejected by drug-using adults, the girls were adaptive, employing what Lopez and colleagues describe as a relational strategy: drug use as "a means for getting closer to unavailable fathers and spending time with partying mothers."[23] Sixteen-year-old Natalie portrays smoking marijuana as a family affair:

> 'Cause half of my family smoke weed, like my aunt, my father, they smoke weed, they smoke a lot of weed . . . . I smoke with them. My cousin, my aunt, my uncle . . . I was used to people around me smoking and like my family being out in the room, catch a contact, so I just started smoking it. . . . I felt like I was already smoking it because I was already in the room where my aunt and uncle were smoking away.

She often left home to be with her biological father, an arrangement that angered her mother, at least in part because the father sold marijuana. But shared drug use was a way for Natalie, who says "I was a Daddy's girl," to get closer to her father both emotionally and physically: "We was always over there together. He was selling his drugs and I was with him." Joanne started smoking marijuana with her mother and older siblings, because it was a way to join in and do something "fun" together. Despite initial warnings from those family members for her not to party with them, Joanne explains, "I guess, if you watch somebody use it for long enough, you are gonna want to try it and see how it is."[24] Michelle recalls with fondness her grandparents in Barbados serving a home remedy of small glasses of rum "for a chest cold, it broke the cold up." She contrasts this with her father serving her beer when she was about 7 years old: "He didn't give it to me for colds, he just gave it to me to drink." Her father also introduced Michelle to marijuana when she was 13 years old, and she then began to use both alcohol and marijuana to get high:

> I used to try to get real drunk. Yeah, but I was an alcoholic. I smoke weed, but that's 'cause I seen my father do that. I was hooked on it some—I wasn't hooked on like that, I was just high almost every day.

The girls' alcohol and marijuana use quickly escalated and expanded beyond the family into peer networks until it was fully integrated into the activities and events of daily life. At home, in school, in the streets, regardless of the context, as one girl notes, "everybody was doing, every teenager used marijuana and alcohol. That was like normal." Marijuana and alcohol were a large part of the girls' social landscape, a regular part of personal celebrations such as birthdays and holidays ("This New Year's that just passed, I smoked, seriously I smoked like 100 blunts back to back, nonstop") as well as stressful and upsetting experiences, of which there were many. Modeling family and other adult coping methods, the girls' substance use provided an avenue of escape from physical and emotional pain and distress. After Joanne's boyfriend was shot and killed, she ritualistically incorporated alcohol into the funeral and burial.

> We all got ripped at the funeral. I mean that was the first time I ever really got so drunk I could hardly even walk, I was so high I couldn't even see straight. That was the first time. They have this thing where you tap a 40 [oz. beer] then you dump it over the casket and then they, um, start to put dirt over the grave and then they put, and then they just, you, we stayed there all night, I cried all night, and then that same night I was already ripped and stuff, I was gone, I was like in another world.

Substance use was also integral to the girls' violent activities. Little empirical evidence has linked problematic marijuana use to violent behaviors in the same manner as problematic alcohol use.[25] But context is critical to understanding violence and "how and why alcohol and drugs are related to violence." Some research has indicated that, among African Americans adolescents, for example, marijuana use is often related to neighborhood disorganization and disadvantage, including violence and drug sales.[26] Kathy regularly used "alcohol and weed" and then started "fistfights with people walking by." Christine describes how she "did robberies when I was high—and fights." Elena, who claims "all the girls in my projects, we fight like boys. We don't do all that scratching stuff," headed a girl gang that consumed copious amounts of alcohol and marijuana when new members were initiated. Identifying with the imagery of tough street gangbangers, Elena's group commemorated members "stepping up" through the ranks with a celebratory ritual: "If you succeed when we did something violent you have to smoke at least 25 blunts so you could move up." Her exaggerated accounting suggests what Richard Majors and Janet Billson refer to as a "cool pose," a presentation of self that sends a message of detached fearlessness, strength, and control.[27] Actual reported amounts were less important than the desire to appear invincible; excessive smoking after attacks on others was calming and served to block psychological distress and feelings of remorse, and to defend against the reactivation of traumatic memories. The disinhibiting effect of combining excessive amounts of alcohol and marijuana may have contributed to the production of interpersonal violence among these girls who were already suffering disrupted attachments and a range of traumagenic effects.

"I Just Felt Like I Had Nothing to Live For"

Attachment theory proposes that children's earliest experiences of "attunement and misattunement" shape their ability to care for themselves and affect whether they feel they are deserving of good care or not.[28] When children's primary caregivers inflict pain on them, the threat of danger or annihilation causes them to develop incompatible working models of the self and attachment figures. Their internal representation of the caregiver splits: separate from the conscious working model that sees the caregiver as good is an internalized, dissociated identification with the aggressor. Self-harming behaviors arise when children develop a disorganized attachment to the source of pain (the still-loved parent) and then strive to maintain the attachment by inflicting pain on themselves. Psychologically altered by abuse, they may cling to the abuser, rather than forgo attachment.[29] In the original LAVIDA study, from which this study draws its data,[30] girls were nearly three times more likely than boys to have tried to harm themselves; a full one-fourth of the girls reported that they tried to hurt themselves prior to being remanded to custody, though, of these, some clarified that they only threatened self-harm. The median initial age was only 11 years.

Self-cutting involves deliberately slicing the skin deeply enough to ensure permanent scars. Maria was the only girl in this study who referenced behavior that Robert Ross et al. suggest may fall along a physically harmful continuum: "Self-mutilation is 'more directly destructive than smoking or heavy drinking but less directly destructive than suicide attempts,' and suicide may actually represent an extreme form of self-injurious behavior."[31] Child abuse and self-mutilation are often linked, and it is a practice common among girls who are held in custody. Maria describes carving her skin as a means of staying in relation: "I tried to hurt myself which you can see I did a 'V' here 'cause my nephew's name is Victor . . . that's my love, I guess, . . . the one that just turned 5." The boy, a small child, is the one person with whom she confides when something is bothering her, and she explains that having his initial on her body comforts her and keeps him close.

Several girls stated that, although they had considered hurting themselves, they did not act on the thought. Several claimed that their actions were misunderstood and misconstrued; they, however, were clear about their emotions and their feelings that what they wanted and needed from adults remained out of reach. Jackie, for example, states that personnel from the housing authority claimed she was suicidal: "They said yeah. They said that 'cause I got on the roof. They said my aunt said I tried to jump off, but I didn't. I was just mad. I was just sitting on the roof." Paula does admit to contemplating jumping off the roof of her apartment building several times, but says she was frightened: "I was gonna jump off the roof, but I couldn't do it. I would sit there, at the edge of the roof, but I never jumped. Just sit there, look down and get scared. I just got too scared—I couldn't do it." Rather than address what might be disturbing or distressful for her, Paula's mother punishes her:

> Yeah, one of my friends from another building saw me on the roof so she told her grandmother, and her grandmother called the housing and they went and they brought me back to my mother's house, then, you know, I got in trouble again. [What did she do?] She beat me!

Certainly parents and city authorities respond with alarm to children on rooftops but, from the girls' perspective, adult responses failed to recognize the attachment needs underlying their anger and motivating their behaviors. Jill, who ran away because "I never thought that I was going to be able to make it in that house," deliberately swallowed a large quantity of prescription pills when she was 13 years old. Unlike Paula, Jill's suicide attempt was not punished, but was equally misunderstood.

I don't remember, but it was prescribed. It was a prescription that the doctor gave me. I felt like I didn't want to live anymore 'cause I had nothing to live for. I didn't have a relationship with my mother and I don't have a father, or like, anyone else I could turn to talk to, so I just felt like I had nothing to live for.

Her despair and sense of detachment were evident but went unnoticed, and the suicidal act itself was misinterpreted as a physical illness: "I just got sick because mostly I didn't take enough of them, so I just got sick. And like, basically, I just got sick. And my mom just thought I had the flu."

The anger that the girls identified as driving their attempts or threats of self-harm was directed at those charged with their care. When she was 10 years old, Valerie threatened to hang herself: "I didn't try to, you know, I just said it. It was like 'I'm gonna hang myself.' I was mad, angry. I don't remember why, but it was my family." Gayle was afraid of the staff at her group home, and angry at the abuse they inflicted: "I tried to hang myself once. 'Cause I didn't like [facility name], 'cause the people there, they used to hit you." When she was 12 years old, Marcella tried to "take an overdose of pills . . . because of all the problems in my house and stuff, and my sister wasn't in the house either, so it was like, it was just me and my mother then." She laughs off her attempt, but says she ingested enough "Baby Tylenol" to require having her stomach pumped. In a separate incident after a fight with her mother, the mother summoned the police.

We [police officer and Marcella] started fightin' . . . they came in, they dragged me in . . . they handcuffed me, she told them what happened and, all of a sudden, I said, "I want to kill myself," and they sent, they put me in a hospital.

Marcella's suicide threat led to her commitment to a psychiatric ward, where her feelings of disconnection and abandonment escalated: "It was like all these adults, and they had all these problems and there was really crazy people there. I wasn't really crazy, I was just very . . . I just had a very bad temper." She missed her mother and found conditions in the adult ward extremely difficult.

Not being with people my own age, and people I can relate to, and nasty food. You couldn't even go outside; you just stay on that one floor all these days and being followed by a person every hour on the hour and things like that, and then, if you act stupid, they put you in this room with only a mattress on the floor.

Marcella was separated from her mother and deprived of her connection with the only caregiver she knew and—despite their violent history together—with whom Marcella felt safe. Her history of disrupted attachments and loss, the original source of her aberrant behavior, was replicated within a punitive framework: paid professionals who did not know her and so were unlikely to develop any attachment. The mother-child separation was completed when, upon her release from the hospital, Marcella was taken to a group home. Within a month, she ran away and back to her mother.

The girls' early relationships and experiences shaped how they learned to cope with stresses and responsibilities. While seeking social supports is generally considered an appropriate problem-focused strategy, the girls found that their attempts to reach out to adults were futile; there were few models and little guidance available to help them manage the traumagenic effects of earlier experiences. With their fragile sense of safety and control overwhelmed, the girls employed strategies of running away, substance use, and, less frequently, deliberate self-harm. At first, avoidant coping was adaptive and appropriate. For example, running away helped to alleviate (at least temporarily) the pain of abusive family dynamics. Leaving home provided a reprieve from rules and regulations and a respite from violent conditions and conflicts while enabling the girls to maintain relationships. Drug use, too, was a way for the girls to psychically distance themselves and gain fleeting relief from traumatic events and stressors. Or, when used in the company of otherwise unavailable caregivers, substance use was a conduit for engagement and a means for developing or preserving emotional bonds. Self-harm, whether enacted or threatened, was also a means of maintaining attachment. A "push-pull" reliance between caregivers and adolescent daughters is demonstrative of girls' needs and desires for attachment and relationship with caregivers, no matter how abusive or unloving these figures might be. Again, the fear of abandonment exceeds the fear of the abuser.[32] In response to loss, separation, and abandonment, they engage in self-directed violence and physically and mentally remove themselves from the source of pain. Still, they are unable to relinquish attachment to those responsible for hurting them. Girls leave home, use drugs, and engage in self-harming behaviors, but continue to return to caregivers, continue to stay in connection with the familiar.[33] This "pattern of habitual disengagement" blocks the reflection and cognitive restructuring needed to "construct adaptive meanings" of their experiences of trauma and abuse.[34]

The avoidant strategies, however, also placed the girls in this study at higher risk for revictimization and increased their contact with service agencies and the justice system. The girls struggled as best they could, but were blamed for what was perceived to be their "bad" personal behavior. Their coping strategies were penalized and criminalized while the genesis of most difficulties—the atrocities committed within the family and the community—persisted unabated and without intervention. The internal dynamics are of great concern because despite their efforts, the girls are not able to defend against psychic distress in the long term. When children's emotional needs are not attended to, and their desire for connection is continually frustrated, their feelings of anger, betrayal, and powerlessness can become intolerable. Without supportive interventions to contain the rage, social detachment and isolation are likely to grow. And when avoidant strategies fail, alternatives must be found. In the context of violent communities, confrontive coping—the use of aggressive tactics to alter a situation—is reframed as a type of problem-focused strategy: an attempt to change the stressful situation by acting on the environment or oneself.[35] Using violence in dangerous environs can provide teenage girls some protection and a sense of "controllability" over present and future events, at least in the short term.[36] It may also satisfy the tremendous, primal human need for attachment, albeit in a distorted manner. In the following chapter, I consider the girls' confrontational coping behaviors within a framework that links psychological trauma and violence: violence as the "reciprocal manifestation of a damaged attachment system."[37]

Notes

1. Lazarus and Folkman, *Stress, Appraisal and Coping,* p. 141.
2. Lazarus, "Coping Theory and Research." Similarly, Simon et al. ("Making Meaning of Traumatic Events," p. 230) describe three strategies that youths use to process experiences of child sexual abuse: constructive, absorbed, and avoidant. To measure how African American and Latino adolescents coped with neighborhood danger in Chicago, Rasmussen et al. ("Adolescent Coping,"

p. 65) used five of Folkman et al.'s ("Dynamics of a Stressful Encounter") sub-scales: confrontive coping, seeking social supports, planful problem solving, positive reappraisal, and escape-avoidance.

3. Shapiro and Levendosky, "Adolescent Survivors."

4. Thoits, "Social Support as Coping Assistance," p. 417. See also Spac-carelli, "Stress, Appraisal and Coping"; Crimmins, *Early Childhood Loss;* Feiring et al., "The Role of Shame and Attribution Style."

5. Holahan et al., "Coping, Stress Resistance, and Growth"; Strack and Feifel, "Age Differences, Coping"; Weisman, *Coping Capacity.*

6. See Robertson et al., "Adverse Events."

7. Lazarus and Folkman, *Stress, Appraisal and Coping,* p. 141.

8. V. Johnson and Pandina, "Effects of Family Environment," p. 72. Also see Cernkovich and Giordano, "Family Relationships"; Denzin, "Toward a Phenomenology." See Cleary ("Adolescent Victimization," p. 680), in which the relative risk of "both suicidal and violent behaviors" was nearly three times greater for victimized youths compared with nonvictimized youths.

9. Goldblatt ("Strategies of Coping," p. 535) cites Zvi Eisikovits, Zeev Winstok, and Guy Enosh, "Children's Experience of Interparental Violence: A Heuristic Model," *Children and Youth Services Review* 20, no. 6 (1998).

10. Rasmussen et al. ("Adolescent Coping," p. 62) references Colder et al. ("The Relation of Perceived Neighborhood Danger") and Garbarino et al. ("What Children Can Tell Us").

11. Costa et al., "Personality and Coping"; McCrae, "Age Differences and Changes"; Vaillant, *Attachment to Life.*

12. Rasmussen et al. ("Adolescent Coping," p. 72) characterize "pseudo-effective" coping as being "simultaneously associated with elevated perceived safety and exposure to violence."

13. The Federal Office of Juvenile Justice and Delinquency Prevention broadly defines a runaway youth as "a child [who] leaves home without per-mission and stays away overnight." Snyder and Sickmund, *Juvenile Offenders and Victims: 2006,* p. 42.

14. Puzzanchera and Sickmund, *Juvenile Court Statistics 2005,* p. 77. In 1996 (the year that the girls in this study were interviewed), girls represented a majority of the approximately 200,000 charges for running away from home that were processed in juvenile courts. This was the pattern between 1980 and 1999; although the total numbers decreased, it continued to hold through 2008. US Department of Justice, *Crime in the United States, 1997,* p. 222; Snyder, "Juvenile Arrests 1999"; Poe-Yamagata and Butts, *Female Offenders;* Puzzanchera, "Juvenile Arrests 2008," p. 3.

15. Alemagno et al., "Juveniles in Detention," pp. 49–50. In a study of female and male juvenile detainees, Kingree et al. ("Psychosocial and Behav-ioral Problems," p. 202) found that those detainees who had run away from home "showed more depression, suicidal ideation, traumatic experiences [and] alcohol use than did detainees who did not report running away."

16. American Correctional Association, *The Female Offender,* p. 8.

17. Carol Stack (*All Our Kin*) depicts the mutually supportive family net-works of low-income African Americans in the early 1970s. By the time that the girls in this study were growing up, however, these traditional supports had

been financially and emotionally strained by long-term unemployment, punitive criminal justice policies, and the ravages of HIV/AIDS—before being further weakened by the crack epidemic of the 1980s. See also Dunlap et al., "The Severely Distressed African-American Family"; W. J. Wilson, *When Work Disappears;* M. Wilson and Tolson, "Familial Support."

18. Kingree et al., "Psychosocial and Behavioral Problems"; Kempf-Leonard and Johansson, "Gender and Runaways."

19. Harlow, *Prior Abuse;* Ireland and Widom, "Childhood Victimization and Risk"; C. Smith and Thornberry, "Childhood Maltreatment and Adolescent Involvement"; Dembo et al., "Physical Abuse"; Dembo et al., "Further Study of Gender Differences"; Kingery, Pruitt, and Hurley, "Violence and Illegal Drug Use"; Widom et al., "Alcohol Abuse."

20. Krystal and Raskin, *Drug Dependence,* p. 11. See also Heide and Solomon, "Responses to Severe Childhood Maltreatment"; Herman, *Trauma and Recovery;* Belknap and Holsinger, "Overview of Delinquent Girls."

21. Some researchers suggest that youths made a conscious choice to avoid crack, having witnessed the devastation it wrought on prior generations and fearing the stigma it had acquired. Curtis, "The Improbable Transformation"; Furst et al., "The Stigmatized Image".

22. Suchman et al., "Early Bonding," p. 434.

23. Lopez et al., "Drug Use with Parents," p. 140.

24. Attempting to make sense of the contradictory messages, 15-year-old Joanne blames herself: "If I had listened to everybody who told me that I shouldn't do it—which is everybody, nobody never wanted me to smoke cigarettes and smoke blunts and drink—I would have been fine, but I just wanted to do what I wanted to do."

25. Widom et al., "Examination of Pathways"; Lambert et al., "Perceptions of Neighborhood Characteristics"; C. Williams et al., "Marijuana Use Among Minority Youths."

26. Parker and Auerhahn, "Alcohol, Drugs, and Violence," p. 311; Brook et al., "Psychosocial Factors"; C. Williams et al., "Marijuana Use Among Minority Youths." For research that complements that of C. Williams et al. ("Marijuana Use Among Minority Youths"), see Cleveland et al. ("The Impact of Parenting"), who found that emotionally supportive family attachments, along with close monitoring and communicating about alcohol and other drugs, were associated with less use of tobacco, alcohol, and other substances among African American youth.

27. Majors and Billson, *Cool Pose.*

28. Farber, "Dissociation, Traumatic Attachments"; Bowlby, *Separation.*

29. Robinson, "'Since I Couldn't.'"

30. Crimmins et al., *Learning About Violence.*

31. Ross et al., "Self-Mutilation," p. 278.

32. Peacock, *Hand-Me-Down Dreams;* Shengold, *Soul Murder Revisited.*

33. Robinson, "It's Not Easy"; Robinson and Ryder, "Psychosocial Perspectives."

34. Simon et al. ("Making Meaning of Traumatic Events," p. 230) cites Anke Ehlers and David Clark, "A Cognitive Model of Posttraumatic Stress Syndrome," *Behavior Research and Therapy* 38, no. 4 (2000); Edna Foa and

Barbara Rothbaum, *Treating the Trauma of Rape: Cognitive-Behavioral Therapy for PTSD* (New York: Guilford Press, 1988); Lizabeth Roemer, Brett Litz, Susan Orsillo, and Amy Wagner, "A Preliminary Investigation of the Role of Strategic Withholding of Emotions in PTSD," *Journal of Traumatic Stress* 14, no. 1 (2001).

35. Rasmussen et al. ("Adolescent Coping," p. 71) found confrontive coping (one of Folkman et al.'s, "Dynamics of a Stressful Encounter," five coping subscales) to be positively correlated with perceived safety for girls. For boys, confrontive coping was positively associated with exposure to violence. The divergent findings may have to do with different roles and meanings afforded to girls and boys in confrontational behavior.

36. Sullivan et al., "Precursors and Correlates of Women's Violence."

37. De Zulueta, *From Pain to Violence,* p. 78.

7

Illegal Acts:
"I Don't Know if You
Consider That as Violence"

This girl, she owed me money and I didn't mean to,
I really didn't, I didn't mean to hit her, but she was talking
about my mother and I was not trying to hear it.
So I mauled her. I just beat her down.
—*Joanne, 15 years old*

We generally assume the vulnerability of the girlchild, an assumption that arouses instincts of nurturance and protectiveness. But when a girl does not fit within or measure up to society's norms and expectations, when she engages in behaviors perceived as violent, her actions quickly provoke our fears and anxieties—and often our wrath.[1] We are not as swift to protect as we are to sanction. It is only when we locate a young woman's violence within the context of her early relationships that we can begin to see how her actions also reflect the traumagenic effects of harm done to her. As I demonstrated in prior chapters, the childhoods of the girls in this study were marked by various, multiple, and repeated experiences of loss and victimization as well as the lack of strong social supports. In this chapter, I examine how trauma-saturated girls, in their attempts to defend against additional harm, come to use violence against others. I describe the situational contexts and characteristics of the girls' violent acts, including the *instant offense* (robbery or assault) that led to their incarceration. And I examine four primary motivations for their actions: the need for respect, the desire for revenge, self-defense, and financial gain. The severity of violence varied, but the contexts of the behaviors and the motivations that the girls attributed to the acts were remarkably similar. Placed within a developmental framework, the girls' stories reveal links between their earliest and closest relationships and their subsequent disruptive behaviors. Just as with their avoidant strategies (substance use, running away, and self-harm), the girls' confrontational strategies ultimately proved pseudoeffective, pulling them into the deep end of the justice system.

Despite official designations, the girls do not see themselves as violent offenders; mainstream adult society's definitions (i.e., legal norms) do not always resonate with these girls, for whom violence is commonplace. Many are unable to separate the instant offense from a repertoire of other illegal and deviant activities, reflecting perhaps their age and the social distance between themselves and adult authorities. Asked generally about the violence that they participated in prior to custody, the girls volunteer a litany of behaviors, a diverse mix that does not discriminate between what is expedient, what is illegal, and what is violent. Royale's response is typical: "We hopped cabs. We used to stole from malls, we jumped girls, robbed people's houses. We sold drugs." From the girls' standpoint, violence is a flexible and ambiguous term. If we are to understand their behaviors, we must broaden our framework to include, as Colette Daiute and Michelle Fine suggest, "youth subjectivity and experience . . . in the contexts of social institutions, dynamic relational processes, and symbolic media."[2] Thus, in this chapter I look beyond the girls' individual illegal actions to consider their subjective experiences of harm. Within the particular and personal context of conflicting peer relationships, for example, Jackie redefines assault as self-defense. She states that she did not do violent things with her friends: "No, not if, if we had, um, if we don't like nobody, if we don't like nobody and that person try to jump one of us, we gonna jump them. I don't know if you consider that as violence, but I don't think it is." Jackie reframes what adults might consider "gang violence" as an understandable (though problematic) means of protection. Significantly, in discussing violent experiences, the young women also describe extensive histories of loss; both loss and violence are part of the equation.

When queried about specific and serious delinquent activities, the girls do acknowledge their participation and indicate some common ground with normative concepts of violence and accountability. Over half of the girls, for example, admit that they deliberately "throw rocks and bats at the cars and stuff while they running, while they driving back and forth," and a third of the group said they had used a weapon or force to rob someone, or had snatched someone's purse or wallet. Though none of the young women were adjudicated for murder or manslaughter, one discloses her role in a gang-related killing. The girls generally do not excuse their behaviors, but some express surprise at their actions and are remorseful. Many struggle with their sense of self and personal responsibility. Describing the injuries she inflicted on another girl during a fight, Royale comments: "I couldn't believe that I did that to her face, 'cause, I didn't know I could punch that hard. . . . I was sad for her even though we hit her." Reflecting on her instant offense, Jill admits: "I just have a hard time talking about what I did. . . . I never thought I could get to the point where I could actually try to take someone's life."

The Situational Context and Characteristics of Violent Offending

Before we examine the girls' motivations, it is helpful to consider the general situational context and characteristics of their violent behaviors. The girls' lives overlap with those of boys in the community but, for the most part, activities are conducted in separate, gendered spheres. The young women are very much enmeshed in a female universe: girls act with peers and those peers are usually female. Only occasionally are boys directly involved in the girls' delinquency (e.g., Alona and a girlfriend robbed and beat up a group-home staff member, and a boy drove the getaway car; Kathy was the driver in a male carjacking ring). In other circumstances, males are the audience "egging" on girl fights or, more insidiously, the instigators of violence. Jill's boyfriend, for example, threatened to leave Jill after the girl's mother argued with him and demanded he leave the home that the three shared. His alternate proposal was for the 14-year-old to kill her mother so that the couple could run away together. Jill was the one who attempted to slit her mother's throat—at her 20-year-old boyfriend's suggestion and under his direction.

> He's the one who gave me the idea. [What did he say to you?] He told me to cut her jugular vein, and my mom had a bunch of money in the back of her trunk and we would take the car and go to Colorado.

The girls may have seen themselves as partnering with boys, but these relationships were often fraught with inequities of power and respect.[3]

Given the arenas in which the girls' lives play out, most victims also are female and nearly as likely to be peers (under 18 years old) as adults. Generally the girls are not well acquainted with their victims, but familiar schoolmates or neighborhood residents are typical targets. Despite the familiarity, the girls make sharp delineations between themselves and the "other," reducing the victim to "nothing, she was nothing." Jennifer assesses it as: "More or less a stranger . . . she was, to me she could have been almost nothing."

Though approximately a third of the girls had at some time in their lives used a weapon or force to rob someone, in their instant offense and adjudication most tended to use only their own body as a weapon: fists, feet, and teeth. Among those who threatened to or did use a weapon, the weapons consisted of blunt objects (a gun handle) or cutting instruments (a box cutter or knife) that required direct physical contact with the victim. Weapon use was secondary and pragmatic, according to Elena:

> If I'm 5'4", if a girl was like 6'2" and I can't really reach her to fight her, and she just constantly punching me in my face and I'm hitting her but it's not working, I would just pull out a blade and just stab her in her side or something like that so she'll come down.

Though alcohol and marijuana use was common, only one-third of the girls indicated that they were using any substance at the time of their instant offense. When asked directly if anything violent ever happened because they were using alcohol or other drugs, approximately half of the girls answered in the affirmative. Adjudicated on an assault charge, Marcella is clear about the influence of drug use on her violent behaviors in general:

> Basically, all my problems that happened is because I was under the influence of drugs. That's when all my bad behaviors really came out. . . . Once, I was on a train, and I would . . . I had already smoked marijuana. And there was this bum on the train, and just me and my friend, and I burned his hair.

Motivations for Violence

This study identified four primary motives for using violence: the need for respect and the desire for revenge were prominent, while self-defense or defense of others and the desire for financial gain were noted to a lesser extent. These categories were not mutually exclusive and often appeared closely intertwined. From an attachment perspective, the categories reflect the girls' difficulties with disrupted or maladaptive attachment relations and the resultant traumagenic effects, including an internalized sense of badness and deficiencies in executive functioning and empathy. Abused and neglected, many believed that they were unloved and unlovable: "bad" girls. This stigmatized identity helped to alleviate self-blame. The conflation is evident in Michelle's description of herself: "I was kinda bad when I was little, but it was because I didn't have what I wanted at the time. So, I started fighting in school, having problems in school and stealing and stuff." Alternately raised by her strict and religious grandmother, her frequently absent mother, and her sexually abusive father, Michelle admits she constantly struggles with feelings of shame and anger and the urge to act: "I'm still trying to be religious, but sometime I get out of control; not out of control, but sometimes I go beat people up." Hypervigilant to any indication of being "dissed," the girls are poised to respond with action; though violence is at times a rational response to an escalating history of conflict, the girls are quick to react to perceived insults and disrespect. In a distorted desire to engage in emotionally significant, interpersonal exchanges, the girls attempt to solve problems with violence. In this, we see disorder of the attachment system—attachment gone wrong.[4] I review the four primary motivations for this violence below.

The Need for Respect

The girls strove to maintain a modicum of self-respect and power in a world hostile to and dangerous for females. Earning and maintaining respect among peers in the neighborhood can be protective: it strengthens friendships and marks boundaries between the group and outsiders. Girlfriends fight one another but consolidate efforts when under attack: "You all can fight, you all can fight each other but, if somebody come try mess with you all, you always protect each other and that's true."

For these girls, growing up in families and neighborhoods that provided few opportunities in which females could thrive and flourish, respect is a zero-sum game and violence a primary means for establishing it.[5]

A child's trust and confidence is significantly undermined by a rejecting and abusive caregiver. As a result, the child often attributes hostile intent to the actions of others—a negative expectation that is associated with greater aggression.[6] Child maltreatment also triggers the over-activation of the attachment system, and children may cling to those who cause them pain; though attachment bonds may be malformed or disrupted, in the eyes of the child these adults remain the first and the most precious relationship. Thus, for several girls in this study, even a verbal affront against their still-loved parents generated a violent response.

Fifteen-year-old Joanne, whose statement opens this chapter, describes how the dynamics of a drug transaction quickly shifts to violence when the buyer disrespects her mother: "She was like, your mother did this, this, and this with this, this, and this person. The ho [whore] did this, this, and this. . . . She got into my personal issues and if it becomes personal—she's not getting up." Despite her long history of fighting with and running away from her drug-using mother, Joanne remains emotionally attached and displaces her anger onto the taunting buyer. Similarly, Paula, abandoned by her parents for her first 3 years, is highly sensitive to and offended by comments about her friend's mother and associated derogatory racial epithets:

> This man was in his front yard and Lovely ask him for a dollar, and he said go ask your mother for a dollar. I was like what did you say? He was like you heard me; I was like you don't speak to nobody like that. He just calling us all different types of black this, that, and a third. . . . He's like go ask your mother for a dollar; her mother is a crackhead. . . . I knew that and I know he didn't know that, but still how you just gonna come out and say that? Because that's disrespectful.

The girls in this study also reacted violently to those who would direct racial epithets, derogatory comments, or even certain looks at them. All such acts were assumed to carry hostile intent, and the girls (even if they had instigated the encounter) were determined not to "back down" once they perceived a threat.

As a child, Michelle was subjected to her father's sexual advances for years, as well as her mother's seeming indifference. At 16 years old, Michelle responds vehemently and with physical violence when a boyfriend calls her a bitch. The fight between the two teenagers escalates and Michelle is charged with assault.

> I was defending myself, 'cause I thought he was disrespecting me. . . . I'm the only girl in here [a group home], why must you call a girl a "B"? Then after that I was like you better not be talking to me. He was like, so what was you gonna do? . . . He pulled me out of the van and started punching me. I was fighting him back; the first time he beat me up, the second time he fell to the floor.

Adele explicitly demanded a demonstration of what she believed to be appropriate respect from an adult stranger. When the woman responds with sexist and racial slurs, Adele punches her.

> We was walking on some block . . . going to the train station. This lady, she was walking by, so we was like, spread out, she got to say "excuse me" to get by. . . . So we spreaded out and the lady had bumped me. I turned around and was like "what you doing?" She was drunk and she came out of her face and was like "you black bitch." So, I looked at her and I just swung on her.

The girls also engaged in staredowns in an effort to force respect from others on the block. The behavior, however, requires the instigator to back up her challenge at any hint of disrespect. Michelle describes one such encounter:

> She was on my block, I was walking and she was looking at me. I was like, what's she looking at? I didn't say it to her, but I was looking at her. I thought she was going to look at me and look away, 'cause I was gonna look away. She kept on looking, so we followed each other's eyes, she walk this way and I walk this way. I was like . . . and she was like, what the fuck you looking at? I was like you was looking at me.

The exchange of defiant stares between the two girls leads first to a verbal squabble and then escalates into a physical battle over status and territory. Paula explains the dynamics: "people be wanting to have people under pressure, I guess. That's just, that's how people be wanting to be: other people scared of them." If successful, the hostile look can prevent, or at least delay, a fight; physical attacks may be a last resort.

> They would swear to God I'm giving them the evil eye. And you know, it's just that they come in my face . . . I'm not one to really walk away from a fight, but I'm gonna give you a chance to just get away from me. . . . And if it don't work no other way, I gotta, I gotta fight you.

Respect among neighborhood peers also is acquired through demonstrations in the public arena. In this context, the girls' violence provides high entertainment value for a primarily male audience: crowds of boys "amp up" the spectacle of physical contests between individual girls. Jackie describes the context of her assault charge:

> I didn't feel like fighting. When I look nice and stuff, I definitely don't feel like fighting somebody. . . . When I came on the street, all my boy cousins and them was on the streets already. It was a lot of people, the street was packed, man. . . . We was just fighting to see who can fight, that's what they wanted to see. They told her I better not back up from her, and I wasn't gonna back up from her so her and me fought. . . . The fight was really about who could beat whoever . . . that's what they all really wanted to see, who was the best fighter.

Despite her ambivalence about the fight, Jackie knows that declining to participate will cause her to lose face and endanger her safety in the neighborhood; the loss of respect in such a public way would have marked her as a vulnerable target.

The Desire for Revenge

Revenge against real and perceived harms was another strong motivator of the girls' violent behaviors. Although a number of the girls' victims were mere acquaintances, others were individuals with whom the girls had a malformed psychological attachment. When, as mentioned above, Jill's mother argues with the girl's boyfriend, Jill becomes highly distressed and—at his insistence—retaliates by trying to cut her mother's throat:

> I didn't really want to kill her, but I didn't want to never see my boyfriend again. So I was very confused, but I didn't know what to do. . . . I got down on my knees and I looked up at her neck, and I just did it without thinking.

The mother-daughter attachment was fragile. Acknowledging that she "didn't have a good relationship" with her mother, Jill is threatened by the possible loss of her only other attachment—that with her boyfriend.

Attacks against friends were often perceived as attacks against the self and typically called for a retaliatory response: "The girl that we beat up, her friends was trying to beat up my friends, so the next day, we all went up there and we was on the bus and we just started fighting them." In another case, though Donna is charged with robbery and admits to taking another girl's earrings by force, her motivation is not financial gain—it is to avenge her sister who had previously fought with the girl.

> So, we went up to their face and was like, you got beef with my sister? She was like nah, we fought and it's over. I said shut up bitch . . . I'm ready to fight that ass again. I'll bust that ass, she's talking about it was a tie; it was not no tie. So, we was gonna fight.

Here, the need to retaliate is tied to status: to who has the "right" to claim a win and therefore express her dominant position, and to consolidate her place in the status hierarchy.[7] This is important to girls with weak attachments and few supports, and a diminished sense of self. Exposure to chronic fear and pain placed the girls on high alert for signs of danger; after multiple or intense experiences, the girls could become hyperaroused at the slightest provocation.[8] Valerie illustrates how a simmering, but not immediately threatening, situation could provide the catalyst for a violent encounter.[9]

> We had this thing going. First they try to jump me, but they didn't succeed. The third day I only see two of them. . . . She wasn't the one I wanted, but it wasn't nobody else there so I

figured, they didn't care who I was, because they had a problem with somebody I knew. They were trying to jump me, because of somebody else.

The desire for revenge also motivated a small number of the girls in this study to use their sexuality to retaliate against boys' harassment and to defend against future assaults. The girls describe how they manipulated stereotypical gender perceptions to their advantage by appearing sexually available to young men—not with the intent of stealing from the victim, as has been reported by others—but to inflict humiliation and harm and to exert power.[10] Impaired executive functioning in traumatized girls can also produce a hypersexuality that serves defensive purposes.[11] Such acts may be attempts at emotional connection, though ill considered and distorted.

Gina describes how her group of friends targeted and sexually enticed young men who had harassed them:

We threatened boys. . . . What's that girl, Lorena Bobbitt? . . . I'd go out to a boy who like liked me a little bit, or just some boy, and we be like, come on, you wanna go to my house, my mother ain't home, and they'd be like yeah, we go in your house. And then they go and as soon as you get 'em in there, you lock the door and then you pull down their pants and everything, and you be like, yeah, remember you said da da da da da . . . and he was like, no I didn't say that, I didn't say that. She was like why you screaming like a little girl now and then they threatened to cut off. . . . I just sat back and laughed so. . . . You know, them knives, they got the little ones and then the bigger ones? Yeah. Like, you know how them people that go real fast [chef's chopping] that's what she had.

Alona describes another scenario wherein girls deliberately used sexual attractiveness in a type of sting: "Suppose my people don't like you and you like me. I saw you and was like, 'what's up baby?' and start feeling up on you. When you get into it, my people just come and beat you up."

These threats and acts of revenge are specifically directed at boys who have expressed a sexual interest in the girls, an interest that manifested in ways that were intrusive, threatening, and demeaning. The girls' retaliatory actions are a defense against unwanted male attention and an attempt at empowerment for those who have endured substantial and cumulative victimizations.[12]

The girls also negotiate volatile situations in their drug market work, and as part of their tutelage learn that violent retaliation is often necessary. Joanne admits she and two others "beat this crackhead up so bad because she wouldn't pay us and she was sending people that we never seen before to our house and stuff, and we just beat her so bad, she almost. . . . She went to the hospital." One of the girls "was charged with attempted murder, I mean it was that bad." Usually, male drug dealers are gatekeepers in criminal social networks, maintaining control over money and drugs by requiring sellers to inflict violence on nonpaying customers. When Gina "was just learning" the trade, she allows another girl to walk away without paying. "This man I was working for" quickly makes it known that Gina cannot afford to let the incident pass. The "manager" orders her to take him to the debtor's residence where he demonstrates how to solve the problem:

> We went to her building and he went upstairs and was like "open up, open up," and she opened it and he just hit her in the head with a bottle, and her boyfriend just laid there watching TV and then we left. He hit her with the bottle and she fell and we left, and her boyfriend didn't do nothing.

It is made abundantly clear that boys provide little protection to girls who break the rules of the game, whether the boy is a romantic partner (to the nonpaying user) or a drug manager. Survival in the drug business depends on established business norms and conventions of timely payments and discretion; anything less requires violent retaliation. Elena says a nonpaying customer put "my life in jeopardy" because her earnings were short. The seller's male manager verbally threatens her, then hands her a gun and tells her that she had "better handle your business." Accompanied by her cousin, Elena finds and demands payment from the customer, but the woman refuses to pay. After three hours of threats ("You couldn't do nothing. She was a crackhead anyway"), Elena tells her cousin, "just shoot her. And my cousin just shot her. That was the end of that."

Violence was a manifestation of traumagenic effects, including impaired executive functioning, and a demonstration of the need for action over reflection. So, when the party directly responsible for a girl's immediate distress was not accessible (i.e., the person was older than the girl or stronger, or was absent), retaliation might be directed elsewhere. Lisa, for example, agreed to watch a neighbor's children for an evening, but became agitated and angry when the woman failed to return home for 3 days. Lisa retaliates against the children:

> And she didn't come back for a whole weekend, so, me and my sister got mad. So we got, um . . . turned on the hot water, we put her kids' hands under the hot water, 'cause it wasn't like for 5 minutes, it was like. . . . We had burnt their hands. 'Cause I was mad that she didn't, she didn't even, she didn't even come in, she didn't even call.

Sometimes the original object of violence was more abstract, not an individual, but a social institution. Alona and her friends, for example, set out to burglarize a group home that had, against Alona's will, moved her to another facility. The unexpected appearance of a staff member during the break-in led to a violent attack.

> I was living in a group home in Queens and they kicked me out. . . . I got upset and told them I was going to get them back 'cause I didn't want to move, so me and [a friend] we robbed the group home. I told them I ain't wanna go to Brooklyn. I told them and they didn't wanna listen to me. We robbed the group home and the person in there. . . . She scared the shit out of me, kid. She scared the shit out of us all. We had went upstairs and she was talking on the phone, but I didn't see her 'cause I had this thing on my face. So she turned around and I screamed and then she screamed, and we then just like beat her up.

Lisa's and Alona's early losses and rejections weakened their attachment bonds with caregivers and left them susceptible to subsequent threats of abandonment. Lisa, one of nine children, was often responsible for the care of her siblings. Soon after her younger sister was diagnosed with brain cancer, a brother was born premature and had to remain in the hospital for a time. Her family moved frequently and, for reasons she could not recall, Lisa spent a year in foster care when she was 10 years old. Alona's father was dead and when she was 12 years old, her mother placed her in a foster home, a home she was kicked out of because of the foster mother's new boyfriend. In an attempt to defend against their feelings of anger and shame reminiscent of prior abandonments, and threatened by yet another rejection or loss, Lisa and Alona, respectively, retaliate against adults who "didn't even come [back] in, she didn't even call" and "didn't wanna listen to me." The need to stay attached, to be counted—and intolerance for additional affronts—provokes anger and despair in the face of powerlessness. The girls alleviate their distress with physical violence.

Self-Defense or Defense of Others

Self-defense, or acting to defend others, was a third important motivation for violence among the girls in this study. Allegiance to friends was particularly important. Maria defends herself and a girlfriend against a drunk woman who insults, argues with, and strikes the friend.

> I was defending myself 'cause I was not trying to let her cut me. . . . And she grabbed me by my throat. I'm like yo, I'm the one that's doing something to this lady. That's my—that was my choice—pick up the bottle and just cut her. . . . But I had to do—I had to defend myself 'cause I was not trying to let her cut me. And that's not fair. How come she got to cut my friend and she ain't in jail? That's not fair. She should be in jail.

In another incident involving a girlfriend, Marcella stabs a boy who, in the course of an argument with another boy, had shoved Marcella's friend to the floor.

> All I know is these two guys are arguing with each other and my friend . . . comes between them, and she's trying to stop them from fighting or whatever and the guy pushes her on the floor. And so that guy pushes her on the floor and I go to help her up and instead . . . she passes me a knife. So I turn around and I'm face to face with the guy who pushed her on the floor. And I push him and I tell [him] watch the knife, and then he steps back in my face and I stabbed him and I ran.

Gina, who habitually runs away from various foster homes and institutions, tries to defend herself from a "sneak" move by officials after responding to a social worker's request to come into the office.

Feeling betrayed, she uses violence to resist police officers.

> I went over there and then she put me in a room and she left, she closed the door and then five minutes later, she came back with like these two or three guys and they sat down on the table by me and they was like we have a warrant out for your arrest. For running away, . . . they was like you're gonna have to go to Tryon [OCFS secure facility]. And then, I tried, I said I ain't going nowhere and I tried to get up, and the man stood up and I kneed him in his genitals whatever, and then the other guy went to go restrain me and then I hit somebody and I scratched somebody and I bit somebody and then they just, they restrained me.

The girls were engulfed in and constantly on guard against any threat of violence. From early ages, most endured violence in their homes and in their communities—both as witnesses and recipients. Fighting to defend a relationship with a friend or to defend oneself from control of powerful institutional forces can suppress emotional pain, if only temporarily; rather than being victimized once again, the girls described feeling powerful and in control during these incidences. As Royale claims, she "got heart" from her gang activities: "I can do a lot of things and don't regret it. Like before I joined that group I was, I wouldn't cut nobody. I was scared, but then when I joined it, I could cut people and it didn't bother me."

The Desire for Financial Gain

The desire for financial gain was also an important, but infrequent, motivation for the girls to act violently. Kathy declares what was obvious for many youth living in poor, disorganized neighborhoods: "It was just the way we grew up—we couldn't make money on our own." Diane claims she was only a bystander, but the girlfriends she hung out with were specific in their intent: "They need some cash, some money, whatever, so they's talking about catching a pocket. Rob somebody for their cash." Robbery was a quick solution to a lack of money. From an attachment perspective, the acquisition of money in this way was also an opportunity for the girls to engage with others and exert their limited power.

The motives that the girls present for using violence need to be understood within the framework of an attachment-based model. In the enactment of various delinquent and criminal behaviors, the girls recklessly placed themselves in the way of danger. They were motivated by a need for respect and a desire for revenge as well as by self-defense and financial needs. But they were also handicapped early in life by disrupted and malformed psychological attachments, traumatic experiences, and an absence of emotional support. Limited in their ability to form social bonds with individuals or social institutions, or to reflect on the consequences of their actions, they turned instead to the physicality of crime to provide "a sense of consolidation and a coherent identity."[13]

Applying an Attachment-Based Model

Labels of robbery and assault serve classification and sentencing purposes, but they truncate an understanding of the girls' actions and behaviors. Such labels cannot provide context or insight into the motivations behind the acts that they are meant to represent and hold little meaning for adolescent girls regularly engaged in an assortment of illegal and violent activities. An examination of the narrative data in this study reveals a complex story and exposes the dissonance between mainstream norms and the girls' perspectives. For these girls *violence* is an elastic term, the meaning dependent on particular contexts and the individual's experiences. When Elena, for example, is asked about drug-related violence in her neighborhood, she describes walking into her building's elevator where a woman was "stabbing him all in his chest. I was standing right there. Blood was all over my shirt." Yet she claims that "I don't see no violence with drug using." Maybe she is making a distinction between general violence and violence specifically related to drug use. Or perhaps, like many of the young women in this study who "don't see no violence" even as they recite incidents of horror, she is numb to the violence all around her and considers a stabbing so commonplace as to be unremarkable.

Violence and trauma are insidious in the girls' lives. And so to understand their behaviors, we need to listen to what they are telling us and consider how their interpretations are tied to family dynamics and the context of the larger community. We need to recognize the connections between disrupted attachments, traumatic histories, and subsequent violent behaviors. Too often, however, when the subject is "violent girls," the public conversation ends with the need to sanction and control behaviors. Left out of the discussion is any acknowledgment of the substantial and cumulative losses and victimizations that such girls experience—events and experiences that interfere with the formation of attachment relationships and diminish the capacity to think about and empathize with the mental state of others. As I detailed in Chapter 2, it is important to note that the disruption of a child's primary relationship may produce traumagenic effects, including interruption of brain development and executive functioning. Absent the intervention of a psychologically attuned, loving caregiver, normal child development is impaired; the addition of other losses and victimizations, witnessed and experienced, can contribute to behaviors deemed antisocial, aggressive, or violent. Defensive in nature, such behaviors are a "by-product of psychological trauma."[14] Ever vigilant for cues that might signal a threat reminiscent of prior losses and victimizations, trauma-saturated girls remain in "a physiological state of preparedness to face the danger."[15] They may employ aggression as a defense, if only temporarily, against their own unpleasant memories and thoughts triggered by a social worker's duplicity, a peer's taunt, or a junkie's insults toward a mother with whom bonds are tenuous.

In a distortion of attachment, the girls in this study sought a connection through the use of their own body. Jackie, the young woman who described jumping certain peers as self-defense and not a form of violence, told of her mother's abandonment in infancy and specifically linked many of her own delinquent actions to her anger at that loss. Responsibility for her upbringing rotated among her father, an aunt, and city and state institutions; as a result, Jackie "just didn't trust nobody" and "don't feel safe." Explaining why she cut a girlfriend, Jackie reveals her vulnerability to yet another loss and betrayal: "She was like one of the . . . friends that tried to jump me. . . . She had just came from my house eating my food, then she think she going 'round the corner and start talking 'bout me." Jackie used violence as a way (albeit problematic) to diffuse the pain of her broken parental attachments and to provoke a friend to stay in relation with her.

The girls in this study engaged in violence, but they also were victims of neglect and violence in their homes, on the streets of their neighborhoods, and in the care of social institutions created to address their needs. They had been beaten and abused, sexually violated, and then ignored, stigmatized, and penalized. Growing up with a deep sense of adult betrayal and alienation, the girls sought alternative means of connecting with others, despite the harmful personal and social consequences. Afforded little in the way of protection as children, they are classified by an offense incurred in adolescence; we label them "violent" and act as if the label itself is the problem. It is not. Though the label may allow powerful adults and institutions to assuage their own fears and impose systems of subordination on female juvenile offenders, such terminology moves us no closer to resolving problematic behaviors.[16] In the concluding chapter, I address the need for policies and praxis that first acknowledge what has come before—what we as a society have done and what we have refused to do—to create the "problem" of girls' violence, and that then assume the responsibility to care for the most vulnerable among us—the girlchild.

Notes

1. Robinson and Ryder, "Psychosocial Perspectives"; Heidensohn, *Women and Crime.*

2. For discussions of feminist standpoint theory, see Hartsock, "Theoretical Bases for Coalition Building"; Collins, *Black Feminist Thought;* Daiute and Fine, "Youth Perspectives on Violence," p. 3.

3. Contreras, "'Damn, Yo—Who's That Girl?'"

4. Fonagy et al., "Morality, Disruptive Behavior," p. 230; see also De Zulueta, *From Pain to Violence.*

5. See Jones, *Between Good and Ghetto.*

6. Karr-Morse and Wiley, *Ghosts from the Nursery,* p. 165.

7. Griffiths et al., "Fighting over Trivial Things."

8. Karr-Morse and Wiley, *Ghosts from the Nursery,* p. 162.

9. Baskin and Sommers, "Female's Initiation."

10. Similar tactics are used by female drug users and robbers, as described in the ethnographic work of Lisa Maher (*Sexed Work,* pp. 95–96) and Jody Miller ("Up It Up," pp. 54–57), but for different purposes.

11. Robinson and Ryder, "Psychosocial Perspectives."

12. Histories of witnessing or experiencing rape and other sexual assaults as young children have been significantly and highly correlated with precocious sexual activity and being used sexually. As Debold and colleagues observe ("Cultivating Hardiness Zones," p. 187), "the realization that their bodies are a site of temptation and conquest provides many girls with a profound sense of anxiety for their own safety and some girls, in addition, with an illusory sense of power that too often backfires."

13. Fonagy et al., "Morality, Disruptive Behavior," p. 258.

14. De Zulueta, *From Pain to Violence,* p. xi.

15. Karr-Morse and Wiley, *Ghosts from the Nursery,* p. 162.

16. Robinson and Ryder, "Psychosocial Perspectives."

8

Rethinking
Violence and Delinquency

I don't think it can be prevented 'cause there are just angry
people out there. Maybe they had a hard life or maybe they
probably don't have nobody there for them, they experience life that's been hurtful and all they do is go out to
hurt other people. They just angry.
—*Diane, 16 years old*

Diane is not hopeful about violence prevention. She knows all about
"life that's been hurtful" and, like the other girls in this study, she is
angry, shamed, and anxious. These girls "don't have nobody there for
them." They have been harmed, often by the persons in whom they
intuitively placed their trust: parents and other primary caregivers.
Growing up in hostile conditions without the intervention of loving
adults, such girls carry their acquired scars forward; subjected to multiple and repeated traumatic events in childhood, they have become
multiproblem adolescents, adjudicated for a robbery or assault.[1] Paula
considers the personal consequences:

I was almost turning 15 and I was in a foster home. . . . I was
thinking that when I was like 12, so I was like what I got to
show for this? I been stabbed, sliced, shot, and stitched up. I
don't need this no more. No wonder they keep telling me I'm
gonna be dead before 19.

Michelle similarly realizes that "there's nothing to show for what
I did. I don't have no education and some of my brain cell[s] are prob-

151

ably gone." To many, they are simply "violent girls." But this generic label does not delineate between and among girls, types of behaviors, or motivations, nor does it provide any context for the girls' actions. The girls' narratives tell a more complicated, nuanced story, exposing the social and psychological terrain that the young women inhabit. Clinging to ragged connections "waved vainly across vast chasms," such "harmed and harming" girls affirm much of what is known about links between female victimization and offending.[2] And of greater significance, the stories of the girls in this study reveal how the process unfolds.

Biologist, psychiatrist, and psychoanalytical therapist Felicity De Zulueta states, "Violence is not a biological instinct: it is the manifestation of both our disrupted attachment bonds and our shattered self."[3] Preventing future violence by and against girls requires us to attend to more than specific acts and to carefully consider how affectional ties, traumagenic dynamics, and violent behaviors are intertwined. An understanding of these relationships redefines the purported problem of "girls' violence" and suggests new approaches to address the mechanisms that lie beneath observed behaviors. While it may be too late to help the 24 girls in this study, what they have to say about the importance of relationships offers direction for what adults and the systems they create can do to protect future generations of girls from harm and the violence that harm produces.

Violence is not beyond solution, but we must be thoughtful and selective about where we expend our efforts. In the psychological thriller *Shutter Island,* Max von Sydow's character, a Dr. Naehring, explains that *trauma* originates from the Greek word for *wound;* in a sinister whisper he adds, "wounds can create monsters. . . . And wouldn't you agree that when you see a monster, you must stop it?"[4] For the past 30 years or so, our approach to youth violence has been to capture the individual "monster" rather than (ad)dress the original wounds. This must change. Key systems and institutions, particularly schools and the juvenile justice system, must act collectively to attend to children's psychological attachment needs. This is a critical piece of the wholistic approach required to reduce violence in our homes and in our communities. I realize that the problems of adolescent girls and their families are numerous and varied; poverty and social marginalization, broken relationships, and violence are too complex, too intimately linked and historically rooted to submit to simple solutions. But even small steps move us forward; to not take them is to condemn the chances of future generations of young women. In this chapter, I discuss recommendations for policies and programs, and provide examples of some innovative approaches.

Support for Girls and Their Families

The first priority is to promote and support the development of healthy early relationships for all children. The attachment literature makes clear the connection between the well-being of parents and that of their children; in his earliest works, John Bowlby stresses the importance of social networks, economic security, and health care in nurturing strong parent-child relationships.[5] Children with loving and psychologically attuned caregivers have a secure base, a foundation from which to thrive and grow, and an internalized model of self as worthy and the world as safe. When family systems are working well, parents and children may be less dependent on other systems and services, but nearly all contemporary families would benefit from policies that place children and their needs at the forefront (e.g., quality daycare, accessible health care, family leave, and paid sick days).

The assumption that all parents and caregivers can function independent of external support is a fallacy that contradicts what we know about economic, social, political, racial, and gendered stratification in society. A large percentage of parents and other primary caregivers, many living in marginalized areas, are ill equipped to provide for even basic child needs. Clearly, the families of girls in this study operated under significant stress and deficient social supports; many of the adults likely suffered from their own experiences of unresolved loss and violation. The social conditions associated with stratification in the mid-1990s when these girls entered the juvenile justice system continue to interfere with effective parenting today. And for a great many, the situation is worse.

To counteract these deprivations and to interrupt the intergenerational transmission of parental problems, we must acknowledge the primacy of early attachment bonds and implement policies that bolster family cohesiveness. Beneficial strategies include reinvestment (or investment) in local public education, housing, and business opportunities. Women, who generally serve as primary caregivers for young children, deserve pay equity, flexible work options, and access to reproductive health services. Many of the mothers of the girls in this study struggled with drug addiction and emotional difficulties. Thus, comprehensive substance abuse treatment and mental health services are often critical to family stability.

When family systems are impaired because primary caregivers are limited in their ability to provide essential loving attention and support, children require additional assistance. Neglected, abandoned, or abused children may either fail to form affective bonds or suffer the disruption or loss of those bonds, and such interference with normal child development can contribute to internal conflicts and social problems later in life. Yet the message that so many girls in this study received, both implicitly and explicitly, was that they were alone and unworthy of love and protection. Failure to satisfy children's essential needs for attachment, love, and security, and failure to comprehensively address traumagenic effects, perpetuates mental health problems and antisocial behaviors, including violence. Thus, if primary caregivers cannot provide children a "felt sense of safety" and social affiliation, the larger community has an obligation and a responsibility to do so.

Collaboration Between and Among Systems

Those who care for children, in any capacity and in any system, must learn to collaborate.[6] Troubled children are frequently passed between systems (e.g., education, child welfare, and juvenile justice) without any sense of continuity. A girl removed from school under a zero-tolerance policy, for example, may be placed in a youth home or juvenile detention facility. Under those conditions, she loses all connection to teachers and peers at school and must attempt to develop new attachments with strangers in an unfamiliar setting. As girls enter each system, they are forced to interact with new personnel and repeat their story. New case files are opened, frequently without the benefit of essential information from the previous agency or institution. For a trauma-saturated girl, this process is frightening and disruptive and may even be dangerous. Consistency is the foundation on which to begin to address children's attachment needs; a single caseworker or advocate knowledgeable about a child's history and needs could help navigate between and among systems to enable streamlined and respectful information sharing. Structurally based disconnections could be minimized with the creation of collaborative and comprehensive protocols in which systems are attuned to the need for stable relationships and act in concert to repair and develop attachments.

Agency personnel at all levels, as well as key community stakeholders, need to be trained to recognize abuse and neglect and the traumagenic effects of these and other potentially damaging experiences. An example of a collaborative project concerned with recognizing and responding to abused children is the National Child Protection Training Center.[7] With the goal of eliminating child abuse in three generations, the center disseminates scholarly and clinical knowledge, develops curricula for undergraduate college students, and conducts training for professionals in the field. Additionally, training in PTSD symptomology is critical for service providers.

Girls similar to those in this study traverse many systems, each of which can either hinder or support loving attachments. Two of the most significant systems for troubled girls are education and juvenile justice, with child welfare often serving as the connecting link. In the following subsections, I present suggestions for addressing individual behaviors and institutional structures in these contexts, ones that are centered on the need for training and collaboration, and the transformation of harsh punitive responses into corrective supports that build attachments and address the detrimental effects of trauma.

Education

Educators and those who make policy within educational systems need training to better understand how behavioral problems are often manifestations of victimization and loss. Resultant traumagenic effects may interrupt brain development and executive functioning; these effects can impair planning and social judgment faculties, abstract reasoning, moral development, and impulse control. Given teachers' close and extensive contact with children in the classroom, they are likely to be among the first to notice a girl's problem behaviors. Specialized training can assist teachers in also recognizing behavioral antecedents and thereby reduce reflexive, punitive responses to "bad" behaviors. Teachers may recognize problems but to better ensure effective and positive outcomes, school administrators must then be ready to provide direct assistance to teachers in their efforts to help students. In addition to personnel training, schools and the children in their care would benefit from praxis and protocols that facilitate collaboration between teachers, school health professionals, and other stakeholders. Together, adults need to identify appropriate interventions, all the while striving to keep the girl in relationship with the supportive adults who know her.

Behavioral problems of individual students cannot be separated from prevailing institutional and structural contexts, and so it is incumbent on school administrators to promote school climates that are sensitive to the safety and relational needs of all students. Administrators simultaneously must counter policies that, in the name of discipline and safety, exacerbate student misbehavior, alienation, and aggression.[8] Zero-tolerance policies, for example, contribute to environments that undermine the development of healthy social relations in schools. These policies impose "predetermined consequences or punishment for particular offenses without consideration of the circumstances or the disciplinary history of the student."[9] Originally designed to intercept guns, and tied to federal funding, zero-tolerance policies are in force in approximately 90 percent of schools nationwide.[10] Individual jurisdictions have broadened the scope of these policies to cover a range of intentional acts, including drug use and threats of violence, often pre-empting actual incidences. The pervasiveness and acceptability of zero-tolerance approaches to disciplinary issues are problematic because they rely on suspensions and expulsions; these types of policies replicate student experiences of abandonment and detachment and fail to confront the underlying problems.

Violence prevention efforts cannot be limited to a concern with bombs, guns, and extreme force. They must also assess more insidious and pervasive forms of aggression and harm. Educators and other guardians (e.g., administrators, hall monitors, bus drivers, and security personnel) may need assistance in identifying verbal and physical violence, interpreting behaviors and bodies, and responding appropriately. Power relations mediate claims of violence in complex ways and often privilege the dominance of boys, whites, and heterosexuals over others. Teachers, for example, may claim that most "kids" (signifying white boys) are only fooling around when they use force (i.e., "normal"), whereas any force by girls is too much (i.e., "unusual, noteworthy, or striking").[11] Sometimes adults are the ones to inflict harm.[12] One ethnographic study, for example, suggests that many urban African American girls, in efforts to gain respect among peers and to establish a reputation as a "strong girl" in the community, may be "enacting a racialized and class-based insistence on toughness that conflicts with teachers' understanding of how girls should behave."[13] Lisa Leitz found that though African American middle school girls may take pride in their academic achievements and consider education critical to their future, teachers often complained about the "loud black girls" and harassed or neglected them in the classroom.[14] As a result of educators' perceptions and hostility, more girls than boys may be identified as involved in fights (as opposed to "roughhousing") and be subjected to disciplinary proceedings; the female "troublemakers" are subsequently suspended, detained, or expelled.[15]

Antiviolence policies enacted to discipline girls for fighting are not similarly employed to protect girls from sexual violence. For example, in the wake of shootings by students who had been teased and harassed, schools began to implement gender-neutral bullying policies. In many cases, these new policies subsumed existing sexual and gender harassment policies. An act as commonplace and purportedly harmless as teasing a girl and snapping her bra, for example, might be construed as bullying by some administrators, but it is also sexual harassment that is humiliating and damaging to young girls' perceptions of self-worth. Such behavior, and similar others, contributes to an environment that condones sexual objectification and fails to protect girls from sexual violence. School personnel need to understand the psychological and legal consequences when harassment is minimized or assault is defined as flirtatious or playful.[16] Conflating illegal gender harassment and sexual violence with bullying deprives victims of legal rights and protections offered by extant antiharassment laws.[17]

Educators also need to consider how gender and race shape student positions in the social structure and affect power differentials and choices. Some teachers, for example, may claim to not see much gender-based sexual violence and to define what they do see as mostly verbal ("You know, like slut, whore, you know, things like that") not "real" physical violence.[18] Or adults may assess any physical adolescent sexual activity that they do observe as "normal" and consensual, overlooking power differentials that exist between the involved students. Coercion may be mistaken for consent ("an appearance of mutuality does not mean that both parties have equal say in what is happening").[19] The behaviors in fact may be both harmful and illegal. Assistance in this area might be found in partnerships with community groups or nonprofits that are knowledgeable in sexual harassment law and skilled in presenting sexual violence prevention programming.

Police in schools also may undercut efforts to develop and sustain a supportive school climate. Ideally, police should be aligned with the educational mission of schools and, like all school officials, should serve as trusted and protective adults. For this reason, officers should not be randomly assigned to work in schools, and those who are school-based must be provided with specialized training in youth development. A police presence in middle and high schools, however, often works in tandem with zero-tolerance policies—a combination that has contributed to increased state intrusion in the lives of minority youths and girls as well as their subsequent involvement in the justice system.[20] This approach to school violence erodes emotional safety and the connection between educators and students, and may precipitate disruptive behaviors. The National Rifle Association's recent set of recommendations (National School Shield Task Force) is alarming in its blatant disregard for the traumagenic effects of structural violence;[21] for children surrounded by violence and subjected to its physical, physiological, and psychological harms, arming school personnel is likely to escalate fear and generate defensive responses that may end in more tragedy. Such approaches are destined to fail as a response to problems that derive from poor attachments. School officials need to work in partnership with law enforcement and other stakeholders to design disciplinary practices that hold students accountable for their actions and behaviors. Disciplinary plans, however, should limit legalistic responses and include collaborative interventions that address children's attachment and security needs. Responding to students solely as potential delinquents and considering all misbehavior as potentially delinquent acts contribute to the "school to prison pipeline" that pushes students into the juvenile and, ultimately, the criminal justice system.[22]

Prior to their current incarcerations, the girls in this study were involved in multiple instances of violence, both as victims and as offenders. If access to *effective* violence prevention and intervention programming had been available to them while they were in school, it is possible that they might have found alternatives to violence. Certainly mainstream adult norms that shun fighting and other aggressive acts did not easily fit with these girls' lives, and the girls did derive some benefits from violence (e.g., respect, revenge, money, and material goods). Thus, a simplistic "just say no" to violence program was unrealistic, not only because of their social environments, but also because their internal relational needs went unnoticed and unaddressed.

Though it is not necessary that prevention and intervention programs all be gender specific, programs do need to be sensitive and responsive to the cultural knowledge and lived experiences of all girls.

Young women desire programs that speak directly to their circumstances and can translate general antiviolence messages into practical skills. Many of the girls in this study suggested that people "think before they get up and try to burn somebody or shoot somebody, or whatever they gonna do, think about it first before you do it." Others believed they could "have prevented the whole thing" if they had, for example, gone "straight home from school." Such advice, however, without relevant and accessible tools, is impractical. Programs need to incorporate space for participants to engage in self-reflection, to make meaningful connections, and to practice alternative ways of handling stressors and resolving conflict. This could include restorative justice principles and practices that aim to repair harm and restore relationships among those affected. Practices that respond to specific acts of harm or misconduct and also address violence that occurs in the larger community have proven effective in schools across the United States and around the world.[23] Praxis will need to be adapted, however, for acts of sexual violence; as we have seen, rather than being supported by families and communities, female victims of sexual abuse and assault often are not believed and continue to be shamed and stigmatized.[24]

Juvenile Justice

A variety of local and state agencies attend to the needs of troubled and troubling children. Generically, services are provided under the auspices of child welfare and juvenile justice systems. Some jurisdictions have merged the functions of these two systems while others have maintained separate structures and processes, but children regularly move between them. For our purposes, I refer to the justice system only.

The original intent of the US juvenile justice system is in many respects similar to that of child welfare, with the state serving as parent or guardian in place of primary caregivers. The foundational doctrine of the juvenile court (parens patriae) gives the court authority over children in need of guidance and protection, allowing the state to act in place of the parents (in loco parentis) to make decisions concerning the best interests of the child. This ideal has never fully materialized, but the past three decades of "get tough" policies have moved us even farther away from the original intent. It is time to revisit the parental role of the state and how best to fulfill the needs of children, especially young female offenders.

All of the girls in this study, adjudicated on violent offenses, also had significant, cumulative experiences with loss, victimization, and violence. Their early experiences were ignored even as their transgressions were harshly penalized. Despite numerous encounters with state officials and institutions, none of the girls received the support that they needed. Their experiences are not unique; a high percentage of children who enter the juvenile justice system have histories of violence and untreated trauma.[25] What is critical is that the justice system not only hold children accountable for their actions, but also take responsibility for correcting the harms done to them. Failure to do so now leaves these children and their communities vulnerable to increased violence and victimization in the future.

While the juvenile justice system often falls short of its goals, it remains in a position to address at least some of the roots of violence among the children in its care. In order to develop a collaborative approach similar to that posited for educational systems, juvenile justice personnel will first need to assess how youths move through and between institutions. Then, they must determine where and how collaboration might be improved to minimize disruptions in young people's attachments to significant others. The various components of the juvenile justice system must find ways to provide coordinated and comprehensive services and treatment for youths, whether they are in the community or in custody, and to maintain consistent communication among practitioners and other stakeholders.

Given that approximately one-half of all youths in the juvenile justice system meet criteria for at least two mental health disorders, coordinated and comprehensive mental health services are critical for this young clientele.[26] The need for mental health services is especially acute among young female offenders who traditionally are overlooked.[27] National mental health advocates have called for major system and policy changes to address the disparity between the growing need and the limited availability of appropriate mental health services for juvenile offenders.[28] And systems need to heed this call to make funding for treatment available despite constricting state and local budgets.

In early 2013, New York City announced the debut of a comprehensive and integrated effort designed to improve child mental health care services. The public-private partnership is a collaboration of the city's Administration for Child Services, the Child Study Center at New York University, and Bellevue Hospital. Together these entities seek to address early childhood trauma and its potentially severe consequences, including PTSD. As the director of the Child Study Center warns, "the nation's child welfare system is the frontline safety net for abused and neglected children, and if it fails, the consequences can be tragic and last well into adulthood."[29] One component of the partnership will provide trauma-focused care at secure juvenile detention centers in New York City; another establishes a Center on Coordinated Trauma Services in Child Welfare and Mental Health to assist children and families across the United States with trauma-related mental health needs. This ambitious initiative serves as a promising model of innovation and collaboration for addressing the health and safety of systems-involved and traumatized children and their families.

To the extent that institutionalization can be detrimental to the health and well-being of troubled children, confinement should be imposed only as a last resort. Whenever possible, graduated, alternative sanctions should be employed. This applies to children in need of temporary housing as well as those who are adjudicated delinquent. When children must be removed from homes, every effort should be made to find housing in close proximity to significant others. Some children might, for example, be able to be placed with other family members or friends to ensure the continuity of relational bonds. If confinement becomes necessary, there may be alternatives to sending youths far away. Recognizing the importance of relational connections, New York City in 2012 created the Close to Home Initiative to keep adjudicated delinquent youth in nonsecure and limited-secure placements close to their communities and available services. This community-based program restructures custodial placement of juvenile offenders and has the potential to limit the negative consequences of disrupted attachments and traumagenic dynamics. It is a model that other jurisdictions might consider.

Researchers and practitioners often recommend transitional and reintegrative supervision and services for those in custody as a means of lowering high recidivism rates among young offenders. Aftercare programming, unfortunately, not only remains underdeveloped in most juvenile justice systems,[30] but also frequently has no direct connection to facility-based services. Thus, a challenge for those working with female juvenile offenders is to develop high-quality, aftercare services that will support girls in their communities on their release. Juvenile intensive aftercare programming for girls should be based on a therapeutic alliance and characterized by continuity of care between residential facilities and community-based aftercare.[31]

Community Development

As I noted at the beginning of this book, the girls in this study described lives of intertwined violence: violence experienced, witnessed, and enacted at home, in school, and on the streets. These experiences cannot be separated from "unequal social structures and relations."[32] Too many of our communities are wounded and unable to bear the burden without assistance. Structural impediments to healthy human development include adverse economic conditions; devastation resulting from HIV/AIDS and the drug trade; and minimal social, educational, and health services. In addition, cultural mores and gender inequalities that sexualize and objectify girls and young women contribute to sexual abuse and interfere with the development of safe communities where they can grow to womanhood.

When traditional institutions of support—extended social networks, religious centers, and schools—are weak or dysfunctional, the damaging effects are ubiquitous and provide fertile ground for violence. Denizens of many urban communities with limited access to resources and power succumb to defensive attitudes and behaviors that condone, support, and replicate violence. Systems purportedly designed to respond to community needs (e.g., education, social service, and justice) often instead impose intrusive and controlling policies on young women of color and their families.[33] For example, mandatory arrest practices in domestic violence incidents increasingly usher into the justice system Latinas and black girls, despite evidence that the behaviors in question may more accurately be characterized as acts of self-defense. Policies of mass incarceration, too, fall disproportionately on African American and other minority groups with detrimental consequences that are both gendered and racialized. In this context, troubled girls' "(mal)adaptive responses to sexual exploitation and other injuries—psychological and physical," become subject to the punitive authority of professionals within these systems where traumagenic effects are often replicated and compounded.[34] To decouple actions and behaviors of individual girls and their families from communities and the larger society is to obscure the systemic violence that girls live with every day.

Recognizing the extensive amount of violence and victimization that young people experience while living in poor and dangerous neighborhoods, and knowing the communal consequences, we cannot now rely on "safe privilege" and turn away. We must instead find ways to support efforts to strengthen community ties and enhance collective responses to violence. Community organizing is a powerful and empowering means of establishing cultural identity and serving local needs. A simple start is the dissemination of information on the traumagenic effects of interpersonal violence and the benefits of positive and healthy relationships. A more expansive initiative would be to develop a project similar to the Chicago-based organization, Cure Violence, which uses public health techniques to respond to gun-related violence.[35] Outreach workers are employed to disrupt conflicts before they erupt and to educate the community about consequences of violent behavior. Many of these highly trained "violence interrupters" are community members: former gang members, former drug dealers, or past perpetrators of violence who now serve as part of the solution. Implemented in over a dozen US cities, the program seeks to prevent violence through identification and detection; interruption, intervention, and risk reduction; and changing behaviors and norms. By treating violence as a learned behavior that can be "unlearned," Cure Violence offers a solution to a problem that often appears unsolvable.

Girls living in violent neighborhoods have limited options for safe recreation or relaxation. Adele, one of the girls in this study, points out that her neighborhood needs "more programs for kids to go to instead of them hanging out on the streets and things like that." One way to actualize this would be to create local spaces for girls, or to add to existing programs services tailored to their needs such as "girl spaces" or "hardiness zones."[36] At a basic and practical level, these spaces can provide a safe setting where girls can hang out or participate in supportive and empowering activities. This is the idea behind the Haiti Adolescent Girls Network, a collaboration among nongovernmental organizations and local women's groups in that country. Created in response to limited programming for girls who are vulnerable to violence and sexual exploitation, these safe spaces provide a location in which girls "regularly meet, find peer mentoring, and build skills."[37] Surely, if this type of collaboration can work in one of the poorest countries in the world, a similar approach can be modeled within US cities.

Recreational and supportive activities are important, but not sufficient to counter the violence, victimization, and loss in girls' lives. A traumatized girl cannot feel empowered if all of her psychic energy is focused on maintaining the self. The girls in this study rarely went to a family member or anyone else in the community when something was bothering them, oftentimes because the people who should have provided nurturance and protection from harm had instead maltreated or neglected them. Thus, youth centers might also provide age-appropriate, trauma-related information and space for girls to safely share traumatic experiences. Appropriate clinical care is necessary to address what underlies girls' behaviors—attachment disruptions and other traumagenic effects—and to help girls build an internal structure of support and self-control.[38] Additional responses might include trauma-informed dance or yoga programs and supervised peer-to-peer support.

Community efforts to decrease violence are inherently limited because of the national scope of the problem. In addition to the need for more community programming, Adele specifically pointed to the role of gun manufacturers and high-level drug traffickers in promoting violence in neighborhoods and suggests that disadvantaged communities would be better served if "they take guns away and stop making all these types of chemicals for drugs." Local communities, on their own, cannot implement effective policies to reduce community gun and drug-related violence; state and possibly federal legislation is required. In the aftermath of the Sandy Hook Elementary School shooting in December 2012, Congress is once again debating the shape and structure of federal gun regulations and controls while a number of states have initiated major overhauls of their laws. New York's legislation is unique in that it imposes certain restrictions not only on individual gun owners but, perhaps more important, on gun manufacturing companies. Connecticut's legislation will create the nation's first statewide registry (available to law enforcement only) of people convicted of crimes involving the use or threat of dangerous weapons; it will also require eligibility certificates for the purchase of any rifle, shotgun, or ammunition. While it is too soon to evaluate the effectiveness of these and other emerging legislative responses, they represent some of the strictest gun control policies in the country and an important step toward reducing community violence.

Just as local communities require state and federal assistance in reducing gun violence, so too do they need help addressing drug-related violence. But this cannot be limited to law enforcement strategies that have not proven successful after decades of a war on drugs. Much of the violence in these communities is directly related to limited legitimate opportunities for economic stability. For girls and families engaged in the distribution and sale of illicit drugs, the primary motivations are financial. Without sustainable economic investments in neighborhoods, in combination with training and jobs that pay a livable wage, drug violence will continue to flourish.

Finally, communities, like the schools, should consider incorporating restorative justice elements into local responses to violence. Restorative justice processes and activities are built on the awareness that offenders need to return to the familiar in order to reestablish or create a new connection and bonds to family, school, and community. In seeking to counter the harm done to the community, this approach reiterates the importance of connections among those who transgress the rules, the victims of those transgressions, and the community as a whole.

Future Research

Future research on youth violence would benefit from a multidisciplinary approach that includes an investigation of attachment theory and its implications. As with control theories, for example, attachment theory considers the early bond between parents and children to be crucial in determining the course of human development. The emphasis, however, is on nurturing and supporting an innate need as opposed to controlling destructive impulses. The long-term consequences of a disruption in secure attachments may be similar to the characteristics of a person with low self-control, a possibility indicative of some affiliation between these two distinct bodies of literature.[39] Although the basic assumptions of human nature in each perspective are very different, as are the implications that flow from those assumptions, a close examination of early childhood traumatic experiences may reveal a foundation for merging developmental psychology and trauma literature with established criminological theories. Such theoretical integration is helpful in understanding the experiences and behaviors of young offenders and offers additional clarification of developmental pathways. It is important, however, to keep in mind a key difference between these theories. While control theories postulate that the construct of low self-control remains fairly stable over a lifetime, attachment theory maintains that, depending on life circumstances and opportunities, "reattachment" is always possible—individuals tend to move toward the natural state of satisfying attachment relationships.[40] This ability to alter relationships provides a hopeful note for intervening programming.

Much of what we know about violent behaviors is based on the study of male offenders. There is a clear need for in-depth, exploratory research that includes the female experience. In addition, given that childhood and adolescence are both periods of tremendous change in cognitive capacities, size, strength, gender differentiation, relationships, and social environments—all of which affect the potential for victimization as well as offending—there is a particular need to expand the study of adolescent female offending. Longitudinal studies are well suited to track changes over time and determine the temporal ordering of experiences and behaviors, and they are critical for charting developmental pathways into, as well as out of, delinquency and crime. Such studies, however, tend to employ structured survey instruments.

As is evidenced in this study, narrative data can enhance our understanding of the nature, context, and meaning of actions. The young women in this study wanted to talk about their lives—perhaps because few adults had ever demonstrated an interest in really listening to them. Thus, it is important that more qualitative, conversational interviewing methods be incorporated into all research endeavors, including longitudinal studies. These types of approaches generate data that assist in the development of new theoretical explanations: they reveal the complexities and nuances of human behaviors about which little is known.

Future studies should include questions on a broad range of experiences and problematic behaviors common among female adolescents as well as questions that capture the potentially hostile environments in which girls come of age.[41] How is it that girls spend years being shuttled among social institutions (family, school, and child welfare) that consistently fail them? What are the long-term consequences of girls' traumatic experiences? How do our social policies—purportedly grounded in the humanitarian intent of protecting children—contribute to alienation, stigmatization, and aggression? And how do harsh responses serve to reify bad behavior?[42]

Research will also benefit from improved methodological techniques. The responses of the girls in this study demonstrate the complexity of language and the need for close attention to wording in interview schedules, particularly when referring to sensitive subjects such as sex and violence. It is possible that young women are exposed to so much violence, and have received so little support in addressing traumagenic effects, that violence is the norm. Personal victimizations are spoken of matter-of-factly, masking any emotion, and minimizing the amount and consequences of violence. If girls are asked about ever having been "physically or sexually abused," for example, interviewers must be cautious when analyzing responses. Questions must be specific about what the interviewer is trying to ask: "abused," for example, has a multitude of meanings for different people within different economic and cultural settings, and traumatized adolescents especially have difficulty naming what has occurred, often minimizing or forgetting events. This also has implications for the training of interviewers. One approach could be to ask about the developmental environment in which girls grew up to learn how they were socialized to violence and how they came to accept as normal loved ones hurting other loved ones. Refinements in language and format ultimately may result in new data for interpreting violent delinquency by both girls and boys.

The current study sought to better understand violence perpetrated by young women, an area sorely in need of empirical study. My findings, however, are also relevant to youth violence in general. The attachment-based model that I describe throughout this book may apply to boys, as it is likely that boys and girls share similar responses to disruptions in parental attachment.[43] But, because children grow up in a gendered world, their choices, opportunities, and experiences are most assuredly different from one another and, therefore, their resultant emotional distress is likely to manifest differently. Young women, for example, are more likely to be sexually harassed, bothered, and assaulted, both within and outside the home. This fact will affect how they are perceived by and how they perceive others, and it will influence their emotional (i.e., level of fear, anxiety, and anger) and physical (i.e., how to dress, act, move, and where to go) states. They are likely to employ different ways of coping with emotions and, perhaps, in a different temporal order. Violence, however, is apt to be one of the outcomes, given the cumulative effect of extensive early detachment, victimization, and loss as well as the lack of support and supervision. Thus, the need for gendered analyses that investigate early childhood trauma and later manifestations remains strong.

The girls who agreed to be interviewed for this research have aged out of the juvenile justice system. So too has Lidia, whose unfolding news story was relayed in the beginning of this book. I cannot know with certainty where any of the girls are today—I can only hope that they have found a way to integrate their traumatic histories into their past and have begun to write new stories for themselves. But without significant interventions, which did not appear eminent, I am not optimistic for their success. Even more discouraging is that an unknown number of girls, who are growing up in ravaged neighborhoods and who "don't have anyone there for them," continue to be subjected to horrific familial and community violence and loss. And thousands of girls, with stories similar to those presented here, continue to enter our juvenile justice systems daily. Girls who engage in violence require supervision and controls but, as human beings, they primarily need consistent, psychologically attuned, and loving relationships. Rather than increased social control in the form of monitoring and punishment, the greater need is for social support—increased adult acceptance, affection, and guidance. It is my hope that each of us will take these girls' stories to heart and, so empowered, will join with others to make the changes necessary to ensure safer, less painful lives for girls everywhere.

Notes

1. Finkelhor et al., "Violence, Abuse, and Crime Exposure"; Finkelhor et al., "Poly-victimization"; Elliott et al., *Multiple Problem Youth.*
2. Banks, *Affliction,* p. 340; Daly, "Women's Pathways to Felony Court," p. 28.
3. De Zulueta, *From Pain to Violence,* p. 295.
4. *Shutter Island*, directed by Martin Scorsese (Hollywood, CA: Paramount Pictures, 2010).
5. Bretherton, "The Origins," p. 766, citing John Bowlby, "Maternal Care and Mental Health," *World Health Organization Monograph,* 1951.
6. Brubaker and Fox, "Urban African American Girls at Risk," p. 253.
7. The National Child Protection Training Center (NCPTC) was established in 2003 as a partnership between Winona State University in Minnesota and the National District Attorneys Association. In 2007, the National Association to Prevent Sexual Abuse of Children, a national coalition of survivors and child protection advocates, became the managing agent of NCPTC.
8. Hyman and Perone, "The Other Side of School Violence"; Stein, "Bullying or Sexual Harassment?"
9. Richards, "Zero Room," p. 91.
10. Richards, "Zero Room," p. 100, citing the US Department of Education; Zernike, "Crackdown on Threats."

11. B. Solomon, "Traditional and Rights-Informed Talk," p. 265.

12. Hyman and Perone, "The Other Side of School Violence."

13. Leitz, "Girl Fights," p. 38. See also Rosenbloom and Way's ("Experiences of Discrimination") description of how teachers' treatment of various racial and ethnic groups feeds antagonism among youth.

14. Leitz, "Girl Fights," p. 31.

15. Ibid.

16. Despite both federal and state laws requiring attention to sex discrimination in the schools, sexual and gender harassment continues to proliferate. American Association of University Women Foundation and Harris Interactive, *Hostile Hallways;* Stein, "What a Difference a Discipline Makes."

17. According to L. Brown et al. ("Patriarchy Matters," p. 1263), though ostensibly designed to protect students, bullying policies may "deflect the school's legal responsibility for the creation of a safe and equitable learning environment" and place the onus of solving the problem on the victim.

18. Solomon, "Traditional and Rights-Informed Talk," p. 278.

19. Ibid., p. 276.

20. See Stein, "What a Difference a Discipline Makes," footnote 60. See also Ayers et al., *Zero Tolerance;* Girouex, "Zero Tolerance, Domestic Militarization"; L. Brown et al., "Patriarchy Matters."

21. Hutchinson, *Report of the National School Shield Task Force.*

22. Raeder, *State of Criminal Justice,* p. 140. See also Morris et al., *Confined in California.*

23. International Institute for Restorative Practices, *Improving School Climate.*

24. Herman, "Justice from the Victim's Perspective."

25. Abram et al., "Posttraumatic Stress Disorder and Trauma"; Blackburn et al., "The Next Generation"; Hennessey et al., *Trauma Among Girls.*

26. Teplin et al., "Psychiatric Disorders in Youth."

27. Golzari et al., "The Health Status of Youth."

28. National Association of State Mental Health Program Directors, *Position Statement on Mental Health Services;* National Mental Health Association, *Mental Health Treatment for Youth.*

29. "Mayor Bloomberg Announces Partnership."

30. Mears and Travis, "Youth Development and Reentry."

31. Altschuler, "Rehabilitating and Reintegrating."

32. Hussain et al., "Violence in the Lives of Girls," p. 59.

33. Nanda, "Blind Discretion."

34. Robinson and Ryder, "Psychosocial Perspectives."

35. Information on Cure Violence is available at http://cureviolence.org.

36. Griffin, *Season of the Witch,* p. 50. See also Debold et al., "Cultivating Hardiness Zones."

37. See Jessica Nieradka, "Safe Spaces for Adolescent Girls in Haiti," International Planned Parenthood Federation, www.ippfwhr.org/en/blog/safe-spaces-adolescent-girls-haiti.

38. Caldwell and Van Rybroek ("Reducing Violence," p. 634) state this is not easily done and "cannot be reduced to a structured program of workbooks

and phases of treatment." The imposition of manualized skills, or other such external controls, may in reality exacerbate extreme defenses already in place.

39. Gottfredson and Hirschi, *General Theory of Crime;* Hayslett-McCall and Bernard, "Attachment, Masculinity, and Self-Control," p. 17.

40. Waters et al., "Attachment Security."

41. The current study was a secondary analysis of data from the larger LAVIDA project and, as such, was limited in its ability to gather gendered data. See Crimmins et al., *Learning About Violence and Drugs Among Adolescents.*

42. Robinson, "'Since I Couldn't,'" p. 202. See also Hyman and Perone, "Other Side of School Violence."

43. Indeed, Hayslett-McCall and Bernard ("Attachment, Masculinity, and Self-Control") propose a theory of disproportionate male offending that contends that the US masculine culture, as promoted by standard parenting practices, contributes to an "aggregate-level effect of disproportionately disrupted early attachment in boys." The girls in this study were subject to similar harsh parenting techniques that resulted in a traumatic failure to meet their attachment needs.

Bibliography

Abbott, Andrew. "Of Time and Space: The Contemporary Relevance of the Chicago School," *Social Forces* 75, no. 4 (1997): 1149–1182.

Abram, Karen, Linda Teplin, Devon Charles, Sandra Longworth, Gary McClelland, and Mina Dulcan. "Posttraumatic Stress Disorder and Trauma in Youth in Juvenile Detention," *Archives of General Psychiatry* 61, no. 4 (2004): 403–410.

Abrantes, Ana, Norman Hoffman, and Ronald Anton. "Prevalence of Co-occurring Disorders Among Juveniles Committed to Detention Centers," *International Journal of Offender Therapy and Comparative Criminology* 49, no. 2 (2005): 179–193.

Ainsworth, Mary. "Infant-Mother Attachment," *American Psychologist* 34, no. 10 (1979): 932–937.

Ainsworth, Mary, Silvia Bell, and Donelda Stayton. "Individual Differences in Strange Situation Behavior of One-year-olds." In *The Origins of Human Social Relations,* edited by H. R. Schaffer, 17–57. London: Academic Press, 1971.

Ainsworth, Mary, Mary Blehar, Everett Waters, and Sally Wall. *Patterns of Attachment: A Psychological Study of the Strange Situation.* Hillsdale, NJ: Lawrence Erlbaum Associates, 1978.

Alder, Christine, and Anne Worrall. *Girls' Violence: Myths and Realities.* Albany: State University of New York Press, 2004.

Alemagno, Sonia, Elizabeth Shaffer-King, and Rachel Hammel. "Juveniles in Detention: How Do Girls Differ from Boys?" *Journal of Correctional Health Care* 12, no. 1 (2006): 45–53.

Alexander, Ruth. *The "Girl Problem": Female Delinquency in New York, 1900–1930.* Ithaca: Cornell University Press, 1995.

Allison, Paul D., and Frank F. Furstenberg. "How Marital Dissolution Affects Children: Variations by Age and Sex," *Developmental Psychology* 25, no. 4 (1989): 540–549.

Altschuler, David. "Rehabilitating and Reintegrating Youth Offenders: Are Residential and Community Aftercare Colliding Worlds and What Can

Be Done About It?" *Justice Policy Journal* 5, no. 1 (2008): 1–26. www.cjcj.org.

Alverez, Julie, and Eugene Emory. "Executive Function and the Frontal Lobes: A Meta-Analytic Review," *Neuropsychology Review* 16, no. 1 (2006): 17–42.

American Association of University Women Foundation and Harris Interactive. *Hostile Hallways: Bullying, Teasing and Sexual Harassment in School.* Washington, DC: American Association of University Women Foundation and Harris Interactive, 2001. www2.huberlin.de/sexology /ECR6/hostilehallways.pdf.

American Bar Association and National Bar Association. *Justice by Gender: The Lack of Appropriate Prevention, Diversion and Treatment Alternatives for Girls in the Justice System.* Washington, DC: American Bar Association and National Bar Association, 2001. www.nttac.org/views /docs/jabg/grpcurriculum/justice_gender.pdf.

American Correctional Association. *The Female Offender: What Does the Future Hold?* Laurel, MD: American Correctional Association, 1990.

American Psychiatric Association. *Diagnostic and Statistical Manual of Mental Disorders,* 4th ed., text revision (*DSM-IV-TR*). Washington, DC: American Psychiatric Association, 2000.

Anderson, Elijah. *Code of the Street: Decency, Violence, and the Moral Life of the Inner City.* New York: W. W. Norton, 1999.

Annie E. Casey Foundation. "Kids Count Data Center." http://datacenter.kids count.org/data/acrossstates/Rankings.aspx?ind=106, accessed March 1, 2011.

Ansbro, Maria. "Using Attachment Theory with Offenders," *Probation Journal* 55, no. 3 (2008): 231–244.

Arditti, Joyce. *Parental Incarceration and the Family: Psychological and Social Effects of Imprisonment on Children, Parents, and Caregivers.* New York: New York University Press, 2012.

Armour, Marilyn. "Experiences of Covictims of Homicide: Implications for Research and Practice," *Trauma, Violence and Abuse* 3, no. 2 (2002): 109–124.

Arnold, Regina. "Processes of Victimization and Criminalization of Black Women." In *The Criminal Justice System and Women: Offenders, Victims and Workers,* edited by Barbara Price and Natalie Sokoloff, 136–146. New York: McGraw-Hill, 1995.

Artz, Sibylle. *Sex, Power and the Violent School Girl.* Toronto, ON: Trifolium Books, 1998.

Ayers, William, Bernardine Dohrn, and Rick Ayers. *Zero Tolerance: Resisting the Drive for Punishment in Our Schools.* New York: The New Press, 2001.

Backhouse, Constance. *Petticoats and Prejudice: Women and Law in 19th Century Canada.* Toronto, ON: Published for the Osgoode Society by Women's Press, 1991.

Balaban, Victor. "Assessment of Children." In *Effective Treatments for PTSD: Practice Guidelines from the International Society for Traumatic*

Stress Studies, edited by Edna B. Foa, Terence M. Keane, Matthew J. Friedman, and Judith A. Cohen, 62–82. New York: Guilford Press, 2010.

Banks, Russell. *Affliction*. New York: Harper and Row, 1990.

Barron, Christie, and Dany Lacombe. "Moral Panic and the Nasty Girl," *Canadian Review of Sociology and Anthropology* 42, no. 1 (2005): 51–69.

Bartollas, Clemens. "Little Girls Grow Up: The Perils of Institutionalization." In *Female Criminality: The State of the Art,* edited by Concetta C. Culliver, 469–482. New York: Garland, 1993.

Baskin, Deborah, and Ira Sommers. *Casualties of Community Disorder: Women's Careers in Violent Crime*. Boulder: Westview, 1998.

Baskin, Deborah, and Ira Sommers. "Female's Initiation into Violent Street Crime," *Justice Quarterly* 10, no. 4 (1993): 559–583.

Batacharya, Sheila. "Racism, 'Girl Violence,' and the Murder of Reena Virk." In *Girls' Violence: Myths and Realities,* edited by Christine Alder and Anne Worrall, 61–80. Albany: State University of New York Press, 2004.

Batchelor, Susan. "Prove Me the Bam!: Victimization and Agency in the Lives of Young Women Who Commit Violent Offenses," *Probation Journal: The Journal of Community and Criminal Justice* 52, no. 4 (2005): 358–375.

Batchelor, Susan, Michelle Burman, and Jane Brown. "Discussing Violence: Let's Hear It from the Girls," *Probation Journal* 48, no. 2 (2001): 125–134.

Baumrind, Diana. "The Influence of Parenting Style on Adolescent Competence and Substance Abuse," *Journal of Early Adolescence* 11, no. 1 (1991): 56–95.

Becker, Howard. *Tricks of the Trade: How to Think About Research While You're Doing It*. Chicago: University of Chicago Press, 1998.

Becker-Blease, Kathryn, and Jennifer Freyd. "Beyond PTSD: An Evolving Relationship Between Trauma Theory and Family Violence Research," *Journal of Interpersonal Violence* 20, no. 4 (2005): 403–411.

Begum, Shelina. "Girl 'Gangstas' Siege on Family," *Asian News,* May 5, 2006. www.theasiannews.co.uk/news/s/513/513554_girl_gangstas_siege_on_family .html, accessed September 5, 2008.

Belknap, Joanne, and Kristi Holsinger. "An Overview of Delinquent Girls: How Theory and Practice Have Failed and the Need for Innovative Changes." In *Female Offenders: Critical Perspectives and Effective Interventions,* edited by Ruth T. Zaplin, 31–64. Gaithersburg, MD: Aspen, 1998.

Belknap, Joanne, Kristi Holsinger, and Melissa Dunn. "Understanding Incarcerated Girls: The Results of a Focus Group Study," *Prison Journal* 77, no. 4 (1997): 381–404.

Bell, Carl, and Esther Jenkins. "Traumatic Stress and Children," *Journal of Health Care for the Poor and Underserved* 2, no. 1 (1991): 175–185.

Bell, Silvia, and Mary Ainsworth. "Infant Crying and Maternal Responsiveness," *Child Development* 42, no. 4 (1972): 1171–1190.

Benekos, Peter, and Alida Merlo. "Juvenile Justice: The Legacy of Punitive Policy," *Youth Violence and Juvenile Justice* 6, no. 1 (2008): 28–46.

Black, Aaron, and Joanne Pedro-Carroll. "Role of Parent-Child Relationships in Mediating the Effects of Marital Disruption," *Journal of the American Academy of Child and Adolescent Psychiatry* 32, no. 5 (1993): 1019–1027.

Blackburn, Ashley, Janet Mullings, James Marquart, and Chad Trulson. "The Next Generation of Prisoners: Toward an Understanding of Violent Institutionalized Delinquents," *Youth Violence and Juvenile Justice* 5, no. 1 (2007): 35–56.

Blizard, Ruth, and Ann Bluhm. "Attachment to the Abuser: Integrating Object-Relations and Trauma Theories in Treatment of Abuse Survivors," *Psychotherapy* 31, no. 3 (1994): 383–390.

Blyth, Dale, and Carol Traeger. "Adolescent Self-Esteem and Perceived Relationships with Parents and Peers." In *Social Networks of Children, Adolescents, and College Students,* edited by Suzanne Salzinger, John Antrobus, and Muriel Hammer, 171–194. Hillsdale, NJ: Erlbaum, 1988.

Boney-McCoy, Sue, and David Finkelhor. "Psychosocial Sequelae of Violent Victimization in a National Youth Sample," *Journal of Consulting and Clinical Psychology* 63, no. 5 (1995): 726–736.

Boulahanis, John, and Martha Heltsley. "Perceived Fears: The Reporting Patterns of Juvenile Homicide in Chicago Newspapers," *Criminal Justice Policy Review* 15, no. 2 (2004): 132–160.

Bourgois, Philippe. "In Search of Horatio Alger: Culture and Ideology in the Crack Economy," *Contemporary Drug Problems* 16, no. 4 (1989): 619–649.

Bourgois, Philippe. *In Search of Respect: Selling Crack in El Barrio.* Cambridge: Cambridge University Press, 1995.

Bowlby, John. *Attachment.* New York: Basic Books, 1969.

Bowlby, John. *Loss, Sadness and Depression.* New York: Basic Books, 1980.

Bowlby, John. *A Secure Base: Parent-Child Attachment and Healthy Human Development.* New York: Basic Books, 1988.

Bowlby, John. *Separation.* New York: Basic Books, 1973.

Breslau, Naomi, Howard Chilcoat, Ronald Kessler, and Glenn Davis. "Previous Exposure to Trauma and PTSD Effects of Subsequent Trauma: Results from the Detroit Area Survey of Trauma," *American Journal of Psychiatry* 156, no. 6 (1999): 902–907.

Breslau, Naomi, Glenn Davis, Patricia Andreski, and Edward Peterson. "Traumatic Events and Posttraumatic Stress Disorder in an Urban Population of Young Adults," *Archives of General Psychiatry* 48, no. 3 (1991): 216–222.

Breslau, Naomi, Glenn Davis, Patricia Andreski, Edward Peterson, and Lonni Schultz. "Sex Differences in Posttraumatic Stress Disorder," *Archives of General Psychiatry* 54, no. 11 (1997): 1044–1048.

Bretherton, Inge. "The Origins of Attachment Theory: John Bowlby and Mary Ainsworth," *Developmental Psychology* 28, no. 5 (1992): 759–775.

Briere, John. "Methodological Issues in the Study of Sexual Abuse Effects," *Journal of Consulting and Clinical Psychology* 60, no. 2 (1992): 196–203.

Brook, Judith, Jung Lee, Stephen Finch, Jonathan Koppel, and David Brook. "Psychosocial Factors Related to Cannabis Use Disorders," *Substance Abuse* 32, no. 4 (2011): 242–251.

Brown, Lyn. *Raising Their Voices: The Politics of Girls' Anger.* Cambridge: Harvard University Press, 1998.

Brown, Lyn, Meda Chesney-Lind, and Nan Stein. "Patriarchy Matters: Toward a Gendered Theory of Teen Violence and Victimization," *Violence Against Women* 13, no. 12 (2007): 1249–1273.

Brown, Lyn, and Carol Gilligan. *Meeting at the Crossroads.* Cambridge: Harvard University Press, 1992.

Brown, Marion. "Discourses of Choice and Experiences of Constraint: Analyses of Girls' Use of Violence," *Girlhood Studies* 5, no. 2 (2012): 65–83.

Brown, Marion. "Negotiations of the Living Space: Life in the Group Home for Girls Who Use Violence." In *Fighting for Girls: New Perspectives on Gender and Violence,* edited by Meda Chesney-Lind and Nikki Jones, 175–199. Albany: State University of New York Press, 2010.

Browne, Angela, and David Finkelhor. "Impact of Child Sexual Abuse: A Review of the Research," *Psychological Bulletin* 99, no. 1 (1986): 66–77.

Brubaker, Sarah, and Kristan Fox. "Urban African American Girls at Risk: An Exploratory Study of Service Needs and Provision," *Youth Violence and Juvenile Justice* 8, no. 3 (2010): 250–265.

Bureau of Justice Statistics. *Correctional Populations in the United States, 1997.* Washington, DC: US Department of Justice, 2000. www.bjs.gov /index.cfm?ty=pbdetail&iid=691.

Burman, Michele, Susan Batchelor, and Jane Brown. "Researching Girls and Violence: Facing the Dilemmas of Fieldwork," *British Journal of Criminology* 41, no. 3 (2001): 443–459.

Burton, Linda. "Childhood Adultification in Economically Disadvantaged Families: An Ethnographic Perspective," *Family Relations* 56 (2007): 329–345.

Buzawa, Eve, and David Hirschel. "Criminalizing Assault: Do Age and Gender Matter?" In *Fighting for Girls: New Perspectives on Gender and Violence,* edited by Meda Chesney-Lind and Nikki Jones, 33–56. Albany: State University of New York Press, 2010.

Buzawa, Eve, and Gerald Hotaling. "The Impact of Relationship Status, Gender, and Minor Status in the Police Response to Domestic Assaults," *Victims and Offenders* 1, no. 4 (2006): 323–360.

Cain, Maureen. "Towards Transgression: New Directions in Feminist Criminology," *International Journal of Sociology of Law* 18, no. 1 (1990): 1–18.

Caldwell, Michael, and Gregory J. Van Rybroek. "Reducing Violence in Serious Juvenile Offenders Using Intensive Treatment," *International Journal of Law and Psychiatry* 28 (2005): 622–636.

Carrington, Kerry. "Does Feminism Spoil Girls? Explanations for Official Rises in Female Delinquency," *Australian and New Zealand Journal of Criminology* 37, no. 11 (2006): 34–53.

Caruth, Cathy. *Unclaimed Experience: Trauma, Narrative and History.* Baltimore: Johns Hopkins University Press, 1996.

Casey, B. J., Jay N. Giedd, and Kathleen M. Thomas. "Structural and Functional Brain Development and Its Relation to Cognitive Development," *Biological Psychology* 54, no. 1 (2000): 241–257.

Cauffman, Elizabeth, Shirley Feldman, Jaime Waterman, and Hans Steiner. "Posttraumatic Stress Disorder Among Female Juvenile Offenders," *Journal of the American Academy of Child and Adolescent Psychiatry* 37, no. 11 (1998): 1209–1216.

Cauffman, Elizabeth, Frances Lexcen, Asha Goldwebwe, Elizabeth Shulman, and Thomas Grisso. "Gender Differences in Mental Health Symptoms Among Delinquent and Community Youth," *Youth Violence and Juvenile Justice* 5, no. 3 (2007): 287–307.

Cernkovich, Stephen, and Peggy Giordano. "Family Relationships and Delinquency," *Criminology* 25, no. 2 (1987): 295–319.

Chesney-Lind, Meda. "Girls' Crime and Woman's Place: Toward a Feminist Model of Female Delinquency," *Crime and Delinquency* 35, no. 1 (1989): 5–29.

Chesney-Lind, Meda. "Jailing 'Bad' Girls: Girls' Violence and Trends in Female Incarceration." In *Fighting for Girls: New Perspectives on Gender and Violence*, edited by Meda Chesney-Lind and Nikki Jones, 57–79. Albany: State University of New York Press, 2010.

Chesney-Lind, Meda, and Joanne Belknap. "Trends in Delinquent Girls' Aggression and Violent Behavior: A Review of the Evidence." In *Aggression, Antisocial Behavior, and Violence Among Girls: A Developmental Perspective,* edited by Martha Putallaz and Karen Bierman, 203–220. New York: Guilford Press, 2004.

Chesney-Lind, Meda, and Michelle Eliason. "From Invisible to Incorrigible: The Demonization of Marginalized Women and Girls," *Crime Media Culture* 2, no. 1 (2006): 29–47.

Clear, Todd, Dina Rose, and Judith Ryder. "Incarceration and the Community: The Problem of Removing and Returning Offenders," *Journal of Research in Crime and Delinquency* 47, no. 3 (2001): 335–351.

Cleary, Sean. "Adolescent Victimization and Associated Suicidal and Violent Behaviors," *Adolescence* 35, no. 140 (2000): 671–682.

Cleveland, Michael, Frederick Gibbons, Meg Gerrard, Elizabeth Pomery, and Gene Brody. "The Impact of Parenting on Risk Cognitions and Risk Behavior: A Study of Mediation and Moderation in a Panel of African American Adolescents," *Child Development* 76, no. 4 (2005): 900–916.

Coble, Helen, Diana Gantt, and Brent Mallinckrodt. "Attachment, Social Competency, and the Capacity to Use Social Support." In *Handbook of Social Support and the Family,* edited by Gregory Pierce, Barbara Sarason, and Irwin Sarason, 141–172. New York: Plenum Press, 1996.

Colder, Craig, Joshua Mott, Susan Levy, and Brian Flay. "The Relation of Perceived Neighborhood Danger to Childhood Aggression: A Test of

Mediating Mechanisms," *American Journal of Community Psychology* 28, no. 11 (2000): 83–104.

Collins, Patricia Hill. *Black Feminist Thought: Knowledge, Consciousness, and the Politics of Empowerment.* Boston: Unwin Hyman, 1990.

Collins, Patricia Hill. "The Meaning of Motherhood in Black Culture and Black Mother-Daughter Relationships." In *Double Stitch: Black Women Write About Mothers and Daughters,* edited by Patricia Bell-Scott, 42–60. New York: Harper Perennial, 1991.

Colvin, Mark. *Crime and Coercion: An Integrated Theory of Chronic Criminality.* New York: St. Martin's, 2000.

Connor, Daniel. *Aggression and Antisocial Behavior in Children and Adolescents: Research and Treatment.* New York: Guilford Press, 2002.

Contreras, Randol. "'Damn, Yo—Who's That Girl?' An Ethnographic Analysis of Masculinity in Drug Robberies," *Journal of Contemporary Ethnography* 38, no. 4 (2009): 465–492.

Cook, Philip, and John Laub. "After the Epidemic: Recent Trends in Youth Violence in the United States." In *Crime and Justice: A Review of Research,* vol. 29, edited by Michael Tonry, 1–39. Chicago: University of Chicago Press, 2002.

Cook, Philip, and John Laub. "The Unprecedented Epidemic in Youth Violence." In *Crime and Justice: A Review of Research,* vol. 24, edited by Michael Tonry and Mark Moore, 27–64. Chicago: University of Chicago Press, 1998.

Corrado, Raymond, Candice Odgers, and Irwin Cohen. "The Incarceration of Young Female Offenders: Protection for Whom?" *Canadian Journal of Criminology* 42, no. 2 (2000): 189–207.

Corrado, Raymond, Ronald Roesch, Stephen Hart, and Jozef Gierowski. *Multi-problem Violent Youth: A Foundation for Comparative Research on Needs, Interventions and Outcomes.* Amsterdam: IOS Press, 2002.

Costa, Paul, Mark Somerfield, and Mark McCrae. "Personality and Coping: A Reconceptualization." In *Handbook of Coping: Theory, Research, Applications,* edited by Moshe Zeidner and Norman Endler, 44–61. New York: Wiley, 1996.

Crenshaw, Kimberle. "From Private Violence to Mass Incarceration: Thinking Intersectionality About Women, Race, and Social Control," *UCLA Law Review* 59, no. 6 (2011): 1418–1472.

Crimmins, Susan. "Early Childhood Loss as a Predisposing Factor in Female Perpetrated Homicides." Unpublished doctoral dissertation, City University of New York, 1995.

Crimmins, Susan, Henry Brownstein, Barry Spunt, Judith Ryder, and Raquel Warley. *Learning About Violence and Drugs Among Adolescents,* Final Report to the National Institute on Drug Abuse, Grant No. R01 DA08679. Washington, DC: National Institutes of Health, 1998.

Crimmins, Susan, Sean Cleary, Henry Brownstein, Barry Spunt, and Raquel Warley. "Trauma, Drugs and Violence Among Juvenile Offenders," *Journal of Psychoactive Drugs* 32, no. 1 (2000): 43–54.

Crimmins, Susan, Sandra Langley, Henry Brownstein, and Barry Spunt. "Convicted Women Who Have Killed Children: A Self-psychology Perspective," *Journal of Interpersonal Violence* 12, no. 1 (1997): 49–69.

Cullen, Francis, James Unnever, John Paul Wright, and Kevin Beaver. "Parenting and Self-Control." In *Out of Control: Assessing the General Theory of Crime,* edited by Erich Goode, 61–74. Stanford: Stanford Social Sciences, 2008.

Curtis, Richard. "The Improbable Transformation of Inner-City Neighborhoods: Crime, Violence, and Drugs in the 1990s," *Journal of Criminal Law and Criminology* 88, no. 4 (1998): 1233–1266.

Daiute, Collette, and Michelle Fine. "Youth Perspectives on Violence and Injustice," *Journal of Social Issues* 59, no. 1 (2003): 1–14.

Daly, Kathleen. "Women's Pathways to Felony Court: Feminist Theories of Lawbreaking and Problems of Representation," *Southern California Review of Law and Women's Studies* 2, no. 11 (1992): 11–51.

Das, Veena, and Ashis Nandy. "Violence, Victimhood and the Language of Silence." In *The Word and the World: Fantasy, Symbol and Record,* edited by Veena Das, 177–195. New Delhi: Sage, 1986.

Davies, Andrew. "'These Viragoes Are No Less Cruel than the Lads': Young Women, Gangs and Violence in Late Victorian Manchester and Salford," *British Journal of Criminology* 39, no. 1 (1999): 72–89.

Debold, Elizabeth, Lyn Brown, Susan Weseen, and Geraldine Brookins. "Cultivating Hardiness Zones for Adolescent Girls: A Reconceptualization of Resilience in Relationships with Caring Adults." In *Beyond Appearance: A New Look at Adolescent Girls,* edited by Norine Johnson, Michael Roberts, and Judith Worell, 181–204. Washington, DC: American Psychological Association, 1999.

Debold, Elizabeth, Marie Wilson, and Idelisse Malavé. *Mother Daughter Revolution: From Good Girls to Great Women.* New York: Bantam Books, 1994.

DeJong, Allan, Arturo Hervada, and Gary Emmett. "Epidemiologic Variations in Childhood Sexual Abuse," *Child Abuse and Neglect* 7, no. 2 (1983): 155–162.

Dembo, Richard, James Schmeidler, Julie Guida, and Atiq Rahman. "A Further Study of Gender Differences in Service Needs Among Youths Entering a Juvenile Assessment Center," *Journal of Child and Adolescent Substance Abuse* 7, no. 4 (1998): 49–77.

Dembo, Richard, Linda Williams, Lawrence Lavoie, and Estrellita Berry. "Physical Abuse, Sexual Victimization, and Illicit Drug Use," *Violence and Victims* 4, no. 2 (1989): 121–138.

Denzin, Norman. "Toward a Phenomenology of Domestic Violence," *American Journal of Sociology* 90, no. 3 (1984): 483–513.

De Zulueta, Felicity. *From Pain to Violence: The Traumatic Roots of Destructiveness.* London: Whurr, 1993.

Didion, Joan. *The White Album.* New York: Farrar, Straus and Giroux, 1990.

DiIulio, John. "The Coming of the Super-Predators," *Weekly Standard,* November 27, 1995, 23–28.

Dise-Lewis, Jeannie. "The Life Events and Coping Inventory: An Assessment of Stress in Children," *Psychosomatic Medicine* 50 (1988): 484–499.

Doka, Kenneth. *Children Mourning, Mourning Children.* Washington, DC: Hospice Foundation of America, 1995.

Doob, Anthony, and Jane Sprott. "Is the 'Quality' of Youth Violence Becoming More Serious?" *Canadian Journal of Criminology and Criminal Justice* 40, no. 2 (1998): 185–194.

Duckworth, Melanie, D. Danielle Hale, Scott Clair, and Henry Adams. "Influences of Interpersonal Violence and Community Chaos on Stress Reactions in Children," *Journal of Interpersonal Violence* 15, no. 8 (2000): 806–826.

Dunlap, Eloise, Andrew Golub, and Bruce Johnson. "The Severely Distressed African-American Family in the Crack Era: Empowerment Is Not Enough," *Journal of Sociology and Social Welfare* 33, no. 1 (2006): 115–139.

Dunlap, Eloise, Andrew Golub, Bruce Johnson, and Ellen Benoit. "Normalization of Violence: Experiences of Childhood Abuse by Inner-City Crack Users," *Journal of Ethnicity in Substance Abuse* 8, no. 1 (2009): 15–34.

Dunlap, Eloise, Gabriele Stürzenhofecker, Harry Sanabria, and Bruce Johnson. "Mothers and Daughters: The Intergenerational Reproduction of Violence and Drug Use in Home and Street Life," *Journal of Ethnicity in Substance Abuse* 3, no. 2 (2004): 1–23.

Egeland, Byron, Mark Kalkoska, Natan Gottesman, and Martha Erikson. "Pre-school Behavior Problems: Stability and Factors Accounting for Change," *Journal of Child Psychology and Psychiatry* 31, no. 6 (1990): 891–909.

Ehlers, Anke, and David Clark. "A Cognitive Model of Posttraumatic Stress Syndrome," *Behaviour Research and Therapy* 38, no. 4 (2000): 319–345.

Eisikovits, Zvi, Zeev Winstok, and Guy Enosh. "Children's Experience of Interparental Violence: A Heuristic Model," *Children and Youth Services Review* 20, no. 6 (1998): 547–568.

Elliott, Delbert. "Serious Violent Offenders: Onset, Developmental Course, and Termination—The American Society of Criminology 1993 Presidential Address," *Criminology* 32, no. 1 (1994): 1–21.

Elliott, Delbert, David Huizinga, and Scott Menard. *Multiple Problem Youth: Delinquency, Substance Use, and Mental Health Problems.* New York: Springer Verlag, 1989.

English, Diana, Cathy Spatz Widom, and Carol Brandford. *Childhood Victimization and Delinquency, Adult Criminality, and Violent Criminal Behavior: A Replication and Extension,* Final Report to the National Institute of Justice, Grant No. 97-IJ-CX-0017. Rockville, MD: National Institute of Justice/NCJRS, 2001.

Erikson, Eric. *Youth and Society.* New York: W. W. Norton, 1965.

Erikson, Kai. *Everything in Its Path: Destruction of a Community in the Buffalo Creek Flood.* New York: Simon and Schuster, 1976.

Erikson, Kai. *A New Species of Trouble: The Human Experience of Modern Disasters.* New York: W. W. Norton, 1994.

Erikson, Martha, L. Allan Sroufe, and Byron Egeland. "The Relationship Between Quality of Attachment and Behavior Problems in Pre-school in a High-risk Sample," *Monographs of the Society of Research in Child Development* 50, no. 1–2 (1985): 147–166.

Eth, Spencer, and Robert Pynoos. "Developmental Perspective on Psychic Trauma in Childhood." In *Trauma and Its Wake,* edited by Charles R. Figley, 36–52. New York: Brunner/Mazel, 1985.

Evans, Heidi. "Young, Female and Turning Deadly," *New York Daily News,* December 19, 1999, 6–7.

Fagan, Abigail. "The Gender Cycle of Violence: Comparing the Effects of Child Abuse and Neglect on Criminal Offending for Males and Females," *Violence and Victims* 16, no. 4 (2001): 457–474.

Failinger, Marie. "Lessons Unlearned: Women Offenders, the Ethics of Care, and the Promise of Restorative Justice," *Fordham Law Review Journal* 33, no. 2 (2006): 487–526.

Fairchild, Sherry. "Introduction to a Special Edition: Attachment Theory and Its Application to Practice," *Child and Adolescent Social Work Journal* 26, no. 4 (2009): 287–289.

Fantuzzo, John, Laura DePaola, Laura Lambert, Tamara Martino, Genevie Anderson, and Sara Sutton. "Effects of Interparental Violence on the Psychological Adjustment and Competencies of Young Children," *Journal of Consulting and Clinical Psychology* 59, no. 2 (1991): 258–265.

Fantuzzo, John, and Carol Lindquist. "The Effects of Observing Conjugal Violence on Children: A Review of Research Methodology," *Journal of Family Violence* 4, no. 1 (1989): 77–94.

Farber, Sharon. "Dissociation, Traumatic Attachments, and Self-Harm: Eating Disorders and Self-Mutilation," *Clinical Social Work Journal* 36, no. 1 (2008): 63–72.

Farrington, David. "Childhood Risk Factors and Risk-Focused Prevention." In *The Oxford Handbook of Criminology,* 4th ed., edited by Mike Maguire, Rodney Morgan, and Robert Reiner, 602–640. Oxford: Oxford University Press, 2007.

Farrington, David. "Developmental and Life-course Criminology: Key Theoretical and Empirical Issues—The 2002 Sutherland Award Address," *Criminology* 41, no. 2 (2003): 221–255.

Farrington, David. "Explaining the Beginning, Progress, and Ending of Antisocial Behavior from Birth to Adulthood." In *Facts, Frameworks and Forecasts: Advances in Criminological Theory,* vol. 3, edited by Joan McCord, 253–287. New Brunswick, NJ: Transaction, 1992.

Feiring, Candice, Shari Miller-Johnson, and Charles Cleland. "Potential Pathways from Stigmatization and Internalizing Symptoms to Delinquency in Sexually Abused Youth," *Child Maltreatment* 12, no. 3 (2007): 220–223.

Feiring, Candice, Lynn Taska, and Michael Lewis. "The Role of Shame and Attribution Style in Children's and Adolescents' Adaptation to Sexual Abuse," *Child Maltreatment* 3, no. 2 (1998): 129–142.

Feld, Barry. "Violent Girls or Relabeled Status Offenders? An Alternative Interpretation of the Data," *Crime and Delinquency* 55, no. 2 (2009): 241–265.

Fergusson, David, Joseph Boden, and L. John Horwood. "Exposure to Childhood Sexual and Physical Abuse and Adjustment in Early Adulthood," *Child Abuse and Neglect* 32, no. 6 (2008): 607–619.

Ferraro, Kathleen. *Neither Angels nor Demons: Women, Crime, and Victimization.* Boston: Northeastern University Press, 2006.

Finkelhor, David. "The Victimization of Children: A Developmental Perspective," *American Journal of Orthopsychiatry* 65, no. 2 (1995): 177–193.

Finkelhor, David, and Angela Browne. "The Traumatic Impact of Child Sexual Abuse: A Conceptualization," *American Journal of Orthopsychiatry* 55, no. 4 (1985): 530–541.

Finkelhor, David, Richard Ormrod, and Heather Turner. "Poly-Victimization: A Neglected Component in Child Victimization," *Child Abuse and Neglect* 31, no. 1 (2007): 7–26.

Finkelhor, David, Heather Turner, Richard Ormrod, and Sherry Hamby. "Violence, Abuse, and Crime Exposure in a National Sample of Children and Youth," *Pediatrics* 124, no. 5 (2009): 1–13.

Finkelhor, David, Heather Turner, Richard Ormrod, Sherry Hamby, and Kristen Kracke. "Children's Exposure to Violence: A Comprehensive National Survey," *Juvenile Justice Bulletin.* Washington DC: Office of Juvenile Justice and Delinquency Prevention, 2009. https://www.ncjrs.gov/pdffiles1/ojjdp/227744.pdf.

Foa, Edna, and Barbara Rothbaum. *Treating the Trauma of Rape: Cognitive-Behavioral Therapy for PTSD.* New York: Guilford Press, 1998.

Foderaro, Lisa. "Violence Is a Symptom of Youth Centers' Struggles," *New York Times,* February 15, 2002. www.nytimes.com/2002/02/15/nyregion /violence-is-a-symptom-of-youth-centers-struggles.html, accessed July 25, 2011.

Folkman, Susan, Richard Lazarus, Christine Dunkel-Schetter, Anita DeLongis, and Rand Gruen. "Dynamics of a Stressful Encounter: Cognitive Appraisal, Coping, and Encounter Outcomes," *Journal of Personality and Social Psychology* 50, no. 5 (1986): 992–1003.

Fonagy, Peter. "Male Perpetrators of Violence Against Women: An Attachment Theory Perspective," *Journal of Applied Psychoanalytic Studies* 1, no. 1 (1999): 7–27.

Fonagy, Peter, Mary Target, Miriam Steele, Howard Steele, Tom Leigh, Alice Levinson, and Roger Kennedy. "Morality, Disruptive Behavior, Borderline Personality Disorder, Crime, and Their Relationships to Security of Attachment." In *Attachment and Psychopathology,* edited by Leslie Atkinson and Kenneth Zucker, 223–274. New York: Guilford Press, 1997.

Fontana, Andrea, and James Frey. "The Interview: From Structured Questions to Negotiated Text." In *Handbook of Qualitative Research,* 2nd ed., edited by Norman Denzin and Yvonna Lincoln, 645–672. Thousand Oaks, CA: Sage, 2000.

Fox, James. *Trends in Juvenile Violence: A Report to the United States Attorney General on Current and Future Rates of Juvenile Offending.* Boston: Northeastern University Press, 1996.

Frazier, Francis, Lara Belliston, Leslie Brower, and Kraig Knudsen. *Placing Black Girls at Promise: A Report of the Rise Sister Rise Study. Executive Summary.* Columbus: Report from the Ohio Department of Mental Health, 2011.

Freeman, Linda, David Shaffner, and Helen Smith. "Neglected Victims of Homicide: The Needs of Young Siblings of Murder Victims," *American Journal of Orthopsychiatry* 66, no. 3 (1996): 337–345.

Freud, Anna. "Comments on Psychic Trauma." In *The Writings of Anna Freud,* vol. 5: *Research at the Hampstead Child-therapy Clinic and Other Papers, 1956–1965,* edited by Anna Freud, 221–241. New York: International Universities Press, 1967.

Fryer, Roland, Paul Heaton, Steven Levitt, and Kevin Murphy. "Measuring the Impact of Crack Cocaine," NBER Working Paper No. 11318. Cambridge, MA: National Bureau of Economic Research, May 2005. http://ssrn.com/abstract=720405.

Fullilove, Mindy. *The House of Joshua: Meditations on Family and Place.* Lincoln: University of Nebraska Press, 1999.

Furst, Terry, Bruce Johnson, Eloise Dunlap, and Richard Curtis. "The Stigmatized Image of the 'Crackhead': A Sociocultural Exploration of a Barrier to Cocaine Smoking Among a Cohort of Youth in New York City," *Deviant Behavior* 20, no. 2 (1999): 153–181.

Gaarder, Emily, and Joanne Belknap. "Tenuous Borders: Girls Transferred to Adult Court," *Criminology* 40, no. 3 (2002): 481–517.

Gadd, David. "Masculinities, Violence and Defended Psychosocial Subjects," *Theoretical Criminology* 4, no. 4 (2000): 429–449.

Gamble, Vanessa. "Under the Shadow of Tuskegee: African Americans and Health Care," *American Journal of Public Health* 87, no. 11 (1997): 1773–1778.

Garbarino, James. "An Ecological Perspective on the Effects of Violence on Children," *Journal of Community Psychology* 29, no. 3 (2001): 361–378.

Garbarino, James. *See Jane Hit: Why Girls Are Growing More Violent and What We Can Do About It.* New York: Penguin Press, 2007.

Garbarino, James, Kathleen Kostelny, and Nancy DuBrow. "What Children Can Tell Us About Living in Danger," *American Psychologist* 46, no. 4 (1991): 376–383.

Garland, David. *The Culture of Control: Crime and Social Order in Contemporary Society.* Chicago: University of Chicago Press, 2002.

Gibson, Mary. "The 'Female Offender' and the Italian School of Criminal Anthropology," *Journal of European Studies* 12, no. 47 (1982): 155–165.

Gilfus, Mary. "From Victims to Survivors to Offenders: Women's Routes of Entry and Immersion in Street Crime," *Women and Criminal Justice* 4, no. 1 (1992): 63–89.

Gilliard, Darrell, and Allen Beck. *Prisoners in 1997*. Washington, DC: Bureau of Justice Statistics, 1998.

Gilligan, Carol. *In a Different Voice: Psychological Theory and Women's Development*. Cambridge: Harvard University Press, 1982.

Gilligan, Carol, Nona Lyons, and Trudy Hanmer. *Making Connections: The Relational Worlds of Adolescent Girls at Emma Willard School*. Cambridge: Harvard University Press, 1990.

Gilligan, Carol, Annie Rogers, and Deborah Tolman. *Women, Girls, and Psychotherapy: Reframing Resistance*. New York: Harrington Park Press, 1991.

Giroux, Henry. "Zero Tolerance, Domestic Militarization, and the War Against Youth," *Social Justice* 30, no. 2 (2003): 59–65.

Glaser, Barney, and Anselm Strauss. *The Discovery of Grounded Theory: Strategies for Qualitative Research*. Chicago: Aldine, 1967.

Glaze, Lauren. *Correctional Populations in the United States, 2010*. Washington, DC: Bureau of Justice Statistics, 2011.

Glenwick, David, and Joel Mowrey. "When Parent Becomes Peer: Loss of Intergenerational Boundaries in Single Parent Families," *Family Relations* 35, no. 1 (1986): 57–62.

Godfrey, Barry. "Rough Girls, 1880–1930: The 'Recent' History of Violent Young Women." In *Girl's Violence: Myths and Realities,* edited by Christine Alder and Anne Worrall, 21–40. Albany: State University of New York Press, 2004.

Goffman, Irving. *Presentation of Self in Everyday Life*. Garden City, NY: Doubleday, 1959.

Gold, Steven. *Not Trauma Alone: Therapy for Child Abuse Survivors in Family and Social Context*. New York: Brunner/Mazel, 2000.

Goldblatt, Hadass. "Strategies of Coping Among Adolescents Experiencing Interparental Violence," *Journal of Interpersonal Violence* 18, no. 2 (2003): 532–552.

Goldstein, Paul. "Drugs and Violent Crime." In *Pathways to Criminal Violence,* edited by Neil Weiner and Marvin Wolfgang, 16–48. Newbury Park, CA: Sage, 1989.

Goldstein, Paul, Patricia Bellucci, Barry Spunt, and Thomas Miller. "Frequency of Cocaine Use and Violence: A Comparison Between Men and Women." In *The Epidemiology of Cocaine Use and Abuse,* edited by Susan Schober and Charles Schade, 113–138. Washington, DC: US Department of Health and Human Services, 1991. http://archives.drugabuse.gov/pdf/monographs/download110.html.

Golzari, Mana, Stephen Hunt, and Arash Anoshiravani. "The Health Status of Youth in Juvenile Detention Facilities," *Journal of Adolescent Health* 38, no. 6 (2006): 776–782.

Goodkind, Sara, Irene Ng, and Rosemary Sarri. "The Impact of Sexual Abuse in the Lives of Young Women Involved or at Risk of Involvement with the Juvenile Justice System," *Violence Against Women* 12, no. 5: (2006): 456–477.

Gottfredson, Michael, and Travis Hirschi. *A General Theory of Crime*. Stanford: Stanford University Press, 1990.

Greenberg, Mark, Michelle DeKlyen, Matthew Speltz, and Marya Endriga. "The Role of Attachment Processes in Externalizing Psychopathology in Young Children." In *Attachment and Psychopathology,* edited by Leslie Atkinson and Kenneth Zucker, 196–222. New York: Guilford Press, 1997.

Griffin, Gail. *Season of the Witch: Border Lines, Marginal Notes.* Pasadena: Trilogy Books, 1995.

Griffiths, Elizabeth, Carolyn Yule, and Rosemary Gartner. "Fighting over Trivial Things: Explaining the Issue of Contention in Violent Altercations," *Criminology* 49, no. 1 (2011): 61–94.

Grossman, Klaus, Karin Grosman, and Everett Waters, editors. *Attachment from Infancy to Adulthood: The Major Longitudinal Studies.* New York: Guilford Press, 2006.

Groves, Betsy, Barry Zuckerman, Steven Marans, and Donald Cohen. "Silent Victims: Children Who Witness Violence," *Journal of the American Medical Association* 269, no. 2 (1993): 262–264.

Guerino, Paul, Paige Harrison, and William Sabol. *Prisoners in 2010.* Washington, DC: Bureau of Justice Statistics, 2011. Revised February 9, 2012.

Hagan, John. *Structural Criminology.* New Brunswick, NJ: Rutgers University Press, 1989.

Hamid, Ansley. "The Developmental Cycle of a Drug Epidemic: The Cocaine Smoking Epidemic of 1981–1991," *Journal of Psychoactive Drugs* 24, no. 4 (1992): 337–348.

Harlow, Caroline. *Prior Abuse Reported by Inmates and Probationers.* Washington, DC: US Department of Justice, Office of Justice Programs, 1999.

Harris, Yvette, James Graham, and Gloria Carpenter. *Children of Incarcerated Parents: Theoretical Developmental and Clinical Issues.* New York: Springer, 2010.

Hartsock, Nancy. "Theoretical Bases for Coalition Building: An Assessment of Postmodernism." In *Feminism and Social Change: Bridging Theory and Practice,* edited by Heidi Gottfried, 256–274. Urbana: University of Illinois Press, 1996.

Hay, Carter, and Walter Forrest. "The Development of Self-Control: Examining Self-Control's Stability Thesis," *Criminology* 44, no. 4 (2006): 739–774.

Hayslett-McCall, Karen, and Thomas Bernard. "Attachment, Masculinity, and Self-control: A Theory of Male Crime Rates," *Theoretical Criminology* 6, no. 1 (2002): 5–33.

Heide, Kathleen, and Eldra Solomon. "Female Juvenile Murderers: Biological and Psychological Dynamics Leading to Homicide," *International Journal of Law and Psychiatry* 32, no. 4 (2009): 244–252.

Heide, Kathleen, and Eldra Solomon. "Responses to Severe Childhood Maltreatment: Homicidal Fantasies and Other Coping Strategies." Paper presented at the meeting of the American Society of Criminology, San Francisco, November 20–23, 1991.

Heidensohn, Frances. *Women and Crime,* 2nd ed. New York: New York University Press, 1995.

Hennessey, Marianne, Julian Ford, Karen Mahoney, Susan Ko, and Christine Siegfried. *Trauma Among Girls in the Juvenile Justice System.* Los Angeles: National Child Traumatic Stress Network, 2004.

Herman, Judith. "Justice from the Victim's Perspective," *Violence Against Women* 11, no. 5 (2005): 571–602.

Herman, Judith. *Trauma and Recovery.* New York: Basic Books, 1997.

Herrenkohl, Todd, Bu Huang, Emiko Tajima, and Stephen Whitney. "Examining the Link Between Child Abuse and Youth Violence: An Analysis of Mediating Mechanisms," *Journal of Interpersonal Violence* 18, no. 10 (2003): 1189–1208.

Hirschi, Travis. *Causes of Delinquency.* Berkeley: University of California Press, 1969.

Hofer, Myron. "Hidden Regulators: Implications for a New Understanding of Attachment, Separation, and Loss." In *Attachment Theory: Social, Developmental, and Clinical Perspectives,* edited by Susan Goldberg, Roy Muir, and John Kerr, 225–256. Hillsdale, NJ: Analytic Press, 1995.

Holahan, Charles, Rudolf Moos, and Jeanne Schaefer. "Coping, Stress Resistance, and Growth: Conceptualizing Adaptive Functioning." In *Handbook of Coping: Theory, Research and Applications,* edited by Moshe Zeider and Norman Endler, 24–43. New York: Wiley, 1996.

Holland, Janet, and Caroline Ramazanoglu. "Coming to Conclusions: Power and Interpretation in Researching Young Women's Sexuality." In *Researching Women's Lives from a Feminist Perspective,* edited by Mary Maynard and June Purvis, 125–148. London: Taylor and Francis, 1994.

Hollway, Wendy, and Tony Jefferson. "Eliciting Narrative Through the In-depth Interview," *Qualitative Inquiry* 3, no. 1 (1997): 53–70.

Holsinger, Kristi. "Differential Pathways to Violence and Self-Injurious Behavior: African American and White Girls in the Juvenile Justice System," *Journal of Research in Crime and Delinquency* 42, no. 2 (2005): 211–242.

Holstein, James, and Jaber Gubrium. *The Active Interview.* Thousand Oaks, CA: Sage, 1995.

Hood, Sarah, and Michele Carter. "A Preliminary Examination of Trauma History, Locus of Control, and PTSD Symptom Severity in African American Women," *Journal of Black Psychology* 34, no. 2 (2008): 179–191.

Horowitz, Karyn, Stevan Wiene, and James Jekel. "PTSD Symptoms in Urban Adolescent Girls: Compounded Community Trauma," *Journal of American Academy of Adolescent Psychiatry* 34, no. 10 (1995): 1353–1361.

Howell, Elizabeth. *The Dissociative Mind.* Hillsdale, NJ: Analytic Press, 2005.

Hoyt, Stephanie, and David Scherer. "Female Juvenile Delinquency: Misunderstood by the Juvenile Justice System, Neglected by Social Science," *Law and Human Behavior* 22, no. 1 (1998): 81–107.

Hughes, Honore. "Psychological and Behavioral Correlates of Family Violence in Child Witnesses and Victims," *American Journal of Orthopsychiatry* 58, no. 1 (1988): 77–90.

Huizinga, David, Rolf Loeber, Terence Thornberry, and Lynn Cothern. "Co-occurrence of Delinquency and Other Problem Behaviors." Washington, DC: Office of Juvenile Justice and Delinquency Prevention, 2000. https://www.ncjrs.gov/pdffiles1/ojjdp/182211.pdf.

Hurvich, Marvin. "The Place of Annihilation Anxieties in Psychoanalytic Theory," *Journal of the American Psychoanalytic Association* 51, no. 2 (2003): 579–616.

Hussain, Yasmin, Helene Berman, Romy Poletti, Rian Lougheed-Smith, Azmina Ladha, Ashley Ward, and Barbara MacQuarre. "Violence in the Lives of Girls in Canada: Creating Spaces of Understanding and Change." In *Girlhood: Redefining the Limits,* edited by Yasmin Jiwani, Candis Steenbergen, and Claudia Mitchell, 53–69. Montreal: Black Rose Books, 2006.

Hutchinson, Asa. *Report of the National School Shield Task Force.* National Rifle Association. April 2, 2013. www.nraschoolshield.com/NSS_Final _FULL.pdf.

Hyman, Irwin, and Donna Perone. "The Other Side of School Violence: Educator Policies and Practices that May Contribute to Student Misbehavior," *Journal of School Psychology* 36, no. 1 (1998): 7–27.

International Institute for Restorative Practices. *Improving School Climate: Findings from Schools Implementing Restorative Practices.* Bethlehem, PA: International Institute for Restorative Practices, 2009.

Ireland, Timothy, and Cathy Spatz Widom. "Childhood Victimization and Risk for Alcohol and Drug Arrests," *International Journal of the Addictions* 29, no. 2 (1994): 235–274.

Irwin, John, and James Austin. *It's About Time: America's Imprisonment Binge.* Belmont, CA: Wadsworth, 1997.

Johnson, Bruce, Eloise Dunlap, and Sylvie Tourigny. "Crack Distribution and Abuse in New York." In *Illegal Drug Markets: From Research to Prevention Policy,* edited by Mangai Natarajan and Mike Hough, 19–57. Monsey, NY: Criminal Justice Press, 2000.

Johnson, Valerie, and Robert Pandina. "Effects of Family Environment on Adolescent Substance Use, Delinquency, and Coping Styles," *American Journal of Drug and Alcohol Abuse* 17, no. 1 (1991): 71–88.

Johnston, Denise. "Effects of Parental Incarceration." In *Children of Incarcerated Parents,* edited by Katherine Gabel and Denise Johnston, 59–88. New York: Lexington Books, 1995.

Jones, Nikki. *Between Good and Ghetto: African American Girls and Inner City Violence.* New Brunswick, NJ: Rutgers University Press, 2010.

Jordon, Judith. "The Meaning of Mutuality." In *Women's Growth in Connection: Writings from the Stone Center,* edited by Judith Jordon, Alexandra Kaplan, Jean Baker Miller, Irene Stiver, and Janet Surrey, 81–96. New York: Guilford Press, 1991.

Kadi, Joanna. *Thinking Class: Sketches from a Cultural Worker.* Boston: South End Press, 1996.

Karr-Morse, Robin, and Meredith Wiley. *Ghosts from the Nursery: Tracing the Roots of Violence.* New York: Atlantic Monthly Press, 1997.

Kelley, Barbara, Rolf Loeber, Kate Keenan, and Mary DeLamatre. "Developmental Pathways in Boys' Disruptive and Delinquent Behavior." Washington, DC: Office of Juvenile Justice and Delinquency Prevention, 1997. https://www.ncjrs.gov/pdffiles/165692.pdf.

Kelly, Joan. "Children's Adjustment in Conflicted Marriage and Divorce: A Decade Review of Research," *Journal of the American Academy of Child and Adolescent Psychiatry* 39, no. 8 (2000): 963–973.

Kempf-Leonard, Kimberly, and Pernilla Johansson. "Gender and Runaways: Risk Factors, Delinquency, and Juvenile Justice Experiences," *Youth Violence and Juvenile Justice* 5, no. 3 (2007): 308–327.

Kendall-Tackett, Kathleen. *Treating the Lifetime Health Effects of Childhood Victimization.* Kingston, NJ: Civic Research Institute, 2003.

Kendall-Tackett, Kathleen, Linda Williams, and David Finkelhor. "Impact of Sexual Abuse on Children: A Review and Synthesis of Recent Empirical Studies," *Psychological Bulletin* 113, no. 1 (1993): 164–180.

Kilty, Jennifer. "Gendering Violence, Remorse and the Role of Restorative Justice: Deconstructing Public Perceptions of Kelly Ellard and Warren Glowatski," *Contemporary Justice Review* 13, no. 2 (2010): 155–172.

Kinetz, Erika. "School Attack," *Seventeen Magazine,* May 2005. www.zinio.com/pages/Seventeen/May-05, accessed June 1, 2010.

Kingery, Paul, B. E. Pruitt, and Robert Hurley. "Violence and Illegal Drug Use Among Adolescents: Evidence from the US National Adolescent Student Health Survey," *International Journal of the Addictions* 27, no. 12 (1992): 1445–1464.

Kingree, J. B., Ronald Braithwaite, and Tammy Woodring. "Psychosocial and Behavioral Problems in Relation to Recent Experience as a Runaway Among Adolescent Detainees," *Criminal Justice and Behavior* 28, no. 2 (2001): 190–205.

Konopka, Gisela. *The Adolescent Girl in Conflict.* Englewood Cliffs, NJ: Prentice Hall, 1966.

Krystal, Henry, and Hebert Raskin. *Drug Dependence: The Disturbances in Personality Functioning that Create the Need for Drugs.* Northvale, NJ: Jason Aronson, 1970.

Lambert, Sharon, Tamara Brown, Clarenda Phillips, and Nicholas Ialongo. "The Relationship Between Perceptions of Neighborhood Characteristics and Substance Use Among Urban African American Adolescents," *American Journal of Community Psychology* 34, nos. 3/4 (2004): 205–218.

Langhinrichsen-Rohling, Jennifer, and Peter Neidig. "Violent Backgrounds of Economically Disadvantaged Youth: Risk Factors for Perpetrating Violence?" *Journal of Family Violence* 10, no. 4 (1995): 379–397.

Lansford, Jennifer, Shari Miller-Johnson, Lisa Berlin, Kenneth Dodge, John Bates, and Gregory Pettit. "Early Physical Abuse and Later Violent Delinquency: A Prospective Longitudinal Study," *Child Maltreatment* 12, no. 3 (2007): 233–245.

Lauritsen, Janet. "How Families and Communities Influence Youth Victim-
    ization." Washington, DC: US Department of Justice, Office of Juvenile
    Justice and Delinquency Prevention, 2003.
Lauritsen, Janet, Karen Heimer, and James Lynch. "Trends in the Gender
    Gap in Violent Offending: New Evidence from the National Crime Vic-
    timization Survey," *Criminology* 47, no. 2 (2009): 361–399.
Lazarus, Richard. "Coping Theory and Research: Past, Present, and Future,"
    Psychosomatic Medicine 55, no. 3 (1993): 234–245.
Lazarus, Richard, and Susan Folkman. *Stress, Appraisal and Coping.* New
    York: Springer, 1984.
Lederman, Cindy, Gayle Dakof, Maria Larrea, and Hua Li. "Characteristics
    of Adolescent Females in Juvenile Detention," *International Journal of
    Law and Psychiatry* 27, no. 4 (2004): 321–337.
Lee, Felica. "For Gold Earrings and Protection, More Girls Take Road to
    Violence," *New York Times,* November 25, 1991. www.nytimes.com
    /1991/11/25/nyregion, accessed January 27, 2012.
Leitz, Lisa. "Girl Fights: Exploring Females' Resistance to Educational
    Structures," *International Journal of Sociology and Social Policy* 23,
    no. 11 (2003): 15–46.
Leschied, Alan, Anne Cummings, Michele Van Brunschot, Alison Cunning-
    ham, and Angela Saunders. "Aggression in Adolescent Girls: Implica-
    tions for Policy, Prevention and Treatment," *Canadian Psychology* 42
    no. 3 (2001): 200–215.
Leslie, Connie, Nina Biddle, Debra Rosenberg, and Joe Wayne. "Girls Will
    Be Girls," *Newsweek,* August 2, 1993.
Levendosky, Alytia, and Sandra Graham-Berman. "Parenting in Battered
    Women: The Effects of Domestic Violence on Women and Their Chil-
    dren," *Journal of Family Violence* 16, no. 2 (2001): 171–192.
Leydesdorff, Selma, Graham Dawson, Natasha Burchardt, and T. G. Ash-
    plant. "Introduction: Trauma and Life Stories." In *Trauma: Life Stories
    of Survivors,* edited by Kim Rogers and Selma Leydesdorff, with Gra-
    ham Dawson, 1–26. New Brunswick, NJ: Transaction, 2004.
Lieberman Alicia, Patricia Van Horn, and Emily Ozer. "Preschooler Witnesses
    of Marital Violence: Predictors and Mediators of Child Behavior Prob-
    lems," *Development and Psychopathology* 17, no. 2 (2005): 385–396.
Liebling, Alison, and Betsy Stanko. "Allegiance and Ambivalence: Some
    Dilemmas in Researching Disorder and Violence," *British Journal of
    Criminology* 41, no. 3 (2001): 421–430.
Liebson, Richard, Shawn Cohen, and Kristoffer Garin. "Counselor Beaten,
    Set on Fire; Teen Girls Arrested," *Journal News,* White Plains, New
    York, February 9, 2002.
Lincoln, Yvonna, and Egon Guba. "Pragmatic Controversies, Contradictions,
    and Emerging Confluences." In *Handbook on Qualitative Research,* 2nd
    ed., edited by Norman Denzin and Yvonna Lincoln, 163–188. Thousand
    Oaks, CA: Sage, 2000.
Loeber, Rolf, and Magda Stouthamer-Loeber. "The Development of Offend-
    ing," *Criminal Justice and Behavior* 23, no. 1 (1996): 12–24.

Lopez, Vera, Yasmina Katsulis, and Alyssa Robillard. "Drug Use with Parents as a Relational Strategy for Incarcerated Female Adolescents," *Family Relations* 58, no. 1 (2009): 135–147.

Luke, Katherine. "Are Girls Really Becoming More Violent? A Critical Analysis," *Affilia* 23, no. 1 (2008): 38–50.

Luke, Katherine. "Girls' Violence: Tracing the Emergence of a Social Problem Through Print Media Analysis from 1980–2004." Paper presented at the meeting of the American Sociological Association, New York, August 11–14, 2007.

Luthar, Suniya, and Edward Zigler. "Vulnerability and Competence: A Review of Research on Resilience in Childhood," *American Journal of Orthopsychiatry* 61, no. 1 (1991): 6–22.

Maher, Lisa. *Sexed Work: Gender, Race and Resistance in a Brooklyn Drug Market*. Oxford: Clarendon Press, 1997.

Maher, Lisa, and Kathleen Daly. "Women in the Street-Level Economy: Continuity or Change?" *Criminology* 34, no. 4 (1996): 465–491.

Main, Mary. "Analysis of a Peculiar Form of Reunion Behavior Seen in Some Day-Care Children." In *Social Development in Childhood*, edited by Roger Webb, 33–78. Baltimore: Johns Hopkins University Press, 1977.

Main, Mary. "Avoidance in the Service of Attachment: A Working Paper." In *Behavioral Development: The Bielefeld Interdisciplinary Project,* edited by Klaus Immelman, George Barlow, Mary Main, and Lewis Petrinovitch, 651–693. Cambridge: Cambridge University Press, 1981.

Main, Mary, Nancy Kaplan, and Jude Cassidy. "Security in Infancy, Childhood, and Adulthood: A Move to the Level of Representation." In *Growing Points in Attachment Theory and Research,* edited by Inge Bretherton and Everett Waters, 66–104. *Monographs of the Society for Research in Child Development* 50, no. 1–2. Chicago: University of Chicago Press, 1985.

Main, Mary, and Judith Solomon. "Procedures for Identifying Disorganized/Disoriented Infants During the Ainsworth Strange Situation." In *Attachment in the Preschool Years: Theory, Research and Intervention,* edited by Mark Greenberg, Dante Cicchetti, and Mark Cummings, 121–160. Chicago: University of Chicago Press, 1990.

Majors, Richard, and Janet Billson. *Cool Pose: The Dilemmas of Black Manhood in America.* New York: Simon and Schuster, 1993.

Makarios, Matthew. "Race, Abuse, and Female Criminal Violence," *Feminist Criminology* 2, no. 2 (2007): 100–116.

Males, Mike. "Have 'Girls Gone Wild'?" In *Fighting for Girls: New Perspectives on Gender and Violence,* edited by Meda Chesney-Lind and Nikki Jones, 13–32. Albany: State University of New York Press, 2010.

Mangold, William, and Patricia Koski. "Gender Comparisons in the Relationship Between Parental and Sibling Violence and Nonfamily Violence," *Journal of Family Violence* 5, no. 3 (1990): 225–235.

Marans, Steven, and Donald Cohen. "Children and Inner-City Violence: Strategies for Intervention." In *Psychological Effects of War and Vio-*

lence on Children, edited by Lewis Leavitt and Nathan Fox, 281–302. Hillsdale, NJ: Erlbaum, 1993.

Margolin, Gayla. "Effects of Domestic Violence on Children." In *Violence Against Children in the Family and in the Community,* edited by Penelope K. Trickett and Cynthia J. Schellenbach, 57–101. Washington, DC: American Psychological Association, 1998.

Margolin, Gayla, and Richard John. "Children's Exposure to Marital Aggression: Direct and Mediated Effects." In *Out of the Darkness: Contemporary Research Perspectives on Family Violence,* edited by Glenda Kaufman Kantor and Jana Jasinski, 90–104. Thousand Oaks, CA: Sage, 1997.

Massey, Douglas, and Nancy Denton. *American Apartheid: Segregation and the Making of the Underclass.* Cambridge: Harvard University Press, 1993.

Masters, Rosemary, Lucy Friedman, and George Getzel. "Helping Families of Homicide Victims: A Multidimensional Approach," *Journal of Traumatic Stress* 1, no. 1 (1988): 109–125.

"Mayor Bloomberg Announces Partnership." Office of the Mayor press release, February 12, 2013. www.nyc.gov/html/hhc/html/pressroom /press-release-201302-12-nyu-bellevue.shtml.

McCrae, Robert. "Age Differences and Changes in the Use of Coping Mechanisms," *Journal of Gerontology: Psychological Sciences* 44, no. 6 (1989): 161–169.

McLeod, Jane D., and Ronald Kessler. "Socioeconomic Status Differences in Vulnerability to Undesirable Life Events," *Journal of Health and Social Behavior* 31, no. 6 (1990): 162–172.

McNulty, Paul. "Natural Born Killers? Preventing the Coming Explosion of Teenage Crime," *Policy Review,* no. 71 (Winter 1995): 84–87.

Mears, Daniel, and Jeremy Travis. "Youth Development and Reentry," *Youth Violence and Juvenile Justice* 2, no. 1 (2004): 3–20.

Melhem, Nadine, Monica Walker, Grace Moritz, and David Brent. "Antecedents and Sequelae of Sudden Parental Death in Offspring and Surviving Caregivers," *Archives of Pediatric and Adolescent Medicine* 162, no. 5 (2008): 403–410.

Menon, Ritu, and Kamla Bhasin. *Borders and Boundaries: Women in India's Partition.* New Brunswick, NJ: Rutgers University Press, 1998.

Messerschmidt, James W. *Crime as Structured Action: Gender, Race, Class, and Crime in the Making.* Thousand Oaks, CA: Sage, 1997.

Messerschmidt, James W. "From Patriarchy to Gender: Feminist Theory, Criminology and the Challenge of Diversity." In *International Perspectives in Criminology: Engendering a Discipline,* edited by N. Rafter and F. Heidensohn, 167–188. Buckingham: Open University Press, 1995.

Mikulincer, Mario, and Victor Florian. "Coping and Adaptation to Trauma and Loss." In *Handbook of Coping: Theory, Research, Applications,* edited by Moshe Zeidner and Norman Endler, 554–572. New York: Wiley, 1996.

Miller, Jean Baker. "The Development of Women's Sense of Self." In *Women's Growth in Connection: Writings from the Stone Center,* edited by Judith Jordan, Alexandra Kaplan, Jean Baker Miller, Irene Stiver, and Janet Surrey, 11–26. New York: Guilford Press, 1991.

Miller, Jean Baker. *Toward a New Psychology of Women.* New York: Beacon Press, 1976.

Miller, Jean Baker, and Irene Stiver. *The Healing Connection: How Women Form Relationships in Therapy and in Life.* Boston: Beacon Press, 1997.

Miller, Jody. *Getting Played: African American Girls, Urban Inequality, and Gendered Violence.* New York: New York University Press, 2008.

Miller, Jody. "Up It Up: Gender and Accomplishment of Street Robbery," *Criminology* 36, no. 1 (1998): 37–66.

Miller, Jody, and Christopher Mullins. "The Status of Feminist Theories in Criminology." In *Taking Stock: The Status of Criminological Theory— Advances in Criminological Theory,* vol. 15, edited by Francis T. Cullen, John Paul Wright, and Kristie Blevins, 217–250. New Brunswick, NJ: Transaction, 2006.

Miller-Cribbs, Julie, and Naomi Farber. "Kin Networks and Poverty Among African-Americans: Past and Present," *Social Work* 53, no. 1 (2008): 43–51.

Mitchell, Kimberly, and David Finkelhor. "Risk of Crime Victimization Among Youth Exposed to Domestic Violence," *Journal of Interpersonal Violence* 16, no. 9 (2001): 944–964.

Mitchell, Stephen. *Relationality: From Attachment to Intersubjectivity.* Hillsdale, NJ: Analytic Press, 2003.

Moffitt, Terrie, and Avshalom Caspi. "Childhood Predictors Differentiate Life-Course Persistent and Adolescence-Limited Antisocial Pathways Among Males and Females," *Developmental Psychopathology* 13, no. 2 (2001): 355–375.

Moffitt, Terrie, Avshalom Caspi, Michael Rutter, and Phil Silva. *Sex Differences in Antisocial Behavior: Conduct Disorder, Delinquency and Violence in the Dunedin Longitudinal Study.* Cambridge: Cambridge University Press, 2001.

Morris, Monique, Stephanie Bush-Baskette, and Kimberle Crenshaw. *Confined in California: Women and Girls of Color in Custody.* New York: African American Policy Forum, 2012.

Morse, Janice. "Designing Funded Qualitative Research." In *Handbook of Qualitative Research,* edited by Norman Denzin and Yvonna Lincoln, 220–235. Newbury Park, CA: Sage, 1994.

Nanda, Jyoti. "Blind Discretion: Girls of Color and Delinquency in the Juvenile Justice System," *UCLA Law Review* 59, no. 6 (2012): 1502–1539.

Naples, Nancy. *Feminism and Method: Ethnography, Discourse Analysis, and Activist Research.* New York: Routledge, 2003.

Nardone, Thomas. "Decline in Youth Population Does Not Lead to Lower Jobless Rates," *Monthly Labor Review* 110 (June 1987): 37–41. www.bls.gov/opub/mlr/1987/06/rpt1full.pdf.

National Association of State Mental Health Program Directors. *Position Statement on Mental Health Services in a Juvenile Justice Population.*

Alexandria, VA: National Association of State Mental Health Program Directors, 2001. www.nasmhpd.org/general_files/position_statement /JuvenileJustice.pdf.

National Mental Health Association. *Mental Health Treatment for Youth in the Juvenile Justice System.* Alexandria,VA: National Mental Health Association, 2004. https://www.nttac.org/views/docs/jabg/mhcurriculum /mh_mht.pdf.

Ness, Cindy. *Why Girls Fight: Female Youth Violence in the Inner City.* New York: New York University Press, 2010.

Newcombe, Nora, and Jeffrey C. Lerner. "Britain Between the Wars: The Historical Context of Bowlby's Theory of Attachment," *Psychiatry: Journal for the Study of Interpersonal Processes* 45, no. 1 (1982): 1–12.

New York State Department of Health. *AIDS in New York State.* Albany: New York State Department of Health, 2002. www.health.ny.gov/diseases /aids/reports/2001/docs/section17.pdf.

O'Connor, Deborah. "Journeying the Quagmire: Exploring the Discourses that Shape the Qualitative Research Process," *Affilia* 16, no. 2 (2001): 138–158.

Office of Juvenile Justice and Delinquency Prevention. *Statistical Briefing Book,* July 31, 2012. www.ojjdp.gov/ojstatbb/offenders.

Okamoto, Scott. "The Challenges of Male Practitioners Working with Female Youth Clients," *Child and Youth Care Forum* 31, no. 4 (2002): 257–268.

Olesen, Virgina. "Feminisms and Models of Qualitative Research." In *The Landscape of Qualitative Research: Theories and Issues,* edited by Norman Denizen and Yvonna Lincoln, 300–332. Thousand Oaks, CA: Sage, 1998.

Osofsky, Joy. "The Effects of Exposure to Violence on Young Children," *American Psychologist* 50, no. 9 (1995): 782–788.

Parker, Robert Nash, and Kathleen Auerhahn. "Alcohol, Drugs, and Violence," *Annual Review of Sociology* 24 (1998): 291–311.

Peacock, Carol. *Hand-Me-Down Dreams.* New York: Schocken Books, 1981.

Perry, Bruce, Ronnie Pollard, Toi Blakley, William Baker, and Domenico Vigilante. "Childhood Trauma, the Neurobiology of Adaptation, and 'Use-dependent' Development of the Brain: How 'States' Become 'Traits,'" *Infant Mental Health Journal* 16, no. 4 (1995): 271–291.

Pettit, Becky, and Bruce Western. "Mass Imprisonment and the Life Course: Race and Class Inequality in US Incarceration," *American Sociological Review* 69, no. 2 (2004): 151–169.

Pizarro, Jesenia, Steven Chermak, and Jeffrey Gruenewald. "Juvenile 'Super-Predators' in the News: A Comparison of Adult and Juvenile Homicides," *Journal of Criminal Justice and Popular Culture* 14, no. 1 (2007): 87–111.

Poe-Yamagata, Eileen, and Jeffrey Butts. *Female Offenders in the Juvenile Justice System: Statistics Summary.* Washington, DC: Office of Juvenile Justice and Delinquency Prevention, 1996.

Presser, Lois. "The Narratives of Offenders," *Theoretical Criminology* 13, no. 2 (2009): 177–200.

Punch, Maurice. "Politics and Ethics in Qualitative Research." In *Handbook of Qualitative Research,* edited by Norman Denzin and Yvonna Lincoln, 83–97. Thousand Oaks, CA: Sage, 1994.

Puzzanchera, Charles. "Juvenile Arrests 2008," *Juvenile Justice Bulletin.* Washington, DC: Office of Juvenile Justice and Delinquency Prevention, 2009. www.ncjrs.gov/pdffiles1/ojjdp/228479.pdf.

Puzzanchera, Charles, Benjamin Adams, and Melissa Sickmund. *Juvenile Court Statistics 2006–2007.* Pittsburgh: National Center for Juvenile Justice, 2010.

Puzzanchera, Charles, and Wei Kang. "Easy Access to the FBI's Supplementary Homicide Reports: 1980–2010." Washington, DC: Office of Juvenile Justice and Delinquency Prevention, 2012. http://ojjdp.gov/ojstatbb /offenders/qa03102.asp?qaDate=2010&text=yes.

Puzzanchera, Charles, and Wei Kang. "Easy Access to Juvenile Court Statistics: 1985–2010." Washington, DC: Office of Juvenile Justice and Delinquency Prevention, 2013. www.ojjdp.gov/ojstatbb/ezajcs.

Puzzanchera, Charles, and Melissa Sickmund. *Juvenile Court Statistics 2005.* Pittsburgh: National Center for Juvenile Justice, 2008.

Pynoos, Richard, and Kathleen Nader. "Prevention of Psychiatric Morbidity in Children After Disasters." In *Prevention of Mental Health Disturbances in Children,* edited by Stephen Goldston, Joel Yager, Christopher Heinicke, and Richard Pynoos, 211–234. Washington, DC: American Psychiatric Press, 1990.

Pynoos, Robert, Alan Steinberg, and Armen Goenjian. "Traumatic Stress in Childhood and Adolescence: Recent Developments and Current Controversies." In *Traumatic Stress: The Effects of Overwhelming Experience on Mind, Body and Society,* edited by Bessel van der Kolk, Alexander McFarlane, and Lars Weisaeth, 331–358. New York: Guilford Press, 2007.

Rae, Leah, and Shawn Cohen. "Lidia's Story: A Troubled Life in Foster Care," *Journal News,* White Plains, New York. June 23, 2002.

Raeder, Myrna. *The State of Criminal Justice: 2011.* Chicago: American Bar Association, 2011.

Rafter, Nicole. "Hard Times: The Evolution of the Women's Prison System and the Example of the New York State Prison for Women at Auburn, 1893–1933." In *Judge, Lawyer, Victim, Thief: Women, Gender Roles, and Criminal Justice,* edited by Nicole Rafter and Elizabeth Stanko, 237–260. Boston: Northeastern University Press, 1982.

Rafter, Nicole. *Partial Justice: Women, Prisons, and Social Control,* 2nd ed. New Brunswick, NJ: Transaction, 1992.

Rajecki, D. W., Michael Lamb, and Pauline Obmascher. "Toward a General Theory of Infantile Attachment: A Comparative Review of Aspects of the Social Bond," *Behavioral and Brain Sciences* 1, no. 3 (1978): 417–464.

Rando, Therese A. "Complications in Mourning Traumatic Death." In *Living with Grief After Sudden Loss: Suicide, Homicide, Accident, Heart Attack, Stroke,* edited by Kenneth Doka, 139–160. Bristol, PA: Taylor and Francis, 1996.

Rasmussen, Andrew, Mark Aber, and Arvinkumar Bhana. "Adolescent Coping and Neighborhood Violence: Perceptions, Exposure, and Urban Youth's Efforts to Deal with Danger," *American Journal of Community Psychology* 33, nos. 1–2 (2004): 61–75.

Rebellion, Cesar. "Reconsidering the Broken Homes/Delinquency Relationship and Exploring Its Mediating Mechanism(s)," *Criminology* 40, no. 1 (2002): 103–135.

Redmond, Lula. "Sudden Violent Death." In *Living with Grief After Sudden Loss: Suicide, Homicide, Accident, Heart Attack, Stroke,* edited by Kenneth Doka, 53–71. Bristol, PA: Taylor and Francis, 1996.

Reed, Diane, and Edward Reed. "Children of Incarcerated Parents," *Social Justice* 24, no. 3 (1997): 152–170.

Reeves, Jimmie, and Richard Campbell. *Cracked Coverage: Television News, the Anticocaine Crusade, and the Reagan Legacy.* Durham: Duke University Press, 1994.

Reinarman, Carl, and Harry Levine. "The Crack Attack: Politics and Media in the Crack Scare." In *Crack in America: Demon Drugs and Social Justice,* edited by Carl Reinarman and Harry Levine, 1–17. Berkeley: University of California Press, 1997.

Richards, Jill. "Zero Room for Zero Tolerance: Rethinking Federal Funding for Zero Tolerance Policies," *University of Dayton Law Review* 30, no. 1 (2004): 91–117.

Richie, Beth. *Compelled to Crime: The Gender Entrapment of Black Battered Women.* New York: Routledge, 1996.

Rivera, Beverly, and Cathy Spatz Widom. "Childhood Victimization and Violent Offending," *Violence and Victims* 5, no. 1 (1990): 19–35.

Robertson, Angela, Xiaohe Xu, and Andrea Stripling. "Adverse Events and Substance Use Among Female Adolescent Offenders: Effects of Coping and Family Support," *Substance Use and Misuse* 45, no. 3 (2010): 451–472.

Robinson, Robin. "'Crystal Virtues': Seeking Reconciliation Between Ideals and Violations of Girlhood," *Contemporary Justice Review* 8, no. 1 (2005): 59–73.

Robinson, Robin. "'It's Not Easy to Know Who I Am': Gender Salience and Cultural Place in the Treatment of a 'Delinquent Adolescent Mother,'" *Feminist Criminology* 2, no. 1 (2007): 31–56.

Robinson, Robin. "'Since I Couldn't Get Out of My Own Skin': What Would a Feminist, Psychoanalytic Perspective of Crime and Justice Look Like?" In *Routledge Handbook of Critical Criminology,* edited by Walter DeKeseredy and Molly Dragiewicz, 194–208. New York: Routledge, 2012.

Robinson, Robin, and Judith Ryder. "Psychosocial Perspectives of Girls and Violence: Implications for Policy and Praxis," *Critical Criminology* 21, no. 4 (2013). DOI 10.1007/s10612-013-9185-4. http://link.springer.com/article/10.1007/s10612-013-9185-4

Roemer, Lizabeth, Brett Litz, Susan Orsillo, and Amy Wagner. "A Preliminary Investigation of the Role of Strategic Withholding of Emotions in PTSD," *Journal of Traumatic Stress* 14, no. 1 (2001): 149–156.

Rogers, Kim Lacy, Selma Leydesdorff, and Graham Dawson. *Trauma: Life Stories of Survivors.* New Brunswick, NJ: Transaction, 2004.

Rose, Lionel. *Massacre of the Innocents: Infanticide in Great Britain, 1800–1939*. London: Routledge and Kegan Paul, 1986.

Rosenbloom, Susan Rakosi, and Niobe Way. "Experiences of Discrimination Among African American, Asian American, and Latino Adolescents in an Urban High School," *Youth and Society* 35, no. 4 (2004): 420–451.

Ross, Robert, H. Brian McKay, William R. T. Palmer, and C. J. Kenny. "Self-Mutilation in Adolescent Female Offenders," *Canadian Journal of Criminology* 20, no. 4 (1978): 375–392.

Rouse, Linda P. "College Students and the Legacy of Spouse Abuse," *New Directions for Student Service,* no. 54 (Summer 1991): 51–62.

Ruchkin, Vladislav, Mary Schwab-Stone, Roman Koposov, Robert Vermeiren, and Hans Steiner. "Violence Exposure, Posttraumatic Stress, and Personality in Juvenile Delinquents," *Journal of the American Academy of Child and Adolescent Psychiatry* 41, no. 3 (2002): 322–329.

Ryder, Judith. "'I Wasn't Really Bonded with My Family': Attachment, Loss, and Violence Among Adolescent Female Offenders," *Critical Criminology: An International Journal* 15, no. 1 (2007): 19–40.

Ryder, Judith, and Regina Brisgone. "Cracked Perspectives: Reflections of Women and Girls in the Aftermath of the Crack Cocaine Era," *Feminist Criminology* 8, no. 1 (2013): 40–62.

Ryder, Judith, Sandra Langley, and Henry Brownstein. "'I've Been Around and Around and Around': Measuring Traumatic Events in the Lives of Incarcerated Girls." In *Women's Mental Health Issues Across the Criminal Justice System,* edited by Rosemary Gido and L. Dalley, 45–70. Upper Saddle River, NJ: Prentice Hall, 2008.

Rynearson, Edward, and Joseph McCreery. "Bereavement After Homicide: A Synergism of Trauma and Loss," *American Journal of Psychiatry* 150, no. 2 (1993): 258–261.

Salzinger, Suzanne, Margaret Rosario, and Richard Feldman. "Physical Child Abuse and Adolescent Violent Delinquency: The Mediating and Moderating Roles of Personal Relationship," *Child Maltreatment* 12, no. 3 (2007): 208–219.

Sampson, Robert. "Urban Black Violence: The Effect of Male Joblessness and Family Disruption," *American Journal of Sociology* 93, no. 2 (1987): 348–382.

Sampson, Robert, and John Laub. "Crime and Deviance over the Life Course: The Salience of Adult Social Bonds," *American Sociological Review* 55, no. 5 (1990): 609–627.

Sampson, Robert, and John Laub. *Crime in the Making: Pathways and Turning Points Through Life*. Cambridge: Harvard University Press, 1993.

Sampson, Robert, Stephen Raudenbush, and Felton Earls. "Neighborhoods and Violent Crime: A Multilevel Study of Collective Efficacy," *Science* 277, no. 5328 (1997): 918–924.

Sander, Louis. "The Regulation of Exchange in the Infant-Caretaker System and Some Aspects of the Context-Content Relationship." In *Interaction, Conversation and the Development of Language,* edited by Michael Lewis and Leonard A. Rosenblum, 133–156. New York: Wiley, 1977.

Scelfo, Julie. "Bad Girls Go Wild," *Newsweek,* June 13, 2005. www.newsweek
.com/id/50082, accessed July 9, 2008.

Schaffner, Laurie. "Violence Against Girls Provokes Girls' Violence: From
Private Injury to Public Harm," *Violence Against Women* 13, no. 12
(2007): 1229–1248.

Scheeringa, Michael, Claire Peebles, Cynthia Cook, and Charles Zeanah.
"Toward Establishing Procedural, Criterion, and Discriminant Validity
for PTSD in Early Childhood," *Journal of the American Academy of
Child and Adolescent Psychiatry* 40, no. 1 (2001): 52–60.

Scheeringa, Michael, and Charles Zeanah. "Reconsideration of Harm's Way:
Onsets and Comorbidity Patterns of Disorders in Preschool Children
and Their Caregivers Following Hurricane Katrina," *Journal of Clinical
Child and Adolescent Psychology* 37, no. 3 (2008): 508–518.

Schirmer, Sarah, Ashley Nellis, and Marc Mauer. "Incarcerated Parents and
Their Children: Trends 1991–2007." Washington, DC: The Sentencing
Project, 2009. www.sentencingproject.org/doc/publications/publications
/inc_incarceratedparents.pdf.

Schore, Judith, and Allan Schore. "Modern Attachment Theory: The Central
Role of Affect Regulation in Development and Treatment," *Clinical
Social Work Journal* 36 (2008): 9–20.

Schur, Edwin. *Labeling Women Deviant: Gender, Stigma, and Social Control.* New York: McGraw-Hill, 1984.

Sedlak, Andrea, and Karla McPherson. "Youth's Needs and Services: Findings
from the Survey of Youth in Residential Placement," *Juvenile Justice Bulletin.* Washington, DC: Office of Juvenile Justice and Delinquency Prevention, 2010. www.ncjrs.gov/pdffiles1/ojjdp/227728.pdf.

Sedlak, Andrea, Jane Mettenburg, Monica Basena, Ian Petta, Karla McPherson, Angela Greene, and Spencer Li. *Fourth National Incidence Study of
Child Abuse and Neglect (NIS–4): Report to Congress.* Washington, DC:
US Department of Health and Human Services, Administration for Children and Families, 2010. www.acf.hhs.gov/programs/opre/abuse_neglect
/natl_incid/reports/natl_incid/nis4_report_congress_full_pdf_jan2010.pdf.

Sentencing Project. "Incarcerated Women Fact Sheet." www.sentencingproject
.org/doc/publications/cc_Incarcerated_Women_Factsheet_Sep24sp.pdf.

Shapiro, Deborah, and Alytia Levendosky. "Adolescent Survivors of Childhood Sexual Abuse: The Mediating Role of Attachment Style and Coping in Psychological and Interpersonal Functioning," *Child Abuse and
Neglect* 23, no. 11 (1999): 1175–1191.

Sharpe, Gilly. *Offending Girls: Young Women and Youth Justice.* New York:
Routledge, 2012.

Shengold, Leonard. *Soul Murder Revisited: Thoughts About Therapy, Hate,
Love, and Memory.* New Haven: Yale University Press, 1999.

Siegel, Jane. *Disrupted Childhoods: Children of Women in Prison.* New
Brunswick, NJ: Rutgers University Press, 2011.

Siegel, Jane, and Linda Williams. "The Relationship Between Child Sexual
Abuse and Female Delinquency and Crime: A Prospective Study," *Journal of Research in Crime and Delinquency* 40, no. 1 (2003): 71–94.

Silverthorn, Persephanie, and Paul Frick. "Developmental Pathways to Antisocial Behavior: The Delayed-Onset Pathway in Girls," *Development and Psychopathology* 11, no. 1 (1999): 101–126.

Simmons, Rachel. *Odd Girl Out: The Hidden Aggression in Girls*. New York: Harcourt, 2003.

Simon, Valerie, Candice Feiring, and Sarah Kobielski McElroy. "Making Meaning of Traumatic Events: Youths' Strategies for Processing Childhood Sexual Abuse Are Associated with Psychosocial Adjustment," *Child Maltreatment* 15, no. 3 (2010): 229–241.

Simons, Ronald, Leslie Gordon Simons, Yi-Fu Chen, Gene Brody, and Kuei-Hsiu Lin. "Identifying the Psychological Factors that Mediate the Association Between Parenting Practices and Delinquency," *Criminology* 45, no. 3 (2007): 481–517.

Simpson, Gaynell, and Claudia Lawrence-Webb. "Responsibility Without Community Resources: Informal Kinship Care Among Low-Income, African American Grandmother Caregivers," *Journal of Black Studies* 39, no. 6 (2009): 825–847.

Singer, Simon. *Recriminalizing Delinquency: Violent Juvenile Crime and Juvenile Justice Reform*. New York: Cambridge University Press, 1997.

Small, Mario Luis, and Katherine Newman. "Urban Poverty After the Truly Disadvantaged: The Rediscovery of the Family, the Neighborhood, and Culture," *Annual Review of Sociology* 27 (2001): 23–45.

Smith, Carolyn, and Terence Thornberry. "The Relationship Between Childhood Maltreatment and Adolescent Involvement in Delinquency," *Criminology* 33, no. 4 (1995): 451–477.

Smith, Dana, Leslie Leve, and Patricia Chamberlain. "Adolescent Girls' Offending and Health-Risking Sexual Behavior: The Predictive Role of Trauma," *Child Maltreatment* 11, no. 4 (2006): 346–353.

Snyder, Howard. "Juvenile Arrests 1995," *Juvenile Justice Bulletin*. Washington, DC: Office of Juvenile Justice and Delinquency Prevention, 1997. www.ncjj.org/pdf/163813.pdf.

Snyder, Howard. "Juvenile Arrests 1999," *Juvenile Justice Bulletin*. Washington, DC: Office of Juvenile Justice and Delinquency Prevention, 2000. www.ncjrs.gov/pdffiles1/ojjdp/185236.pdf.

Snyder, Howard, and Melissa Sickmund. *Juvenile Offenders and Victims: 1999 National Report*. Washington, DC: US Department of Justice, Office of Juvenile Justice and Delinquency Prevention, 1999. www.ncjrs.gov/html/ojjdp/nationalreport99/toc.html.

Snyder, Howard, and Melissa Sickmund. *Juvenile Offenders and Victims: 2006 National Report*. Washington, DC: US Department of Justice, Office of Justice Programs, Office of Juvenile Justice and Delinquency Prevention, 2006.

Solomon, Brenda. "Traditional and Rights-Informed Talk About Violence: High School Educator's Discursive Production of Student Violence," *Youth and Society* 37, no. 3 (2006): 251–286.

Solomon, Eldra, and Kathleen Heide. "Type III Trauma: Toward a More Effective Conceptualization of Psychological Trauma," *International Journal of Offender Therapy and Comparative Criminology* 43, no. 2 (1999): 202–210.

Sommers, Ira, and Deborah Baskin. "The Situational Context of Violent Female Offending," *Journal of Research in Crime and Delinquency* 30, no. 2 (1993): 136–162.

Spaccarelli, Steve. "Stress, Appraisal, and Coping in Child Sexual Abuse: A Theoretical and Empirical Review," *Psychological Bulletin* 116, no. 2 (1994): 340–362.

Spector, Malcolm, and John Kitsuse. *Constructing Social Problems.* Menlo Park, CA: Cummings, 1977.

Spungen, Deborah. *Homicide: The Hidden Victims.* Thousand Oaks, CA: Sage, 1988.

Sroufe, L. Alan, Elizabeth Carlson, Alissa Levy, and Byron Egeland. "Implications of Attachment Theory for Developmental Psychopathology," *Development and Psychopathology* 11, no. 1 (1999): 1–13.

Sroufe, L. Alan, and June Fleeson. "Attachment and the Construction of Relationships." In *Relationships and Development,* edited by Willard Hartup and Zick Rubin, 51–71. Mahwah, NJ: Erlbaum, 1986.

Sroufe, L. Alan, and Everett Waters. "Heart Rate as a Convergent Measure in Clinical and Developmental Research," *Merrill-Palmer Quarterly* 23, no. 1 (1977): 3–27.

Stack, Carol. *All Our Kin: Strategies for Survival in a Black Community.* New York: Harper and Row, 1975.

Steffensmeier, Darrell, Jennifer Schwartz, Hua Zhong, and Jeff Ackerman. "An Assessment of Recent Trends in Girls' Violence Using Diverse Longitudinal Sources: Is the Gender Gap Closing?" *Criminology* 43, no. 2 (2005): 355–406.

Stein, Nan. "Bullying or Sexual Harassment? The Missing Discourse of Rights in an Era of Zero Tolerance," *Arizona Law Review* 45, no. 3 (2003): 783–799.

Stein, Nan. "Introduction—What a Difference a Discipline Makes: Bullying Research and Future Directions," *Journal of Emotional Abuse* 2, no. 2/3 (2001): 1–5.

Steinburg, Laurence. "Autonomy, Conflict, and Harmony in the Family Relationship." In *Adolescent Behavior: Readings and Interpretations,* edited by Elizabeth Aries, 352–371. New York: McGraw-Hill/Dushkin, 2001.

Steiner, Hans, Ivan G. Garcia, and Zakee Matthews. "Posttraumatic Stress Disorder in Incarcerated Juvenile Delinquents," *Journal of the American Academy of Child and Adolescent Psychiatry* 36, no. 3 (1997): 357–365.

Sterk, Claire. *Fast Lives: Women Who Use Crack Cocaine.* Philadelphia: Temple University Press, 1999.

Stern, Lori. "Disavowing the Self in Female Adolescence." In *Women, Girls, and Psychotherapy: Reframing Resistance,* edited by Carol Gilligan, Annie Rogers, and Deborah Tolman, 105–117. Binghamton, NY: Harrington Park Press, 1991.

Stevens, Tia, Merry Morash, and Meda Chesney-Lind. "Are Girls Getting Tougher, or Are We Tougher on Girls? Probability of Arrest and Juvenile Court Oversight in 1980 and 2000," *Justice Quarterly* 28, no. 5 (2011): 719–744.

Stoppelbein, Laura, and Leilani Greening. "Posttraumatic Stress Symptoms in Parentally Bereaved Children and Adolescents," *Journal of the American Academy of Child and Adolescent Psychiatry* 39, no. 9 (2000): 1112–1119.

Stover, Carla, and Steven Berkowitz. "Assessing Violence Exposure and Trauma Symptoms in Young Children: A Critical Review of Measures," *Journal of Traumatic Stress* 18, no. 6 (2005): 707–717.

Strack, Stephen, and Herman Feifel. "Age Differences, Coping and the Adult Life Span." In *Handbook of Coping: Theory, Research, Applications,* edited by Moshe Zeidner and Norman Endler, 485–501. New York: Wiley, 1996.

Strand, Virgina, Teresa Sarmiento, and Lina Pasquale. "Assessment and Screening Tools for Trauma in Children and Adolescents: A Review," *Trauma, Violence and Abuse* 6, no. 1 (2005): 55–78.

Stuckless, Noreen. *The Influence of Anger, Perceived Injustice, Revenge, and Time on the Quality of Life of Survivor-Victims.* Toronto, ON: York University, 1996.

Suchman, Nancy, Thomas McMahon, Arietta Slade, and Suniya Luthar. "How Early Bonding, Depression, Illicit Drug Use, and Perceived Support Work Together to Influence Drug-dependent Mothers' Caregiving," *American Journal of Orthopsychiatry* 75, no. 3 (2005): 431–445.

Sullivan, Tami, Katherine Meese, Suzane Swan, Carolyn Mazure, and David Snow. "Precusors and Correlates of Women's Violence: Child Abuse Traumatization, Victimization of Women, Avoidance Coping and Psychological Symptoms," *Psychology of Women Quarterly* 29, no. 3 (2005): 290–301.

Swann, Christopher, and Michelle Sylvester. "The Foster Care Crisis: What Caused Caseloads to Grow?" *Demography* 43, no. 2 (2006): 309–335.

Taylor, Angela. *How Drug Dealers Settle Disputes: Violent and Nonviolent Outcomes.* Monsey, NY: Criminal Justice Press, 2007.

Templeton, Robin. "Superscapegoating." Fairness and Accuracy in Reporting (FAIR), January/February 1998. www.fair.org, accessed January 11, 2011.

Teplin, Linda, Karen Abram, Gary McClelland, Mina Dulcan, and Amy Mericle. "Psychiatric Disorders in Youth in Juvenile Detention," *Archives of General Psychiatry* 59, no. 12 (2002): 1133–1143.

Terr, Lenore. *Too Scared to Cry.* New York: HarperCollins, 1990.

Thoits, Peggy. "Social Support as Coping Assistance," *Journal of Consulting and Clinical Psychology* 54, no. 4 (1986): 416–423.

Thornberry, Terrence. "Introduction: Some Advantages of Developmental and Life-Course Perspectives for the Study of Crime and Delinquency." In *Developmental Theories of Crime and Delinquency,* vol. 7: *Advances in Criminological Theory,* edited by Terrance Thornberry, 1–10. New Brunswick, NJ: Transaction, 2004.

Thornberry, Terrence, Timothy Ireland, and Carolyn Smith. "The Importance of Timing: The Varying Impact of Childhood and Adolescent Maltreatment on Multiple Problem Outcomes," *Development and Psychopathology* 13, no. 4 (2001): 957–979.

Tisdale, E. Kay. "The Rising Tide of Female Violence? Researching Girls' Own Understandings and Experiences of Violent Behavior." In *Researching Violence: Essays on Methodology and Measurement*, edited by Raymond Lee and Elizabeth Stanko, 137–153. New York: Routledge, 2003.

Tyner, James. *Space, Place and Violence: Violence and the Embodied Geographies of Race, Sex, and Gender*. New York: Routledge, 2012.

US Department of Health and Human Services, Administration for Children and Families, Administration on Children, Youth, and Families, Children's Bureau. *Child Maltreatment 2010*, 2011. www.acf.hhs.gov/programs/cb/stats_research/index.htm#can.

US Department of Justice. *Crime in the United States, 1997*. Washington, DC: US Government Printing Office, 1998.

Vaillant, George. *Attachment to Life*. Boston: Little, Brown, 1977.

van der Kolk, Bessel. "Trauma and Memory." In *Traumatic Stress: The Effects of Overwhelming Experience on Mind, Body and Society*, edited by Bessel van der Kolk, Alexander McFarlane, and Lars Weisaeth, 279–303. New York: Guilford Press, 2007.

Villalón, Roberta. *Violence Against Latina Immigrants: Citizenship, Inequality, and Community*. New York: New York University Press, 2010.

Wasserman, Gail, Susan Ko, and Larkin McReynolds. "Assessing the Mental Health Needs of Youth in Juvenile Justice Settings," *Juvenile Justice Bulletin*. Washington, DC: Office of Juvenile Justice and Delinquency Prevention, 2004. www.ncjrs.gov/pdffiles1/ojjdp/202713.pdf.

Waters, Everett, Susan Merrick, Domnique Treboux, Judith Crowell, and Leah Albersheim. "Attachment Security in Infancy and Early Adulthood: A Twenty-Year Longitudinal Study," *Child Development* 71, no. 3 (2000): 684–689.

Weisman, Avery. *Coping Capacity: On the Extent of Being Mortal*. New York: Human Sciences Press, 1984.

Wenar, Charles. *Developmental Psychopathology: From Infancy Through Adolescence*, 3rd ed. New York: McGraw-Hill, 1994.

Western, Bruce, and Christopher Wildeman. "The Black Family and Mass Incarceration," *ANNALS of the American Academy of Political and Social Science* 621, no. 1 (2009): 221–242.

Widom, Cathy Spatz. "The Cycle of Violence," *Science* 244, no. 4901 (1989): 160–166.

Widom, Cathy Spatz. "Does Violence Beget Violence? A Critical Examination of the Literature," *Psychological Bulletin* 106, no. 1 (1989): 3–28.

Widom, Cathy Spatz, and M. Ashley Ames. "Criminal Consequences of Childhood Sexual Victimization," *Child Abuse and Neglect* 18, no. 4 (1994): 303–318.

Widom, Cathy Spatz, Timothy Ireland, and Patricia Glynn. "Alcohol Abuse in Abused and Neglected Children Followed-Up: Are They at Increased Risk?" *Journal of Studies on Alcohol* 56, no. 2 (1995): 207–217.

Widom, Cathy Spatz, and Michael Maxfield. *An Update on the "Cycle of Violence."* Washington, DC: US Department of Justice, National Institute of Justice, 2001. www.ncjrs.gov/pdffiles1/nij/184894.pdf.

Widom, Cathy Spatz, Aime M. Schuck, and Helene R. White. "An Examination of Pathways from Childhood Victimization to Violence: The Role of Early Aggression and Problematic Alcohol Use," *Violence and Victims* 21, no. 6 (2006): 675–690.

Wildeman, Christopher, Jason Schnittker, and Kristin Turney. "Despair by Association? The Mental Health of Mothers with Children by Recently Incarcerated Fathers," *American Sociological Review* 77, no. 2 (2012): 216–243.

Williams, Christopher, Jennifer Epstein, Gilbert Botvin, and Michelle Ifill-Williams. "Marijuana Use Among Minority Youths Living in Public Housing Developments," *Journal of Urban Health* 76, no. 1 (1999): 85–101.

Williams, Donald. "Employment in Recession and Recovery: A Demographic Flow Analysis," *Monthly Labor Review* 108, no. 3 (March 1985): 35–42.

Wilson, Melvin, and Timothy Tolson. "Familial Support in the Black Community," *Journal of Clinical Child and Adolescent Psychology* 19, no. 4 (1990): 347–355.

Wilson, William Julius. *The Truly Disadvantaged: The Inner City, the Underclass, and Public Policy.* Chicago: University of Chicago Press, 1987.

Wilson, William Julius. *When Work Disappears: The World of the New Urban Poor.* New York: Alfred A. Knopf, 1996.

Wohl, Amy, Sharon Lu, Sylvia Odem, Frank Sorvillo, Clare Pegues, and Peter Kerndt. "Sociodemographic and Behavioral Characteristics of African-American Women with HIV and AIDS in Los Angeles County, 1990–1997," *Journal of Acquired Immune Deficiency Syndromes and Human Retrovirology* 19, no. 4 (1998): 413–420.

Wood, Jennifer, David Foy, Carole Goguen, Robert Pynoos, and C. Boyd James. "Violence Exposure and PTSD Among Delinquent Girls," *Journal of Aggression, Maltreatment and Trauma* 6, no. 1 (2002): 109–126.

Wright, John Paul, and Frances Cullen. "Parental Efficacy and Delinquent Behaviors: Do Control and Support Matter?" *Criminology* 39, no. 3 (2001): 677–707.

Zernike, Katie. "Crackdown on Threats in Schools Fails a Test," *New York Times,* May 15, 2001.

Index

abandonment, fear of, 13, 27, 128
adolescence: attachment behaviors, changes in, 44; brain development in, 63; relational transformations in, 39–40
Adoption and Safe Families Act (ASFA), 19–20n45
adultification, 49, 57; "parenting" others, 50
African American children: in foster care, 11; maltreatment rates, 87n46; runaway rates, 115; substance use and, 124. *See also* girls of color
aftercare, 161
aggression, 138, 148: as dysfunctional anger (J. Bowlby), 27. *See also* anger
AIDS: African American and Hispanic women and, 43; demise of kinship networks and, 11, 131–132n17
Ainsworth, Mary, 26, 40. *See also* attachment; attachment theory
alcohol and drug use. *See* substance use
anger: attachment patterns and, 40, 57; coping strategies and, 122, 126–127; directed at other girls, 34n14; response to insecurity, 26;

violence and, 27, 145. *See also* aggression
arrests, violent, 3–4; gender variation, 18n16; mandatory (domestic violence), 87n47, 162; and selection bias, 18n22
Artz, Sibylle, 34n14
assault: as instant offense, 9, 15, 133; and violence arrest rates, 3; as self-defense, 134. *See also* offense labels, official
attachment: environmental factors and, 42; maltreatment and, 28; patterns, 27, 35n32, 40, 58n8; as protective bond, 12; representations in study sample, 43–48. *See also* Ainsworth; attachment theory; Bowlby
attachment-based model, 12, 16, 25, 147. *See also* policy recommendations
attachment theory, 25–27; adolescence and, 39–40, 44; control theories and, 165–166; detachment, 29, 39, 72; life course and developmental criminology and, 26; representation of parent-child relationship in, 14; sensitive/responsive parenting

203

85n17, 95; detained versus community juveniles and, 85n21; racial variation among adult females and, 64; and terror, 84n9
poverty: adultification and, 49, 57; segregation and, 42, 66
psychological unavailability. *See* losses
PTSD. *See* posttraumatic stress disorder
punitive strategies: legislative, 4, 11, 21; need to transform, 155; and systems personnel, 128, 106, 162

racial epithets, violent responses to, 138–139
rape, 149n12. *See also* exposure to violence
relational model, women's psychology, 23–24
residential instability, 52, 103
respect. *See* motives for violent behavior
restorative justice: community and, 165; schools and, 159. *See also* policy recommendations
revenge. *See* motives for violent behavior
Ritchie, Beth, 23
robbery, official label, 9,15, 133
Robertson, James, 35n30
Robinson, Robin, 23, 33n6, 36n52, 88n53, 162
running away, 115–121; definitions of, 116, 130n13. *See also* coping strategies
Ryder, Judith, 33n6, 36n43, 60n41, 86n27, 162

safe privilege, 2, 16; African American and Hispanic girls without, 5
sample characteristics, 6–7; alcohol and drug use, 122; weapon use, 136
Sandy Hook Elementary School, 164. *See also* policy recommendations

schools: gendered violence and harassment in, 157; power relations in, 156; restorative justice and, 159; school-to-prison pipeline, 158. *See also* policy recommendations
Schur, Edwin, 33n6
secure base, 12–13, 153. *See also* attachment theory
self-defense. *See* motives for violent behavior
self-harm, 125–128. *See also* coping strategies
September 11, 2001, 19n28
sexual abuse, traumagenic dynamics of, 79. *See also* exposure to violence; sexual assault
sexual assault: effects of, 149n12. *See also* dating and violence; exposure to violence
sexual enticement, as retaliation, 142
sexual harassment: in the community, 78; construed as flirtation, 157; in drug trade, 70; schools and, 157. *See also* policy recommendations
sex work, 42–43
Shengold, Leonard, 62, 65. *See also* "soul murder"
social networks (kinship networks), 11, 106
social support: child development and, 48; and mitigation of stress, trauma, 114
Solomon, Eldra, 84n14
"soul murder," 86n34
Stack, Carol, 130n17
staredowns, 139. *See also* motives for violent behavior
stigma: crack cocaine and, 131n21; identity and, 137; sexual abuse and, 79
"strange situation" behavior. *See* Ainsworth; attachment theory
Stuckless, Noreen, 95
study methodology, 6, 8. *See also* policy recommendations
substance use, 122–125; instant offense and, 136; as relational

strategy, 15, 123. *See also* coping
strategies
suicide attempts, misunderstood or
ignored, 126–127. *See also*
coping strategies
superpredators, 4, 33n3
supervision, representations in study
sample, 51–57
support, representations in study
sample, 48–51

trauma, 28–29; definitions, 62;
gendered response to, 22, 63–64;
population-specific inventory of,
86n31; recalling, 8
traumatic sexualization, 79

victimization. *See* exposure to
violence
violence: contested term, 17n1; as
defensive response, 29, 31, 65,
72, 79, 96, 148; interactional
nature of, 65; and parental social
control, 43. *See also* drug trade;
girl-on-girl violence; motives for
violent behavior; youth violence
violence against women and girls:
perceived as bullying, 157;

witnessing, 67–68. *See also*
dating and violence
"violent girls," 17n1, 148, 149, 152
violent offender, label, 21–22, 33n7

weapons, 135, 136; body as, 136. *See
also* guns; instant offense
women: crack use and, 11, 59n41,
110n21; criminal images of, 33n4;
as heads of household, 11;
incarceration and, 11, 98, 110n18
working models, internal, 13; in
adolescence, 59n27; dissociation
and, 29–30, 125; future
relationships and, 27; trauma-
impaired, 30. *See also* attachment
theory
Wright, John, 48

youth violence: and attachment
model, 167; punitive approaches
to, 21, 152

zero-tolerance policies: failure to
address underlying problems,
156; original intent broadened,
156. *See also* policy
recommendations; schools

About the Book

Seeking to better understand the processes that push teenage girls to acts of criminal violence, Judith Ryder explores the relationship between disrupted emotional bonds and exposure to violence as well as adolescent delinquency.

Ryder draws on intimate interviews to show how teenage girls navigate experiences of physical abuse, emotional loss, and parental abandonment, revealing how their violent acts become a means of connecting with others—however maladaptive and misplaced those connections may be. Her work suggests viable strategies for early interventions to keep at-risk young women out of the criminal justice system.

Judith A. Ryder is associate professor of sociology at St. John's University.